The Kh

by

P. R. T. Gurdon

The Echo Library 2006

Published by

The Echo Library

Echo Library
131 High St.
Teddington
Middlesex TW11 8HH

www.echo-library.com

Please report serious faults in the text to complaints@echo-library.com

ISBN 1-40681-024-X

The Khasis

By

Major P.R.T. Gurdon, I.A.

Deputy Commissioner Eastern Bengal and Assam

Commission, and Superintendent of

Ethnography in Assam.

With an Introduction by

Sir Charles Lyall, K.C.S.I.

(Published under the orders of the Government of

Eastern Bengal and Assam)

Preface

    This book is an attempt to give a systematic account of the Khasi people, their manners and customs, their ethnological affinities, their laws and institutions, their religious beliefs, their folk-lore, their theories as to their origin, and their language.

    This account would perhaps have assumed a more elaborate and ambitious form were it not that the author has been able to give to it only the scanty leisure of a busy district officer. He has been somewhat hampered by the fact that his work forms part of a series of official publications issued at the expense of the Government of Eastern Bengal and Assam, and that it had to be completed within a prescribed period of time.

    The author gladly takes this opportunity to record his grateful thanks to many kind friends who have helped him either with actual contributions to his material, or with not less valued suggestions and criticisms. The arrangement of the subjects discussed is due to Sir Bampfylde Fuller, lately Lieutenant-Governor of the Province, whose kindly interest in the Khasis will long be remembered by them with affectionate gratitude. The Introduction is from the accomplished pen of Sir Charles Lyall, to whom the author is also indebted for much other help and encouragement. It is now many years since Sir Charles Lyall served in Assam, but his continued regard for the Khasi people bears eloquent testimony to the attractiveness of their character, and to the charm which the homely beauty of their native hills exercises over the minds of all who have had the good fortune to know them.

    To Mr. N. L. Hallward thanks are due for the revision of the proof sheets, and to the Revd. H. P. Knapton for the large share he took in the preparation of the index. The section dealing with folk-lore could hardly have been written but for the generosity of the Revd. Doctor Roberts, of the Welsh Calvinistic Mission in the Khasi and Jaintia Hills, in placing at the author's disposal his collection of the legends current among the people. Many others have helped, but the following names may be specially mentioned, viz.: Mr. J. B. Shadwell, Mr. S. E. Rita, the Revd. C. H. Jenkins, Mr. C. Shadwell, Mr. Dohory Ropmay, U Hormu Roy Diengdoh, U Rai Mohan Diengdoh, U Job Solomon, U Suttra Singh Bordoloi, U San Mawthoh, U Hajam Kishore Singh, U Nissor Singh, and U Sabor Roy.

A bibliography of the Khasis, which the author has attempted to make as complete as possible, has been added. The coloured plates, with one exception, viz., that taken from a sketch by the late Colonel Woodthorpe, have been reproduced from the pictures of Miss Eirene Scott-O'Connor (Mrs. Philip Rogers). The reproductions are the work of Messrs W. Griggs and Sons, as are also the monochromes from photographs by Mrs. Muriel, Messrs. Ghosal Brothers, and the author. Lastly, the author wishes to express his thanks to Srijut Jagat Chandra Goswami, his painstaking assistant, for his care in arranging the author's somewhat voluminous records, and for his work generally in connection with this monograph.

P. R. G.

Bibliography

Agricultural Bulletin No. 5 of 1898.
Allen, B. C.—Assam Census Report, 1901.
Allen, W. J.—Report on the Khasi and Jaintia Hill Territory, 1868.
Aymonier, Monsieur—"Le Cambodge."
Bivar, Colonel H. S.—Administration Report on the Khasi and Jaintia Hills District of 1876.
Buchanan Hamilton—"Eastern India." Edited by Montgomery Martin
Dalton, Colonel E. T.—Descriptive Ethnology of Bengal.
Gait, E. A.—Human Sacrifices in Assam, vol. i., J.A.S.B. of 1898.
Grierson, Doctor G. A.—"Linguistic Survey of India," vol. ii.
Henniker, F. C.—Monograph on gold and silver wares in Assam.
Hooker, Sir Joseph—Himalayan Journals.
Hunter, Sir William—Statistical Account of Assam.
Jeebon Roy, U.—*Ka Niam Khasi*
Jenkins, The Rev. Mr.—"Life and Work in Khasia."
Khasi Mynta—A monthly journal published at Shillong in the Khasi language.
Kuhn, Professor E.—*Über Herkunft und Sprache der transgangetischen Völker*. 1883
Kuhn, Professor E.—*Beiträge zur Sprachenkunde Hinterindiens*. 1889.
Lindsay, Lord—"Lives of the Lindsays."
Logan, J. R A—series of papers on the Ethnology of the Indo-Pacific Islands which appeared in the "Journal of the Indian Archipelago."
Mackenzie, Sir Alexander.—Account of the North-Eastern Frontier
Mills, A. J. M.—Report on the Khasi and Jaintia Hills, 1853
Nissor Singh, U—Hints on the study of the Khasi language.
Nissor Singh, U—Khasi-English dictionary.
Oldham, Thomas—On the geological structure of a portion of the Khasi Hills, Bengal.
Oldham, Thomas—Geology of the Khasi Hills.
Peal, S. E.—On some traces of the Kol-Mon-Anam in the Eastern Naga Hills.
Pryse, Rev. W.—Introduction to the Khasis language, comprising a grammar, selections for reading, and a vocabulary.
Records of the Eastern Bengal and Assam Secretariat.
Roberts, The Rev. H.—Khasi grammar.
Robinson—Assam.
Scott, Sir George—Upper Burma Gazetteer.
Shadwell, J. B.—Notes on the Khasis.
Stack E.—Notes on silk in Assam.
Waddell, Colonel—Account of the Assam tribes.J.A S.B.
Ward, Sir William—Introduction to the Assam Land Revenue Manual.

Weinberg, E.—Report on Excise in Assam.
Yule, Sir Henry—Notes on the Khasi Hills and people.

Contents

Introduction xv-xxvii

Section I.—General.
   Habitat -
   Appearance -
   Physical and General Characteristics -
   Geographical Distribution -
   Origin -
   Affinities -
   Dress -
   Tattooing
   Jewellery -
   Weapons -

Section II.--Domestic Life.
   Occupation -
   Apiculture -
   Houses -
   Villages -
   Furniture and Household Utensils -
   Musical Instruments -
   Agriculture -
   Crops -
   Hunting -
   Fishing -
   Food -
   Drink -
   Games -
   Manufactures -

Section III.--Laws and Customs.
   Tribal Organization -
   State Organization -
   Marriage -
   Divorce -
   Inheritance -
   Adoption -
   Tenure of Land and Laws regarding Land -

Laws regarding other Property
Decision of Disputes -
War -
Human Sacrifices -

Section IV.--Religion.
   General Character of Popular Beliefs -
   Ancestor Worship -
   Worship of Natural Forces and of Deities -
   Religious Rites and Sacrifices, Divination -
   Priesthood -
   Ceremonies and Customs attending Birth and Naming of Children -
   Marriage -
   Ceremonies attending Death -
   Disposal of the Dead -
   Khasi Memorial Stones -
   Festivities, Domestic and Tribal -
   Genna -

Section V.--Folk-Lore.
   Folk-tales -

Section VI.--Miscellaneous.
   Teknonomy
   Khasi Method of Calculating Time -
   The Lynngams -

Section VII.—Language -
Appendices.
   A—Exogamous Clans in the Cherra State -
   B—Exogamous Clans in the Khyrim State -
   C—Divination by Egg-Breaking -

Introduction

In 1908 Sir Bampfylde Fuller, then Chief Commissioner of Amman, proposed and the Government of India sanctioned, the preparation of a series of monographs on the more important tribes and castes of the Province, of which this volume is the first. They were to be undertaken by writers who had special and intimate experience of the races to be described, the accounts of earlier observers being at the same time studied and incorporated; a uniform scheme of treatment was laid down which was to be adhered to in each monograph, and certain limits of size were prescribed.

Major Gurdon, the author of the following pages, who is also, as Superintendent of Ethnography in Assam, editor of the whole series, has enjoyed a long and close acquaintance with the Khasi race, whose institutions he has here undertaken to describe. Thoroughly familiar with their language, he has for three years been in charge as Deputy-Commissioner of the district where they dwell, continually moving among them, and visiting every part of the beautiful region which is called by their name. The administration of the Khasi and Jaintia Hills is an exceptionally interesting field of official responsibility. About half of the district, including the country around the capital, Shillong, is outside the limits of British India, consisting of a collection of small states in political relations, regulated by treaty with the Government of India, which enjoy almost complete autonomy in the management of their local affairs. In the remainder, called the Jaintia Hills, which became British in 1835, it has been the wise policy of the Government to maintain the indigenous system of administration through officers named *dolois*, who preside over large areas of country with very little interference. All the British portion of the hills is what is called a "Scheduled District" under Acts XIV and XV of 1874, and legislation which may be inappropriate to the conditions of the people can be, and is, excluded from operation within it. In these circumstances the administration is carried on in a manner well calculated to win the confidence and attachment of the people, who have to hear few of the burdens which press upon the population elsewhere, and, with the peace and protection guaranteed by British rule, are able to develop their institutions upon indigenous lines. It is now more than forty years since any military operations have been necessary within the hills, and the advance of the district in prosperity and civilization during the last half-century has been very striking.

The first contact between the British and the inhabitants of the Khasi Hills followed upon the acquisition by the East India Company, in consequence of the grant of the *Diwani* of Bengal in 1765, of the district of Sylhet. The Khasis were our neighbours on the north of that district, and to the north-east was the State of Jaintia, [1] ruled over by a chief of Khasi lineage, whose capital, Jaintiapur, was situated in the plain between the Surma river and the hills. Along this frontier, the Khasis, though not averse from trade, and in possession of the quarries which furnished the chief supply of lime to deltaic Bengal, were also known as troublesome marauders, whose raids were a terror to the inhabitants of the plains. Captain R.B. Pemberton, in his Report on the Eastern Frontier (1835), mentions [2] an attack on Jaintia by a force under Major Henniker in 1774, supposed to have been made in retaliation for aggression by the Raja in Sylhet; and Robert Lindsay, who was Resident and Collector of Sylhet about 1778, has an interesting account of the hill tribes and the Raja of Jaintia in the lively narrative embodied in the "Lives of the Lindsays." [3] Lindsay, who made a large fortune by working the lime quarries and thus converting into cash the millions of cowries in which the land-revenue of Sylhet was paid, appears to have imagined that the Khasis, whom he calls "a tribe of independent Tartars," were in direct relations with China, and imported thence the silk cloths [4] which they brought down for sale in the Sylhet markets. A line of forts was established along the foot of the hills to hold the mountaineers in check, and a Regulation, No. 1 of 1799, was passed declaring freedom of trade between them and Sylhet, but prohibiting the supply to them of arms and ammunition, and forbidding any one to pass the Company's frontier towards the hills with arms in his hands.

The outbreak of the first Burma War, in 1824, brought us into closer relations with the Raja of Jaintia, and in April of that year Mr. David Scott, the Governor-General's Agent on the frontier, marched through his territory from Sylhet to Assam, emerging at Raha on the Kalang river, in what is now the Nowgong district. This was the first occasion on which Europeans had entered the hill territory of the Khasi tribes, and the account of the march, quoted in Pemberton's Report, [5] is the earliest authentic information which we possess of the institutions of the Khasi race. Dr. Buchanan-Hamilton, who spent several years at the beginning of the 19th Century in collecting information regarding the people of Eastern India, during which he lived for some time at Goalpara in the Brahmaputra Valley, confused the Khasis with the Garos, and his descriptions apply only to the latter people. The name Garo, however, is still used by the inhabitants of Kamrup in speaking of their Khasi neighbours to the South, and Hamilton only followed the local usage. In 1826 Mr. David Scott, after the expulsion of the Burmese from Assam and the occupation of that province by the Company, entered the Khasi Hills in order to negotiate for the construction of a road through the territory of the Khasi Siem or Chief of Nongkhlaw, which should unite Sylhet with Gauhati. A treaty was concluded with the chief, and the construction of the road began. At Cherrapunji Mr. Scott built for himself a house on the plateau which, two years later, was acquired from the Siem by exchange for land in the plains, as the site of a sanitarium. [6] Everything seemed to promise well, when the peace was suddenly broken by an attack made, in April 1829, by the people of Nongkhlaw on the survey party engaged in laying out the road, resulting in the massacre of two British officers and between fifty and sixty natives. This led to a general confederacy of most or the neighbouring chiefs to resist the British, and a long and harassing war, which was not brought to a close till 1833. Cherrapunji then became the headquarters of the Sylhet Light Infantry, whose commandant was placed in political charge of the district, including the former dominions in the hills of the Raja of Jaintia, which he voluntarily relinquished in 1835 on the confiscation of his territory in the plains.

Cherrapunji, celebrated as the place which has the greatest measured rainfall on the globe, became a popular station, and the discovery of coal there, and at several other places in the hills, attracted to it many visitors, some of whom published accounts of the country and people. The first detailed description was apparently that of the Rev. W. Lish, a Baptist missionary, which appeared in a missionary journal in 1838. In 1840 Capt. Fisher, an officer of the Survey Department, published in the Journal of the Asiatic Society of Bengal [7] an account which showed that the leading characteristics of the Khasi race had already been apprehended; he mentions the prevalence of matriarchy or mother-kinship, notes the absence of polyandry, except in so far as its place was taken by facile divorce, describes the religion as a worship of gods of valleys and hills, draws attention to the system of augury used to ascertain the will of the gods, and gives an account of the remarkable megalithic monuments which everywhere stud the higher plateaus. He also recognizes the fact that the Khasis as a race are totally distinct from the neighbouring hill tribes. In 1841 Mr. W. Robinson, Inspector of Schools in Assam, included an account of the Khasis in a volume on that province which was printed at Calcutta. In 1844 Lieut. Yule (afterwards Sir Henry Yule) published in the Journal of the Bengal Asiatic Society [8] a much more detailed description of the hills and their inhabitants than had been given by Fisher. This formed the basis of many subsequent descriptions, the best known of which is the attractive account contained in the second volume of Sir Joseph Hooker's *Himalayan Journals* [9] published in London in 1854. Sir Joseph visited Cherrapunji in June 1850, and stayed in the hills until the middle of the following November.

Meanwhile the Welsh Calvinistic Methodist Mission, originally located at Sylhet, had extended their operations to Cherrapunji, and in 1842 established a branch there. They applied themselves to the study of the Khasi language, for which, after a trial of the Bengali, they resolved to adopt the Roman character. Their system of expressing the sounds of Khasi has since that time continued in use, and after sixty years' prescription it would be difficult to make a change. Their Welsh nationality led them to use the vowel *y* for the obscure sound represented elsewhere in India by a short *a* (the *u* in the English *but*), and for the consonantal *y* to substitute the vowel *i* : *w* is also used as a vowel, but only in diphthongs (*aw, ew, iw, ow*); in other respects the system agrees fairly well with the standard adopted elsewhere. Primers for the study of the language were printed at Calcutta in 1846 and 1852, and in 1855 appeared the excellent "Introduction to the Khasia language, comprising a grammar, selections for reading, and a Khasi-English vocabulary," of the Rev. W. Pryse. There now exists a somewhat extensive literature in Khasi, both religious and secular. An exhaustive grammar, by the Rev. H. Roberts, was published in Trübner's series of "Simplified Grammars" in 1891, and there are dictionaries, English-Khasi (1875} and Khasi-English (1906), besides many other aids to the study of the language which need not be mentioned here. It is recognized by the Calcutta University as sufficiently cultivated to be offered for the examinations of that body. Two monthly periodicals are published in it at Shillong, to which place the headquarters of the district were removed from Cherrapunji in 1864, and which has been the permanent seat of the Assam Government since the Province was separated from Bengal in 1874.

The isolation of the Khasi race, in the midst of a great encircling population all of whom belong to the Tibeto-Burman stock, and the remarkable features presented by their language and institutions, soon attracted the attention of comparative philologists and ethnologists. An account of their researches will be found in Dr. Grierson's *Linguistic Survey of India*, vol. ii. Here it will be sufficient to mention the important work of Mr. J. R. Logan, who, in a series of papers published at Singapore between 1850 and 1857 in the *Journal of the Indian Archipelago* (of which he was the editor), demonstrated the relationship which exists between the Khasis and certain peoples of Further India, the chief representatives of whom are the Mons or Talaings of Pegu and Tenasserim, the Khmers of Cambodia, and the majority of the inhabitants of Annam. He was even able, through the means of vocabularies furnished to him by the late Bishop Bigandet, to discover the nearest kinsmen of the Khasis in the Palaungs, a tribe inhabiting one of the Shan States to the north-east of Mandalay on the middle Salween. With the progress of research it became apparent that the Mon-Khmer group of Indo-China thus constituted, to which the Khasis belong, was in some way connected with the large linguistic family in the Indian Peninsula once called Kolarian, but now more generally known as *Munda*, who inhabit the hilly region of Chutia Nagpur and parts of the Satpura range in the Central Provinces. Of these tribes the principal are the Santhals, the Mundas, and the Korkus. In physical characters they differ greatly from the Indo-Chinese Khasis, but the points of resemblance in their languages and in some of their institutions cannot be denied; and the exact nature of the relation between them is as yet one of the unsolved problems of ethnology.

The work of Logan was carried further by Prof. Ernst Kuhn, of Munich, who in 1888 and 1889 published important contributions to our knowledge of the languages and peoples of Further India. More recently our acquaintance with the phonology of Khasi and its relatives has been still further advanced by the labours of Pater W. Schmidt, of Vienna, whose latest work, *Die Mon-Khmer Völker, ein Bindeglied zwischen Völkern Zentralasiens und Austronesiens* (Braunschweig, 1906), has established the relationship of Khasi not only to the Mon-Khmer languages, but also to Nicobarese and several dialects spoken by wild tribes in the Malay Peninsula.

There still remains much to be done before the speech of the Khasi nation can be considered to have been thoroughly investigated. In the *Linguistic Survey* four dialects are dealt with, the standard literary form, founded on the language of Cherrapunji, the *Pnar* or *Synteng*, of Jowai, the *War*, spoken in the valleys on the southern face of the hills, and the *Lyngngam*, spoken in the tract adjacent to the Garos on the west. Major Gurdon (p. 203) mentions a fifth, that of Jirang or Mynnar, spoken in the extreme north, and there may be others. A great desideratum for linguistic purposes is a more adequate method of recording sounds, and especially differences of tone, than that adopted for the standard speech, which though sufficient for practical purposes, does not accurately represent either the quantity or the quality of the vowels, and leaves something to be desired as regards the consonants (especially those only faintly sounded or suppressed). These things, no doubt, will come in time. The immense advance which has been made in education by the Khasis during the last half-century has enabled some among them to appreciate the interesting field for exploration and study which their own country and people afford; and there is reason to hope that with European guidance the work of record will progress by the agency of indigenous students.

It remains to summarize briefly the principal distinctive features of this vigorous and sturdy race, who have preserved their independence and their ancestral institutions through many centuries in the face of the attractions offered by the alien forms of culture around them.

In the first place, their social organization presents one of the most perfect examples still surviving of matriarchal institutions, carried out with a logic and thoroughness which, to those accustomed to regard the status and authority of the father as the foundation of society, are exceedingly remarkable. Not only is the mother the head and source, and only bond of union, of the family: in the most primitive part of the hills, the Synteng country, she is the only owner of real property, and through her alone is inheritance transmitted. The father has no kinship with his children, who belong to their mother's clan; what he earns goes to his own matriarchal stock, and at his death his bones are deposited in the cromlech of his mother's kin. In Jowai he neither lives nor eats in his wife's house, but visits it only after dark (p. 76). In the veneration of ancestors, which is the foundation of the tribal piety, the primal ancestress (*Ka Iawbei*) and her brother are the only persons regarded. The flat memorial stones set up to perpetuate the memory of the dead are called after the woman who represents the clan (*maw kynthei* p. 150), and the standing stones ranged behind them are dedicated to the male kinsmen on the mother's side.

In harmony with this scheme of ancestor worship, the other spirits to whom propitiation is offered are mainly female, though here male personages also figure (pp. 106-109). The powers of sickness and death are all female, and these are those most frequently worshipped (p. 107). The two protectors of the household are goddesses (p. 112), though with them is also revered the first father of the clan, *U Thawlang*.

Priestesses assist at all sacrifices, and the male officiants are only their deputies (p. 121); in one important state, Khyrim, the High Priestess and actual head of the State is a woman, who combines in her person sacerdotal and regal functions (p. 70).

The Khasi language, so far as known, is the only member of the Mon-Khmer family which possesses a grammatical gender, distinguishing all nouns as masculine and feminine; and here also the feminine nouns immensely preponderate (p. 206). The pronouns of the second (me, pha) and third person (u, ka) have separate forms for the sexes in the singular, but in the plural only one is used (phi, ki), and this is the plural form of the feminine singular.

It may perhaps be ascribed to the pre-eminence accorded by the Khasis to the female sex that successive censuses have shown that the women of this race considerably exceed the men in number. According to the census of 1901, there are 1,118 females to every 1,000 male Khasis. This excess, however, is surpassed by that of the Lushais, 1,191 to 1,000, and it may possibly be due to the greater risks to life encountered by the men, who venture far into the plains as traders and porters, while the women stay at home. Habits of intemperance, which are confined to the male sex, may also explain a greater mortality among them.

It would be interesting to investigate the effect on reproduction of the system of matriarchy which governs Khasi family life. The increase of the race is very slow. In the census of 1891 there were enumerated only 117 children under 5 to every hundred married women between 15 and 40, and in 1901 this number fell to 108. It has been suggested that the independence of the wife, and the facilities which exist for divorce, lead to restrictions upon child-bearing, and thus keep the population stationary. The question might with advantage be examined at the census of 1911.

The next characteristic of the Khasis which marks them out for special notice is their method of divination for ascertaining the causes of misfortune and the remedies to be applied. All forms of animistic religion make it their chief business to avert the wrath of the gods, to which calamities of all kinds—sickness, storm, murrain, loss of harvest—are ascribed, by some kind of propitiation; and in this the Khasis are not singular. But it is somewhat surprising to find among them the identical method of *extispicium* which was in use among the Romans, as well as an analogous development in the shape of egg-breaking, fully described by Major Gurdon (p. 221), which seems to have been known to diviners in ancient Hellas. [10] This method has (with much else in Khasi practice) been adopted by the former subjects of the Khasis, the Mikirs; but it does not appear to be prevalent among any other of the animistic tribes within the boundaries of India.

The third remarkable feature of Khasi usage is the custom, which prevails to this day, of setting up great memorials of rough stone, of the same style and character as the *menhirs* and *cromlechs* which are found in Western Europe, Northern Africa, and Western Asia. It is very surprising to a visitor, unprepared for the sight by previous information, to find himself on arrival at the plateau in the midst of great groups of standing and table stones exactly like those he may have seen in Brittany, the Channel Islands, the south of England, or the Western Isles. Unfortunately the great earthquake of June 1897 overthrew many of the finest of these megalithic monuments; but several still remain, and of these Major Gurdon has given an excellent description (pp. 144 sqq.), with an explanation of the different forms which they assume and the objects with which they are erected. Other races in India besides the Khasis set up stone memorials; but none, perhaps, to the same extent or with the same systematic purpose and arrangement.

In conclusion, I have only to commend this work to the consideration of all interested in the accurate and detailed description of primitive custom. I lived myself for many years among the Khasis, and endeavoured to find out what I could about them; but much of what Major Gurdon records is new to me, though the book generally agrees with what I was able to gather of their institutions and characteristics. It is, I think, an excellent example of research, and well fitted to stand at the head of a series which may be expected to make an important contribution to the data of anthropology.

C. J. Lyall.

November, **1906.**

THE KHASIS

CHAPTER I

General

Habitat.
The Khasis reside in the Khasi and Jaintia Hills district of Assam. They number 176,614 souls, which total is made up of:—

Khasis	107,515
Syntengs	47,883
Christian Khasis	17,125
Khasis inhabiting other districts	4,091
	176,614

The Khasi and Jaintia Hills district is situated between 25° 1' and 26° 5' North Latitude, and between 90° 47' and 92° 52' East Longitude. It contains an area of 6,157 square miles, with a total population at the Census of 1901 of 202,250 souls. In addition to the Khasis there are some members of Bodo tribes inhabiting parts of the district.

The Lynngam tribe appears to have been reckoned in 1901 as Khasi, there being no separate record at the last Census of these people.

The district is split up into two divisions, the Khasi Hills proper and the Jaintia Hills. The Khasi Hills form the western portion of the district and the Jaintia Hills the eastern. The Khasis inhabit the Khasi Hills proper, and the Syntengs, or Pnars, the Jaintia Hills. The latter hills take their name from the Rajas of Jaintia, the former rulers of this part of the country, who had as their capital Jaintiapur, a place situated at the foot of the Jaintia Hills on the southern side, which now falls within the boundaries of the Sylhet district. The Lynngams inhabit the western portion of the Khasi Hills proper. A line drawn north and south through the village of Nongstoin may be said to form their eastern boundary, and the Kamrup and Sylhet districts their northern and southern boundaries, respectively. The people known as *Bhois* in these hills, who are many of them really Mikirs, live in the low hills to the north and north-east of the district, the term "Bhoi" being a territorial name rather than tribal. The eastern boundary of the Lynngam country may be said to form their north-western boundary. The Wárs inhabit the precipitous slopes and deep valleys to the south of the district. Their country extends along the entire southern boundary of the district to the Jadukata, or Kenchi-iong, river where the Lynngam territory may be said to commence towards the south. There are some Hadem colonies in the extreme eastern portions of the Jaintia Hills. It is these colonies which are sometimes referred to by other writers as "Kuki Colonies." They are settlers from the North Cachar Sub-division of the Cachar district within recent years. It is possible that the title Hadem may have some connection with *Hidimba*, the ancient name for the North Cachar Hills.

Appearance.

The colour of the Khasi skin may be described as being usually brown, varying from dark to a light yellowish brown, according to locality. The complexion of the people who inhabit the uplands is of a somewhat lighter shade, and many of the women, especially those who live at Nongkrem, Laitlyngkot, Mawphlang, and other villages of the surrounding high plateaux possess that pretty gipsy complexion that is seen in the South of Europe amongst the peasants. The people of Cherrapunji village are specially fair. The Syntengs of the Jaintia Hills are darker than the Khasi uplanders. The Wárs who live in the low valleys are frequently more swarthy than the Khasis. The Bhois have the flabby-looking yellow skin of the Mikirs, and the Lynngams are darker than the Khakis. The Lynngams are probably the darkest complexioned people in the hills, and if one met them in the plains one would not be able to distinguish them from the ordinary Kachari or Rabha. The nose in the Khasi is somewhat depressed, the nostrils being often large and prominent. The forehead is broad and the space between the eyes is often considerable. The skull may be said to be almost brachy-cephalic, the average cephalic index of 77 Khasi subjects, measured by Col. Waddell and Major Hare, I.M.S., being as high as 77.3 and 77.9, respectively. According to these data the Khasis are more brachy-cephalic than the Aryans, whose measurements appear in Crooke's tables, more brachy-cephalic than the 100 Mundas whose measurements appear in Risley's tables, more brachy-cephalic than the Dravidians, but less brachy-cephalic than the Burmans, whose measurements also appear in Crooke's tables. It would be interesting to compare some head measurements of Khasis with Japanese, but unfortunately the necessary data are not available in the case of the latter people. The Khasi head may be styled sub-brachy-cephalic. Eyes are of medium size, in colour black or brown. In the Jaintia Hills hazel eyes are not uncommon, especially amongst females. Eyelids are somewhat obliquely set, but not so acutely as in the Chinese and some other Mongols. Jaws frequently are prognathous, mouth large, with sometimes rather thick lips. Hair black, straight, and worn long, the hair of people who adopt the old style being caught up in a knot at the back. Some males cut the hair short with the exception of a single lock at the back, which is called *u niuhtrong* or *u niuh-' iawbei* (i.e. the grandmother's lock.) The forepart of the head is often shaven. It is quite the exception to see a beard, although the moustache is not infrequently worn. The Lynngams pull out the hairs of the moustache with the exception of a few hairs an either side of the upper lip.

Physical and General Characteristics

The Khasis are usually short in stature, with bodies well nourished, and the males are extremely muscular. The trunk is long in proportion to the rest of the body, and broad at the waist; calves are very highly developed. The women, when young are comely, of a buxom type, and, like the men, with highly-developed calves, the latter always being considered a beauty. The children are frequently remarkably pretty. Khasis carry very heavy burdens, it being the custom for the coolie of the country to carry a maund, or 82 lbs. weight, or even more occasionally, on his back, the load being fixed by means of a cane band which is worn across the forehead; women carry almost as heavy loads as the men. The coolies, both male and female, commonly do the journey between Cherrapunji and Shillong, or between Shillong and Jowai, in one day, carrying the heavy loads above mentioned. Each of the above journeys is some thirty miles. They carry their great loads of rice and salt from Therria to Cherrapunji, an ascent of about 4,000 feet in some three to four miles, in the day. The Khasis are probably the best porters in the north of India, and have frequently been requisitioned for transport purposes on military expeditions.

The people are cheerful in disposition, and are light-hearted by nature, and, unlike the plains people, seem to thoroughly appreciate a joke. It is pleasant to hear on the road down to Theriaghat from Cherrapunji, in the early morning the whole hillside resounding with the scraps of song and peals of laughter of the coolies, as they run nimbly down the short cuts on their way to market. The women are specially cheerful, and pass the time of day and bandy jokes with passers-by with quite an absence of reserve. The Khasis are certainly more industrious than the Assamese, are generally good-tempered, but are occasionally prone to sudden outbursts of anger, accompanied by violence. They are fond of music, and rapidly learn the hymn tunes which are taught them by the Welsh missionaries. Khasis are devoted to their offspring, and the women make excellent nurses for European children, frequently becoming much attached to their little charges. The people, like the Japanese, are fond of nature. A Khasi loves a day out in the woods, where he thoroughly enjoys himself. If he does not go out shooting or fishing, he is content to sit still and contemplate nature. He has a separate name for each of the commoner birds and flowers. He also has names for many butterflies and moths. These are traits which are not found usually in the people of India. He is not above manual labour, and even the Khasi clerk in the Government offices is quite ready to take his turn at the hoe in his potato garden. The men make excellent stonemasons and carpenters, and are ready to learn fancy carpentry and mechanical work. They are inveterate chewers of *supari* and the pan leaf (when they can get the latter), both men, women, and children; distances in the interior being often measured by the number of betel-nuts that are usually chewed on a journey. They are not addicted usually to the use of opium or other intoxicating drugs. They are, however, hard drinkers, and consume large quantities of spirit distilled from rice or millet. Rice beer is also manufactured; this is used not only as a beverage, but also for ceremonial purposes. Spirit drinking is confined more to the inhabitants of the high plateaux and to the people of the Wár country, the Bhois and Lynngams being content to partake of rice beer. The Mikirs who inhabit what is known as the "Bhoi" country, lying to the north of the district, consume a good deal of opium, but it must be remembered that they reside in a malarious *terai* country, and that the use of opium, or some other prophylactic, is probably beneficial as a preventive of fever. The Khasis, like other people of Indo-Chinese origin, are much addicted to gambling. The people, and especially those who inhabit the Wár country, are fond of litigation. Col. Bivar remarks, "As regards truthfulness the people do not excel, for they rarely speak the truth unless to suit their own interests." Col. Bivar might have confined this observation to the people who live in the larger centres of population, or who have been much in contact with the denizens of the plains. The inhabitants of the far interior are, as a rule, simple and straightforward people, and are quite as truthful and honest as peasants one meets in other countries. My impression is that the Khasis are not less truthful certainly than other Indian communities. McCosh, writing in 1837, speaks well of the Khasis. The following is his opinion of them:—"They are a powerful, athletic race of men, rather below the middle size, with a manliness of gait and demeanour. They are fond of their mountains, and look down with contempt upon the degenerate race of the plains, jealous of their power, brave in action, and have an aversion to falsehood."

Khasis of the interior who have adopted Christianity are generally cleaner in their persons than the non-Christians, and their women dress better than the latter and have an air of self-respect about them. The houses in a Christian village are also far superior, especially where there are resident European missionaries. Khasis who have become Christians often take to religion with much earnestness (witness the recent religious revival in these hills, which is estimated by the Welsh missionaries to have added between 4,000 and 5,000 converts to Christianity), and are model Sabbatarians, it being a pleasing sight to see men, women, and children trooping to church on a Sunday dressed in their best, and with quite the Sunday expression on their faces one sees in England. It is a pleasure to hear the sound of the distant church bell on the hill-side on a Sunday evening, soon to be succeeded by the beautiful Welsh hymn tunes which, when wafted across the valleys, carry one's thoughts far away. The Welsh missionaries have done, and continue to do, an immense amount of good amongst these people. It would be an evil day for the Khasis if anything should occur to arrest the progress of the mission work in the Khasi Hills.

Geographical Distribution.

The Khasis inhabit the Khasi and Jaintia Hills, although there are a few Khasi settlers in the neighbouring plains districts. The Census Report of 1901 gives the following figures of Khasi residents in the plains:

Cachar	333
Sylbet	3,083
Goalpara	4
Kamrup	191
Darrong	90
Nowgong	29
Sibnagar	62
Lakhimpur	22
Lushai Hills	77
North Cachar	32
Naga Hills	82
Garo Hills	117
Manipur	69
Total	4,091 [11]

The following information regarding the general aspect of the Khasi and Jaintia Hills district, with some additions, is derived from Sir William Hunter's Statistical Account of Assam. The district consists almost entirely of hills, only a very small portion lying in the plains. The slope of the hills on the southern side is very steep until a table-land is met with at an elevation of about 4,000 feet at Cherrapunji. Higher up there is another plateau at Mawphlang. This is the highest portion of the hills, some villages being found at as high an elevation as close on 6,000 feet above see level. Fifteen miles to the east of Mawphlang, and in the same range, is situated the civil station of Shillong, at an average elevation of about 4,900 feet. The elevation of the Shillong Peak, the highest hill in the district, is 6,450 feet above sea level. On the northern side of the hills are two plateaux, one between 1,000 and 2,000 feet below the level of Shillong, and another at an elevation of about 2,000 feet above sea level. In general features all these plateaux are much alike, and consist of a succession of undulating downs, broken here and there by the valleys of the larger hill streams. In the higher ranges, where the hills have been denuded of forest, the country is covered with short grass, which becomes longer and more rank in the lower elevations. This denudation of forest has been largely due to the wood being used by the Khasis for fuel for iron smelting in days gone by. The Government, however, has taken steps to protect the remaining forests from further spoliation. A remarkable feature is the presence of numerous sacred groves situated generally just below the brows of the hills. In these woods are to be found principally oak and rhododendron trees. The fir-tree (Pinus Khasia) is first met with on the road from Gauhati to Shillong, at Umsning, at an elevation of about 2,500 feet. In the neighbourhood of Shillong the fir grows profusely, but the finest fir-trees are to be seen in the Jowai sub-division. In the vicinity of Nongpoh is observed the beautiful *nahor* or *nageswar*, the iron-wood tree. The latter is also to be found on the southern slopes of the hills in the Jowai sub-division. There are some *sal* forests to the west and south of Nongpoh, where the *sal* trees are almost as large as those to be found in the Garo Hills. Between Shillong and Jowai there are forests of oak, the country being beautifully wooded. Chestnuts and birches are also fairly common. The low hills on the northern and western sides of the district are clad with dense forests of bamboo, of which there are many varieties. The Pandanus or screw-pine is to be met with on the southern slopes. Regarding the geological formation of the hills, I extract a few general remarks from the Physical and Political Geography of Assam. The Shillong plateau consists of a great mass of gneiss, bare on the northern border, where it is broken into hills, for the most part low and very irregular in outline, with numerous outliers in the Lower Assam Valley, even close up to the Himalayas. In the central region the gneiss is covered by transition or sub-metamorphic rocks, consisting of a strong band of quartzites overlying a mass of earthy schists. In the very centre of the range, where the table-land attains its highest elevation, great masses of intrusive diorite and granite occur; and the latter is found in dykes piercing the gneiss and sub-metamorphic series throughout the southern half of the boundary of the plains. To the south, in contact with the gneiss and sub-metamorphics is a great volcanic outburst of trap, which is stratified, and is brought to the surface with the general rise of elevation along the face of the hills between Shella and Theriaghat south of Cherrapunji. This has been described as the "Sylhet trap." South of the main axis of this metamorphic and volcanic mass are to be found strata of two well defined series: (1) the cretaceous, and (2) nummulitic. The cretaceous contains several important coalfields. The nummulitic series, which overlies the cretaceous, attains a thickness of 900 feet in the Theria river, consisting of alternating strata of compact limestones and sandstones. It is at the exposure of these rocks on their downward dip from the edge of the plateau that are situated the extensive limestone quarries of the Khasi Hills. There are numerous limestone caves and underground water-courses on the southern face of the hills. This series contains coal-beds, e.g. the Cherrafield and that at Lakadong in the Jaintia Hills. Some description of the remarkable Kyllang Rock may not be out of place. Sir Joseph Hooker describes it as a dome of red granite, 5,400 feet above sea level, accessible from the north and east, but almost perpendicular to the southward where the slope is 80° for 600 feet. The elevation is said by Hooker to be 400 feet above the mean level of the surrounding ridges and 700 feet above the bottom of the valleys. The south or steepest side is encumbered with enormous detached blocks, while the north is clothed with forests containing red tree-rhododendrons and oaks. Hooker says that on its skirts grows a "white bushy rhododendron" which he found nowhere else. There is, however, a specimen of it now in the Shillong Lake garden. Numerous orchids are to be found in the Kyllang wood, notably a beautiful white one, called by the Khasis *u'tiw kyllang synrai*, which blooms in the autumn. The view from the top of the rock is very extensive, especially towards the north, where a magnificent panorama of the Himalayas is obtained in the autumn. The most remarkable phenomenon of any kind in the country is undoubtedly the enormous quantity of rain which falls at Cherrapunji. [12] Practically the whole of the rainfall occurs in the rains, i.e. from May to October. The remainder of the district is less rainy. The climate of the central plateau of the Shillong range is very salubrious, but the low hills in parts of the district are malarious. The effect of the different climates can at once be seen by examining the physique of the inhabitants. The Khasis who live in the high central plateaux are exceptionally healthy and strong, but those who live in the unhealthy "Bhoi country" to the north, and in the Lynngam portion to the west of the district, are often stunted and sickly. Not so, however, the Wárs who live on the southern slopes, for although their country is very hot at certain times of the year, it does not appear to be abnormally unhealthy except in certain villages, such as Shella, Borpunji, Umniuh, and in Narpuh in the Jaintia Hills.

Origin.

The origin of the Khasis is a very vexed question. Although it is probable that the Khasis have inhabited their present abode for at any rate a considerable period, there seems to be a fairly general belief amongst them that they originally came from elsewhere. The Rev. H. Roberts, in the introduction to his Khasi Grammar, states that "tradition, such as it is, connects them politically with the Burmese, to whose king they were up to a comparatively recent date rendering homage, by sending him an annual tribute in the shape of an axe, as an emblem merely of submission." Another tradition points out the north as the direction from which they migrated, and Sylhet as the terminus of their wanderings, from which they were ultimately driven back into their present hill fastnesses by a great flood, after a more or less peaceful occupation of that district. It was on the occasion of this great flood, the legend runs, that the Khasi lost the art of writing, the Khasi losing his book whilst he was swimming at the time of this flood, whereas the Bengali managed to preserve his. Owing to the Khasis having possessed no written character before the advent of the Welsh missionaries there are no histories as is the case with the Ahoms of the Assam Valley, and therefore no record of their journeys. Mr. Shadwell, the oldest living authority we have on the Khasis, and one who has been in close touch with the people for more than half a century, mentions a tradition amongst them that they originally came into Assam from Burma via the Patkoi range, having followed the route of one of the Burmese invasions. Mr. Shadwell has heard them mention the name Patkoi as a hill they met with on their journey. All this sort of thing is, however, inexpressibly vague. In the chapter dealing with "Affinities" have been given some reasons for supposing that the Khasis and other tribes of the Mon-Anam family, originally occupied a large portion of the Indian continent. Where the actual cradle of the Mon-Anam race was, is as impossible to state, as it is to fix upon the exact tract of country from which the Aryans sprang. With reference to the Khasi branch of the Mon-Anam family, it would seem reasonable to suppose that if they are not the autochthons of a portion of the hills on the southern bank of the Brahmaputra, and if they migrated to Assam from some other country, it is not unlikely that they followed the direction of the different irruptions of foreign peoples into Assam of which we have authentic data, i.e.

from south-east to north-west, as was the case with the Ahom invaders of Assam who invaded Assam from their settlements in the Shan States via the Patkoi range, the different Burmese invasions, the movements of the Khamtis and, again, the Singphos, from the country to the east of the Hukong Valley. Whether the first cousins of the Khasis, the Mons, moved to their present abode from China, whether they are the aborigines of the portion of Burma they at present occupy, or were one of the races "of Turanian origin" who, as Forbes thinks, originally occupied the valley of the Ganges before the Aryan invasion, must be left to others more qualified than myself to determine. Further, it is difficult to clear up the mystery of the survival, in an isolated position, of people like the Ho-Mundas, whose language and certain customs exhibit points of similarity with those of the Khasis, in close proximity to the Dravidian tribes and at a great distance from the Khasis, there being no people who exhibit similar characteristics inhabiting countries situated in between; but we can, I think, reasonably suppose that the Khasis are an offshoot of the Mon people of Further India in the light of the historical fact I have quoted, i.e. that the movements of races into Assam have usually, although not invariably, taken place from the east, and not from the west. The tendency for outside people to move into Assam from the east still continues.

Affinities.

The late Mr. S. E. Peal, F.R.G.S., in an interesting and suggestive paper published in the Journal of the Asiatic Society of Bengal in 1896, drew attention to certain illustrations of "singular shoulder-headed celts," found only in the Malay Peninsula till the year 1875, when they were also discovered in Chota Nagpur, and figured in the Journal of the Asiatic Society of Bengal for June of that year. These "celts" are, as the name implies, ancient stone implements. Mr. Peal goes on to state the interesting fact that when he was at Ledo and Tikak, Naga villages, east of Makum, on the south-east frontier of the Lakhimpur district of Assam, in 1895, he found iron implements, miniature hoes, used by the Nagas, of a similar shape to the "shoulder-headed celts" which had been found in the Malay Peninsula and Chota Nagpur. Now the peculiarly shaped Khasi hoe or *mo-khiw*, a sketch of which is given, with its far projecting shoulders, is merely an enlarged edition of the Naga hoe described by Peal, and may therefore be regarded as a modern representative in iron, although on an enlarged scale, of the "shoulder-headed celts." Another interesting point is that, according to Forbes, the Burmese name for these stone celts is *mo-gyo*. Now the Khasi name for the hoe is *mo-khiw*. The similarity between the two words seems very strong. Forbes says the name *mo-gyo* in Burmese means "cloud or sky chain," which he interprets "thunderbolt," the popular belief there, as in other countries, being that these palaeolithic implements fell from heaven. Although the Khasi name *mo-khiw* has no connection whatsoever with aerolites, it is a singular coincidence that the name for the Khasi hoe of the present day should almost exactly correspond with the Burmese name for the palaeolithic implement found in Burma and the Malay Peninsula, and when it is remembered that these stone celts are of a different shape from that of the stone implements which have been found in India (with the exception of Chota Nagpur), there would seem to be some grounds for believing that the Khasis are connected with people who inhabited the Malay Peninsula and Chota Nagpur at the time of the Stone Age. [13] That these people were what Logan calls the Mon-Anam, may possibly be the case. Mr. Peal goes on to state, "the discovery is interesting for other reasons, it possibly amounts to a demonstration that Logan (who it is believed was the first to draw attention to the points of resemblance between the languages of the Mon-Anam or Mon-Khmêr and those of the Mundas and the Khasis), was correct in assuming that at one time the Mon-Anam races and influence extended from the Vindyas all over the Ganges Basin, even over Assam, the northern border of the Ultra Indian Peninsula." Mr. Peal then remarks that the Eastern Nagas of the Tirap, Namstik, and Sonkap group "are strikingly like them (i.e. the Mon-Anam races), in many respects, the women being particularly robust, with pale colour and at times rosy cheeks." The interesting statement follows that the men wear the Khasi-Mikir sleeveless coat. Under the heading of dress this will be found described as a garment which leaves the neck and arms bare, with a fringe at the bottom and with a row of tassels across the chest, the coat being fastened by frogs in front. It is a garment of a distinctive character and cannot be mistaken; it used to be worn largely by the Khasis, and is still used extensively by the Syntengs and Lynngams and by the Mikirs, and that it should have been found amongst these Eastern Nagas is certainly remarkable. It is to be regretted that the investigations of the Ethnographical Survey, as at present conducted, have not extended to these Eastern Nagas, who inhabit tracts either outside British territory or in very remote places on its confines, so that we are at present unable to state whether any of these tribes possess other points of affinity, as regards social customs, with the Khasis, but it will be noticed in the chapter dealing with memorial stones that some of the Naga tribes are in the habit of erecting monoliths somewhat similar in character to those of the Khasis, and that the Mikirs (who wear the Khasi sleeveless coat), erect memorial stones exactly similar to those of the Khasis. The evidence seems to suggest a theory that the Mon-Anam race, including of course the Khasis, occupied at one time a much larger area in the mountainous country to the south of the Brahmaputra in Assam than it does at present. Further references will be found to this point in the section dealing with memorial stones. The fact that the Ho-Mundas of Chota Nagpur also erect memorial stones and that they possess death customs very similar to those of the Khasis, has also been noticed in the same chapter. We have, therefore, the following points of similarity as regards customs between the Khasis on the one hand, certain Eastern Naga tribes, the Mikirs, and the ancient inhabitants of the Malay Peninsula on the other:—

(a) Peculiarly shaped hoe, i.e. the hoe with far projecting shoulders

1. Khasis.
2. Certain Eastern Naga tribes.

3. The ancient inhabitants of the Malay Peninsula.
   4. The ancient inhabitants of Chota Nagpur (the Ho-Mundas?).

(b) Sleeveless coat

   1. Khasis.
   2. Mikirs.
   3. Certain Eastern Naga tribes.

(c) Memorial stones

   1. Khasis.
   2. Mikirs.
   3. Certain Eastern Naga tribes.
   4. Ho-Mundas of Chota Nagpur.

I wish to draw no definite conclusions from the above facts, but they are certainly worth considering with reference to Logan's theory as stated by Peal; the theory being based on Logan's philological inquiries. Thanks to the labours of Grierson, Logan, and Kuhn in the linguistic field, we know that the languages of the Mon-Khmêr group in Burma and the Malay Peninsula are intimately connected with Khasi. I say, intimately, advisedly, for not only are roots of words seen to be similar, but the order of the words in the sentence is found to be the same, indicating that both these people think in the same order when wishing to express themselves by speech. There are also syntactical agreements. We may take it as finally proved by Dr. Grierson and Professor Kuhn that the Mon-Khmêr, Palaung, Wa, and Khasi languages are closely connected. In the section of the Monograph which deals with language some striking similarities between the languages of these tribes will be pointed out. We have not so far been able to discover social customs common to the Palaungs and the Khasis; this is probably due to the conversion of the Palaungs to Buddhism, the change in the religion of the people having possibly caused the abandonment of the primitive customs of the tribe. In a few years' time, if the progressive rate of conversions of Khasis to Christianity continues, probably the greater number of the Khasi social customs will have disappeared and others will have taken their place, so that it cannot be argued that because no manifest social customs can now be found common to the Khasis and the Palaungs, there is no connection between these two tribes. The strong linguistic affinity between these two peoples and the wild *Was* of Burma points to an intimate connection between all three in the past. As knowledge of the habits of the wild *Was* improves, it is quite possible that social customs of this tribe may be found to be held in common with the Khasis. With regard to social affinities it will be interesting to note the Palaung folk-tale of the origin of their Sawbwa, which is reproduced in Sir George Scott's Upper Burma Gazetteer. The Sawbwa, it is related, is descended from the Naga Princess Thusandi who lived in the *Nat* tank on the

Mongok hills and who laid three eggs, from one of which was born the ancestor of the Palaung Sawbwa. Here we see how the Palaung regards the egg, and it is noteworthy that the Khasis lay great stress on its potency in divination for the purposes of religious sacrifices, and that at death it is placed on the stomach of the deceased and is afterwards broken at the funeral pyre. Amongst some of the tribes of the Malay Archipelago also the *Gaji-Guru* or medicine-man "can see from the yolk of an egg, broken whilst sacramentally counting from one to seven, from what illness a man is suffering and what has caused it." Here we have an almost exactly parallel case to the Khasi custom of egg-breaking.

In the Palaung folk-tale above referred to the importance of the egg in the eyes of Palaung is demonstrated, and we know how the Khasi regards it. But the folk-tale is also important as suggesting that the ancient people of Pagan were originally serpent-worshippers, i.e. Nágás, and it is interesting to note that the Rumai or Palaung women of the present day "wear a dress which is like the skin of the Naga (snake)." Is it possible that the Khasi superstition of the *thlen*, or serpent demon, and its worship, an account of which will be found under the heading of "Human Sacrifices" in the Monograph, has anything to do with the ancient snake-worship of the people of Pagan, and also of the ancient inhabitants of Naga-Dwipa, and that amongst the wild *Was* the custom of head-hunting may have taken the place of the Khasi human sacrifices to the *thlen*?

Notwithstanding that Sir George Scott says the story has very Burman characteristics, the Palaung folk-tale is further interesting in that it speaks of the Sawbwa of the Palaungs being descended from a *princess*. This might be a suggestion of the matriarchate.

It can well be imagined how important a matter it is also, in the light of Grierson's and Kuhn's linguistic conclusions, to ascertain whether any of the Mon-Khmêr people in Anam and Cambodia and neighbouring countries possess social customs in common with the Khasis. In case it may be possible for French and Siamese ethnologists in Further India to follow up these inquiries at some subsequent date, it may be stated that information regarding social customs is required with reference to the people who speak the following languages in Anam and Cambodia and Cochin China which belong to the Mon-Khmêr group—*Suk, Stieng, Bahnar, Anamese, Khamen-Boran, Xong, Samre, Khmu,* and *Lamet*.

Notwithstanding our failure up till now to find any patent and direct social customs in common between the Khasis and the Palaungs, I am in hopes that we may yet discover some such affinities. Mr. Lowis, the Superintendent of Ethnography in Burma, states that there is no vestige of the matriarchal system among the Palaungs; but there is the folk-tale I have quoted above. In matters of succession, inheritance, &c., the Palaungs, Mr. Lowis, says, profess to follow the Shans, whose customs in this regard have a Buddhistic basis. The Palaungs are devout Buddhists, and, like the Burmans and Shans, bury their lay dead, whereas the Khasis invariably burn. There is nothing in the shape of memorial stones amongst the Palaungs. *Primâ facie* these appear to be points of differentiation between the Palaungs and the Khasis; but they should not, as has already been stated, be regarded as proof positive that the tribes are not connected, and it is possible that under the influence of Buddhism the Palaungs may have almost entirely abandoned their ancient customs, like the Christian Khasis.

Having noticed some similarities as regards birth customs, as described in Dr. Frazer's "Golden Bough," between the Khasis and certain inhabitants of the Dutch East Indies, I wrote to the Dutch authorities in Batavia requesting certain further information. My application was treated with the greatest courtesy, and I am indebted to the kindness of the President, his secretary, and Mr. C. M. Pleyte, Lecturer of Indonesian Ethnology at the Gymnasium of William III., at Batavia, for some interesting as well as valuable information. With reference to possible Malay influence in the countries inhabited by the people who speak the Mon-Khmêr group of languages in Further India, it was thought desirable to ascertain whether any of the people inhabiting the Dutch East Indies possessed anything in common with the Khasis, who also belong to the Mon-Khmêr group. There are, according to Mr. Pleyte, pure matriarchal customs to be found amongst the Minangkabe Malays inhabiting the Padang uplands and adjacent countries, in Sumatra, in Agam, the fifty Kotas, and Tanah Datar, more or less mixed with patriarchal institutions; they are equally followed by the tribes inhabiting parts of Korinchi and other places. The apparently strong survival of the matriarchate in parts of the island of Sumatra, as compared with this corresponding most characteristic feature of the Khasis, is a point for consideration. Mr. Pleyte goes on to state "regarding ancestor-worship, it may be said that this is found everywhere throughout the whole Archipelago; even the tribes that have already adopted Islam, venerate the spirits of their departed." The same might be said of some of the Khasis who have accepted Christianity, and much more of the Japanese. I would here refer the reader to the chapter on "Ancestor-worship." In the Southern Moluccas the placenta is mixed with ashes, placed in a pot, and hung on a tree; a similar custom is observed in Mandeling, on the west coast of Sumatra. This is a custom universally observed amongst the Khasis at births. Teknonomy to some extent prevails amongst some of these Malay tribes as with the Khasis. It will be seen from the above notes that there are some interesting points of affinity between the Khasis and some of the Malay tribes, and if we add that the Khasis are decidedly Malay in appearance, we cannot but wonder whether the Malays have any connection not only with the Mon-Khmêr family, but also with the Khasis, with the Ho-Mundas, and with the Naga tribes mentioned by Mr. Peal in his interesting paper published in the Journal of the Asiatic Society of Bengal, already referred to. We will study the strong linguistic affinities between these peoples in the section which deals with language.

M. Aymonier in "Le Cambodge" mentions the matriarchate as having been prevalent apparently amongst the primitive races of Cambodia, and notes that the ancient Chinese writers spoke of Queens in Fou-nan (Cambodia). If the Khmêrs were the ancient people of Cambodia, here we have an important landmark in common between them and the Khasis. M. Aymonier goes on to speak of priestesses, and the Cambodian taboo, *tam* or *trenam*, which Mr. Lowis, the Superintendent of Ethnography in Burma, suggests may be akin to the Khasi *sang*.

Dress.

Dress may be divided into two divisions, ancient and modern. It will be convenient to take the former division first. The Khasi males of the interior wear the sleeveless coat or *jymphong*, which is a garment leaving the neck and arms bare, with a fringe at the bottom, and with a row of tassels across the chest; it is fastened by frogs in front. This coat, however, may be said to be going out of fashion in the Khasi Hills, its place being taken by coats of European pattern in the more civilized centres and by all sorts of nondescript garments in the interior. The sleeveless coat, however, is still worn by many Syntengs in the interior and by the Bhois and Lynngams. The men in the Khasi Hills wear a cap with ear-flaps. The elderly men, or other men when smartness is desired, wear a white turban, which is fairly large and is well tied on the head. Males in the Siemship of Nongstoin and in the North-Western corner of the district wear knitted worsted caps which are often of a red colour. These are sold at Nongstoin market at about 8 or 9 annas each. They are brought to Nongstoin by traders from the Synteng country, and from Shillong, where they are knitted generally by Synteng women. A small cloth is worn round the waist and between the legs, one end of which hangs down in front like a small apron. The Syntengs wear a somewhat differently shaped cap, having no ear-flaps and with a high-peaked crown. Both Khasi and Synteng caps are generally of black cloth, having, as often as not, a thick coating of grease. The old-fashioned Khasi female's dress, which is that worn by people of the cultivator class of the present day, is the following:—Next to the skin is worn a garment called *ka jympien*, which is a piece of cloth wound round the body and fastened at the loins with a kind of cloth belt, and which hangs down from the waist to the knee or a little above it. Over this is worn a long piece of cloth, sometimes of muga silk, called *ka jainsem*. This is not worn like the Assamese *mekhela* or Bengali *sari*, for it hangs loosely from the shoulders down to a little above the ankles, and is not caught in at the waist—in fact, Khasi women have no waist. It is kept in position by knotting it over both the shoulders. Over the *jainsem* another garment called *ka jain kup* is worn. This is thrown over the shoulders like a cloak, the two ends being knotted in front, it hangs loosely down the back and sides to the ankles. It is frequently of some gay colour, the fashion in Mawkhar and Cherrapunji being some pretty shade of French gray or maroon. Over the head and shoulders is worn a wrapper called *ka tap-moh-khlieh*. This, again, is frequently of some bright colour, but is often white. There is a fold in the *jainsem* which serves as a pocket for keeping odds and ends. Khasi women in cold weather wear gaiters which are often long stockings without feet, or, in the case of the poor, pieces of cloth wound round the legs like putties, or cloth gaiters. I have seen women at Nongstoin wearing gaiters of leaves. It was explained to me that these were worn to keep off the leeches. The Khasi women might almost be said to be excessively clothed—they wear the cloak in such a way as to hide entirely the graceful contours of the figure. The women are infinitely more decently clothed than Bengali coolie women, for instance; but their dress cannot be described as becoming or graceful, although they show taste as regards the blending of colours in their different garments.

The dress of the Synteng women is a little different. With them the *jain khrywang* takes the place of the Khasi *jainsem*, and is worn by them in the following manner:—One of the two ends is passed under one armpit and its two corners are knotted on the opposite shoulder. The other end is then wound round the body and fastened at the waist, from which it hangs half way down the calf. Over this they wear a sort of apron, generally of *muga* silk. They have the cloak and the head-wrapper just the same as the Khasi women. The Synteng striped cloth may be observed in the picture of the Synteng girl in the plate. Khasi women on festive occasions, such as the annual Nongkrem puja, do not cover the head. The hair is then decked with jewellery or with flowers; but on all ordinary occasions Khasi women cover the head. Wár women, however, often have their heads uncovered.

Modern dress.—The up-to-date Khasi male wears knickerbockers made by a tailor, stockings, and boots; also a tailor-made coat and waistcoat, a collar without a tie, and a cloth peaked cap. The young lady of fashion dons a chemise, also often a short coat of cloth or velvet, stockings, and smart shoes. Of course she wears the *jainsem* and cloak, but occasionally she may be seen without the latter when the weather is warm. It should be mentioned that the Khasi males are seldom seen without a haversack in which betel-nut, lime, and other odds and ends are kept; and the female has her purse, which, however, is not visible, being concealed within the folds of her lower garment. The haversack of the men is of cloth in the high plateau and in the Bhoi country, but it is of knitted fibre in the Wár country. The Syntengs have a cloth bag, which they call *ka muna*.

The Wár men dress very much the same as the neighbouring Sylheti Hindus. The Wár women, especially the Shella women, wear very pretty yellow and red checked and striped cloths. The cloak is not so frequently worn as amongst Khasis, except in cold weather. The Lynngam dress is very similar to that of the neighbouring Garos. The males wear the sleeveless coat, or *phong marong*, of cotton striped red and blue, red and white, or blue and white, fastened in the same manner as the Khasi coat and with tassels. A small cloth, generally red or blue, is tied between the legs, one end of it being allowed to hang down, as with the Khasis, like an apron in front. A round cap is commonly worn; but the elderly men and people of importance wear turbans. The females wear short cloths of cotton striped red and blue, the cloth reaching just above the knee, like the Garos; married women wear no upper clothing, except in winter, when a red or blue cotton cloth is thrown loosely across the shoulders. The women wear a profusion of blue bead necklaces and brass earrings like the Garos. Unmarried girls wear a cloth tightly tied round the figure, similar to that worn by the Kacharis. A bag of cloth for odds and ends is carried by the men slung across the shoulder. It should be mentioned that even in ancient times great people amongst the Khasis, like Siems, wore waist-cloths, and people of lees consequence on great occasions, such as dances. The use of waist-cloths among the Khasis is on the increase, especially among those who live in Shillong and the neighbouring villages and in Jowai and Cherrapunji.

Tattooing.

None of the Khasis tattoo; the only people in the hills who tattoo are certain tribes of the Bhoi country which are really Mikir. These tattoo females on the forehead when they attain the age of puberty, a straight horizontal line being drawn from the parting of the hair down the forehead and nose. The line is one-eighth to one-quarter of an inch broad. The Lynngams occasionally tattoo a ring round the wrist of females.

Jewellery.

The Khasis, as a people, may be said to be fond of jewellery. The women are specially partial to gold and coral bead necklaces. The beads are round and large, and are usually unornamented with filigree or other work. The coral is imported from Calcutta. The gold bead is not solid, but a hollow sphere filled with lac. These necklaces are worn by men as well as women, especially on gala occasions. Some of the necklaces are comparatively valuable, e.g. that in the possession of the Mylliem Siem family. The gold and coral beads are prepared locally by Khasi as well as by foreign goldsmiths. The latter derive considerable profits from the trade. The Assam Census Report of 1901 shows 133 goldsmiths in the Khasi and Jaintia Hills district, but does not distinguish between Khasis and foreigners. There are Khasi goldsmiths to be found in Mawkhar, Cherrapunji, Mawlai, and other villages. Sylheti goldsmiths are, however, more largely employed than Khasi in Mawsynram and certain other places on the south side of the hills. In Mr. Henniker's monograph on "gold and silver wares of Assam" it is stated that the goldsmiths of Karimganj in Sylhet make specially for Khasis certain articles of jewellery, such as men's and women's earrings, &c. An article of jewellery which is believed to be peculiar to the Khasis is the silver or gold crown. This crown is worn by the young women at dances, such as the annual Nongkrem dance. An illustration of one will be seen by referring to the plate. These crowns are circlets of silver or gold ornamented with filigree work. There is a peak or, strictly speaking, a spike at the back, called *u'tiew-lasubon*, which stands up some six inches above the crown. There are long ropes or tassels of silver hanging from the crown down the back. Earrings are worn both by men and women. The former affect a pattern peculiar to themselves, viz. large gold pendants of a circular or oval shape. Women wear different patterns of earrings, according to locality. An ornament which I believe is also peculiar to the Khasis is the *rupa-tylli*, or silver collar. This is a broad flat silver collar which is allowed to hang down over the neck in front, and which is secured by a fastening behind. Silver chains are worn by men as well as by women. The men wear them round the waist like a belt, and the women hang them round their necks, the chains being allowed to depend as low as the waist. Bracelets are worn by women; these are either of gold or of silver. The Lynngam males wear bead necklaces, the beads being sometimes of cornelian gathered from the beds of the local hill streams, and sometimes of glass obtained from the plains markets of Damra and Moiskhola. The cornelian necklaces are much prized by the Lynngams, and are called by them *'pieng blei*, or gods' necklaces. Like the Garos, the Lynngams wear as many brass earrings as possible, the lobes of the ears of the females being frequently greatly distended by their weight. These earrings are made out of brass wire obtained from the plains markets. The Lynngams wear silver armlets above the elbow and also on the wrists. It is only a man who has given a great feast who can wear silver armlets above the elbows. These armlets are taken off as a sign of mourning, but never on ordinary occasions. The Lynngams do not wear Khasi jewellery, but jewellery of a pattern to be seen in the Garo Hills. A distinctive feature of the Lynngam women is the very large number of blue bead necklaces they wear. They put on such a large number as to give them almost the appearance of wearing horse collars. These beads are obtained from the plains markets, and are of glass. Further detailed information regarding this subject can be obtained from Mr. Henniker's monograph, which contains a good plate illustrating the different articles of jewellery.

Weapons.

The weapons of the Khasis are swords, spears, bows and arrows, and a circular shield which was used formerly for purposes of defence. The swords are usually of wrought iron, occasionally of steel, and are forged in the local smithies. The Khasi sword is of considerable length, and possesses the peculiarity of not having a handle of different material from that which is used for the blade. In the Khasi sword the handle is never made of wood or bone, or of anything except iron or steel, the result being that the sword is most awkward to hold, and could never have been of much use as a weapon of offence.

The same spear is used for thrusting and casting. The spear is not decorated with wool or hair like the spears of the Naga tribes, but it is nevertheless a serviceable weapon, and would be formidable in the hand of a resolute man at close quarters. The length of the spear is about 6 1/2 feet. The shaft is generally of bamboo, although sometimes of ordinary wood. The spear heads are forged in the local smithies.

The Khasi weapon *par excellence* is the bow. Although no "Robin Hoods," the Khasis are very fair archers, and they use the bow largely for hunting. The Khasi bow (*ka ryntieh*) is of bamboo, and is about 5 feet in height. The longest bow in use is said to be about the height of a man, the average height amongst the Khasis being about about 5 feet 2 inches to 5 feet 4 inches. The bowstring is of split bamboo, the bamboos that are used being *u spit, u shken*, and *u siej-lieh*.

The arrows (*ki khnam*) are of two kinds: (*a*) the barbed-headed (*ki pliang*), and (*b*) the plain-headed (*sop*). Both are made out of bamboo. The first kind is used for hunting, the latter for archery matches only. Archery may be styled the Khasi national game. A description of Khasi archery will be found under the heading "Games." The feathers of the following birds are used for arrows:— Vultures, geese, cranes, cormorants, and hornbills. Arrow-heads are made of iron or steel, and are forged locally. The distance a Khasi arrow will carry, shot from the ordinary bow by a man of medium strength, is 150 to 180 yards. The

Khasi shield is circular in shape, of hide, and studded with brass or silver. In former days shields of rhinoceros hide are said to have been used, but nowadays buffalo skin is used. The shields would stop an arrow or turn aside a spear or sword thrust. The present-day shield is used merely for purposes of display.

Before the advent of the British into the hills the Khasis are said to have been acquainted with the art of manufacturing gunpowder, which was prepared in the neighbourhood of Mawsanram, Kynchi, and Cherra. The gunpowder used to be manufactured of saltpetre, sulphur, and charcoal, the three ingredients being pounded together in a mortar. The Jaintia Rajas possessed cannon, two specimens of which are still to be seen at Jaintiapur. Their dimensions are as follows:—

Length, 9 feet; circumference in the middle, 3 feet 2 inches; diameter of the bore 3 inches. There are some old cannon also at Lyngkyrdem and at Kyndiar in the Khyrim State, of the same description as above. These cannons were captured from the Jaintia Raja by the Siem of Nongkrem. No specimens of the cannon ball used are unfortunately available. There are also small mortars, specimens of which are to be seen in the house of the Siem of Mylliem.

The weapons of the Syntengs are the same as those of the Khasis, although some of them are called by different names. At Nartiang I saw an old Khasi gun, which the people say was fired from the shoulder. I also saw a mortar of the same pattern as the one described amongst the Khasi weapons.

The Wár and Lynngam weapons are also the same, but with different names. The only weapons used by the Bhois (Mikirs) are the spear and bill-hook for cutting down jungle. Butler, writing of the Mikirs 1854, says, "Unlike any other hill tribes of whom we have any knowledge, the Mikirs seem devoid of anything approaching to a martial spirit. They are a quiet, industrious, race of cultivators, and the only weapons used by them are the spear and *da* hand-bill for cutting down jungle. It is said, after an attempt to revolt from the Assamese rule, they were made to forswear the use of arms, which is the cause of the present generation having no predilection for war."

CHAPTER II

Domestic Life

Occupation.

The greater proportion of the population subsists by cultivation. Cultivation of rice may be divided under two headings, high land or dry cultivation and low land or wet cultivation. The total number of persons who subsist by agriculture generally in the hills, is given is the last Census Report as 154,907, but the term agriculture includes the cultivation of the potato, the orange, betel-nut and *pán*. A full description of the different forms of agriculture will be given under the heading "Agriculture." A considerable number of Khasis earn their livelihood as porters, carrying potatoes to the markets on the Sylhet side of the district, from whence the crop is conveyed by means of country boats to the different places of call of river-steamers in the Surma Valley, the steamers carrying the potatoes to Calcutta. Potatoes are also largely carried to Shillong by porters, where the tuber is readily bought by Marwari merchants, who load it in carts to be conveyed by road to Gauhati, from which station it is again shipped to Calcutta and Upper Assam. Many persons are also employed in carrying rice up the hill from Theria to Cherrapunji, Shillong, and on to other places. Salt is also carried by porters by this route. Many Khasis, both male and female, live by daily labour in this way, earning as much as eight annas, and six annas a day, respectively. The Census Report of 1901 shows some 14,000 "general labourers" in the district, the greater number of whom are porters and coolies, both male and female, employed on road work and on building. In Shillong the Government Offices and the printing press give employment to a certain number of Khasis. There is also a fair demand for Khasi domestic servants, both among the Europeans and the Bengali and Assamese clerks who are employed at the headquarters of the Administration. The manufacture of country spirit gives employment to a considerable number of persons, most of whom are females. At a recent census of the country stills in the district, undertaken by the district officials, the number of stills has been found to be 1,530. There must be at least one person employed at each still, so that the number of distillers is probably not less than 2,000, possibly more. The spirit is distilled both for home consumption and for purposes of sale, in some villages almost entirely for sale. In, the Jaintia Hills stock-breeding and dealing in cattle provides occupation for 1,295 people, according to the last census. The cattle are reared in the Jaintia Hills and are driven down to the plains when they reach the age of maturity, where they find a ready market amongst the Sylhetis. Cattle are also driven into Shillong for sale from the Jaintia Hills. Another place for rearing cattle is the Siemship of Nongkhlaw, where there is good pasturage in the neighbourhood of Mairang. These cattle are either sold in Shillong or find their way to the Kamrup district by the old Nongkhlaw road. Cattle-breeding is an industry which is capable of expansion in these hills. There are a few carpenters to be found in Shillong and its neighbourhood. The Khasis are said by Col. Waddell to be unacquainted with the art of weaving; but the fact that a considerable weaving industry exists amongst the Khyrwang villages of the Syntengs, and at Mynso and Suhtnga, has been overlooked by him. The Khyrwangs weave a special pattern of cotton and silk cloth, striped red and white. In Mynso and Suhtnga similar cloths are woven, also the sleeveless coat. In former days this industry is said to have been considerable, but it has been displaced to a large extent of late years by Manchester piece goods. The number of weavers returned at the last census in the district was 533. The Khasis and Mikirs of the low country, or Bhois as they are called, weave cotton cloths which they dye with the leaves of a plant called *u noli*. This is perhaps the wild indigo, or *ram*, of the Shan settlers in the Assam Valley. The weavers are almost always females. An important means of subsistence is road and building work; a considerable number of coolies, both male and female, are employed under Government, practically throughout the year, in this manner, the males earning on an average 8 annas and the females 6 annas a day. Col Bivar writes that in 1875 the wages for ordinary male labourers were 4 to 8 annas a day, and for females 2 1/2 to 4 annas, so that the wages rates have almost doubled in the last thirty years. Contractors, however, often manage to obtain daily labour at lower rates than those paid by Government. Stonemasons and skilled labourers are able to get higher rates. It is easier to obtain coolies in the Khasi than in the Jaintia Hills, where a large proportion of the population is employed in cultivation. The Khasis are excellent labourers, and cheerful and willing, but they at once resent bad treatment, and are then intractable and hard to manage. Khasis are averse to working in the plains in the hot-weather months.

Apiculture.

I am indebted to Mr. Rita for the following remarks on apiculture in the Khasi and Jaintia Hills.

There are two kinds of indigenous bees in the Khasi Hills: one domesticated, called *u ngap* (*apis Indica*), and the other *u lywai*, which is never domesticated, and is very pugnacious; its hives are difficult of access, being always located in very high cliffs. A few hives of a third class of bee are now-a-days to be found in and around the station of Shillong, i.e. the Italian. This bee was imported into the hills by Messrs. Dobbie and Rita, and the species became propagated in the following manner. The bees had been just established in a hive, where they had constructed a brood comb, when the hive was robbed by some Khasis for the sake of the *larvæ* it contained, which they wished to consume as food; but the queen bee escaped and established other colonies, one of which was afterwards captured by Mr. Rita, the others establishing themselves at places in the neighbourhood. The hive used by the Khasis is of a very primitive description. It is usually a hollow piece of wood, about 2 1/2 to 3 ft. in length and 10 or 12 in. in diameter. A small door is placed at each end of the log, one for the bees to go in and out, and the other for the removal of the honey when wanted. The honey-combs are broken and the honey is extracted by squeezing the comb with the hand. Wax is obtained by placing the comb in boiling water and allowing it to cool, when the wax floats to the surface. The Khasis do not systematically tend their bees, as they do not understand how to prevent swarming, and as the Khasi bee is a prolific swarmer, hives become weak very soon and a new hive has to be started from a captured natural swarm. The villages in which bees are regularly kept to any large extent in the Khasi and Jaintia Hills are Thied-dieng, Mawphoo, Nongwar, Mawlong, Pynter, Tyrna, and Kongthong, but most of the Wár villagers rear bees and sell the honey at the neighbouring markets. The collection of the honey of the wild bee, or *u lywai*, is a hazardous occupation, the services of some six or seven persons being required, as the combs of this bee are generally built in the crevices of precipitous rocks, and sometimes weigh more than half a maund each. When such hives are discovered the bees are driven out by the smoke of a smouldering fire lit at the foot of the rock below the hive. Two or three men get to the top of the precipice, leaving two or three of their companions at the base. One of the men on the top of the rock is then lowered down in a sling tied to a strong rope, which is made fast by his companions above to a tree or boulder. The man in the sling is supplied with material to light a torch which gives out a thick smoke, with the aid of which the bees are expelled. The man then cuts out the comb, which he places in a leather bucket or bag, which, when filled, he lowers down to the persons in waiting at the foot of the rock. The wild honey may be distinguished from that of the domestic bee by being of a reddish colour. Honey from the last-mentioned bee is gathered twice or thrice in the year, once in the autumn and once or twice in the spring; that gathered in early spring is not so matured as that collected in autumn. The flora of the Khasi Hills being so numerous, there is no necessity for providing bees with artificial food. The bees are generally able to obtain their sustenance from clover, anemonies, "golden rod," bush honeysuckle, and numerous shrubs such as andromeda, daphne, &c., which abound about Shillong. There seem to be facilities for apiculture on a large scale in these hills, and certainly the honey which is brought round by the Khasis for sale in Shillong is excellent, the flavour being quite as good as that of English honey. Under "Miscellaneous Customs connected with Death" will be found a reference to the statement that the dead bodies of Siems used to be embalmed in honey. The existence of the custom is generally denied by Khasis, but its former prevalence is probable, as several trustworthy authors have quoted it.

Houses.

The houses of the people are cleaner than might be supposed after taking into consideration the dirtiness of the clothes and persons of those who inhabit them. They are as a rule substantial thatched cottages with plank or stone walls, and raised on a plinth some 2 to 3 ft. from the ground. The only window is a small opening on one side of the house, which admits but a dim light into the smoke-begrimed interior. The beams are so low that it is impossible for a person of ordinary stature to stand erect within. The fire is always burning on an earthen or stone hearth in the centre. There is no chimney, the smoke finding its exit as best it can. The firewood is placed to dry on a swinging frame above the hearth. In the porch are stacked fuel and odds and ends. The pigs and calves are generally kept in little houses just outside the main building. The Khasi house is oval-shaped, and is divided into three rooms, a porch, a centre room, and a retiring-room.

In olden days the Khasis considered nails *sang*, or taboo, and only used a certain kind of timber for the fender which surrounds the hearth; but they are not so particular now-a-days. In Mawkhar, Cherrapunji, and other large villages, the walls of houses are generally of stone. In Cherrapunji the houses are frequently large, but the largest house I have seen in the hills is that of the Doloi of Suhtnga in the Jaintia Hills which measures 74 ft. in length. The house of the Siem Priestess at Smit in the Khasi Hills is another large one, being 61 ft. long by 30 ft. broad. In front of the Khasi house is a little space fenced in on two sides, but open towards the village street. The Syntengs plaster the space in front of the house with red earth and cow-dung, this custom being probably a remnant of Hindu influences. The Khasis have some peculiar customs when they build a new house. When the house is completed they perform a ceremony, *kynjoh-hka-skain*, when they tie three pieces of dried fish to the ridge pole of the house and then jump up and try to pull them down again. Or they kill a pig, cut a piece of the flesh with the skin attached, and fix it to the ridge pole, and then endeavour to dislodge it. The Syntengs at Nartiang worship *U Biskurom* (Biswakarma) and *Ka Siem Synshar* when a house is completed, two fowls being sacrificed, one to the former, the other to the latter. The feathers of the fowls are affixed to the centre post of the house, which must be of *u dieng sning*, a variety of the Khasi oak. The worship of a Hindu god (Biswakarma), the architect of the Hindu gods, alongside the Khasi deity *Ka Siem Synshar*, is interesting, and may be explained by the fact that Nartiang was at one time the summer capital of the kings of Jaintia, who were Hindus latterly and disseminated Hindu customs largely amongst the Syntengs. Mr. Rita says that amongst the Syntengs, a house, the walls of which have been plastered with mud, is a sign that the householder has an enemy. The plastering no doubt is executed as a preventive of fire, arson in these hills being a common form of revenge.

Amongst the Khasis, when a daughter leaves her mother's house and builds a house in the mother's compound, it is considered *sang*, or taboo, for the daughter's house to be built on the right-hand side of the mother's house, it should be built either on the left hand or at the back of the mother's house.

In Nongstoin it is customary to worship a deity called *u'lei lap* (Khasi, *u phan*), by nailing up branches of the Khasi oak, interspersed with jaw-bones of cattle and the feathers of fowls, to the principal post, which must be of *u dieng sning*. The Siem priestess of the Nongkrem State at Smit and the ladies of the Siem family perform a ceremonial dance before a large post of oak in the midst of the Siem priestesses' house on the occasion of the annual goat-killing ceremony. This oak post is furnished according to custom by the *lyngskor* or official spokesman of the Siem's Durbar. Another post of oak in this house is furnished by the people of the State.

The houses of the well-to-do Khasis of the present day in Mawkhar and Cherrapunji are built after the modern style with iron roofs, chimneys, glass windows and doors. In Jowai the well-to-do traders have excellent houses of the European pattern, which are as comfortable as many of the European subordinates' quarters in Shillong. Some up-to-date families in Shillong and at Cherra allow themselves muslin curtains and European furniture.

The houses of the Pnar-Wárs are peculiar. The roof, which is thatched with the leaves of a palm called *u tynriew*, is hog-backed and the eaves come down almost to the ground. There are three rooms in the War as in the Khasi house, although called by different names in the Wár dialect. The hearth is in the centre room. The houses are built flush with the ground and are made of bamboos. In the Wár villages of Nongjri and Umniuh there are small houses erected in the compounds of the ordinary dwelling-houses called *ieng ksuid* (spirit houses). In these houses offerings to the spirits of departed family ancestors are placed at intervals, this practice being very similar to the more ancient form of Shintoism. In some Wár villages there are also separate bachelors' quarters. This custom is in accordance with that of the Naga tribes. There is no such custom amongst the Khasi Uplanders. The Wár houses are similar to those of the Pnar Wárs, except that a portion of the house is generally built on a platform, the main house resting on the hill-side and the portion on the platform projecting therefrom, the object being to obtain more space, the area for houses in the village sites being often limited owing to the steepness of the hill-sides.

The Bhoi and Lynngam houses are practically similar, and may be described together. They are generally built on fairly high platforms of bamboo, are frequently 30 to 40 ft. in length, and are divided into various compartments in order to suit the needs of the family. The hearth, which is of earth, is in the centre room. There is a platform at the back of the Lynngam house, and in front of the Bhoi house, used for drying paddy, spreading chillies, &c., and for sitting on when the day's work is done. In order to ascend to a Bhoi house, yon have to climb up a notched pole. The Bhois sacrifice a he-goat and a fowl to *Rèk-ànglong* (Khasi, *Ramiew iing*), the household god, when they build a new house.

Villages.

Unlike the Nagas and Kukis, the Khasis do not build their villages on the extreme summits of hills, but a little below the tops, generally in small depressions; in order to obtain some protection from the strong winds and storms which prevail in these hills at certain times of the year. According to the late U Jeebon Roy, it is *sang*, or taboo, to the Khasis to build a house on the last eminence of a range of hills, this custom having perhaps arisen owing to the necessity of locating villages with reference to their defence against an enemy. Khasis build their houses fairly close together, but not as close as houses in the Bhoi and Lynngam villages. Khasis seldom change the sites of their villages, to which they are very much attached, where, as a rule, the family tombs are standing and the *máwbynna* or memorial stones. In many villages stone cromlechs and memorial stones are to be seen which from their appearance show that the villages have been there for many generations. During the Jaintia rebellion the village of Jowai was almost entirely destroyed, but as soon as the rebellion was over the people returned to the old site and rebuilt their village. Similarly, after the earthquake, the ancient village sites were not abandoned in many cases, but the people rebuilt their houses in their former positions, although in Shillong and Cherrapunji they rebuilt the walls of the houses of wooden materials instead of stone. There is no such thing as a specially reserved area in the village for the Siem and the nobility, all the people, rich or poor, living together in one village, their houses being scattered about indiscriminately. To the democratic Khasi the ides of the Siem living apart from his people would be repugnant. In the vicinity of the Khasi village, often just below the brow of the hill to the leeward side, are to be seen dark woods of oak and other trees. These are the sacred groves. Here the villagers worship U *ryngkew* U *basa*, the tutelary deity of the village. These groves are taboo, and it is an offence to cut trees therein for any purpose other than for performing funeral obsequies. The groves are generally not more than a few hundred yards away from the villages. The villages of the Syntengs are similar in character to those of the Khasis. The Wár villages nestle on the hillsides of the southern border, and are to be seen peeping out from the green foliage with which the southern slopes are clad. In the vicinity of, and actually up to the houses, in the Wár villages, are to be observed large groves of areca-nut, often twined with the *pan* creeper, and of plantain trees, which much enhance the beauty of the scene. Looking at a Wár village from a distance, a darker shade of green is seen; this denotes the limits of the extensive groves where the justly celebrated Khasi orange is grown, which is the source of so much profit to these people. The houses in the Wár villages are generally closer together than those of the Khasis, probably owing to apace being limited, and to the villages being located on the slopes of hills. Generally up the narrow village street, and from house to house, there are rough steep stone steps, the upper portion of a village being frequently situated at as high an elevation as 200 to 300 ft. above the lower. In a convenient spot in a Wár village a clear space is to be seen neatly swept and kept free from weeds, and surrounded with a stone wall, where the village tribunals sit, and the elders meet in solemn conclave. Dances also are held here on festive occasions. At Nongjri village there is a fine rubber tree, under whose hollow trunk there are certain sacred stones where the priest performs the village ceremonies.

 The Bhoi and Lynngam villages are built in small clearings in the forest, the houses are close together and are built often in parallel lines, a fairly broad space being reserved between the lines of houses to serve as a street. One misses the pretty gardens of the Wár villages, for Bhois and Lynngams attempt nothing of the sort, probably because, unlike the Khasi, a Bhoi or Lynngam village never remains more than two or three years in one spot; generally the villages of these people are in the vicinity of the forest clearings, sometimes actually in the midst of them, more especially when the latter are situated in places where jungle is dense, and there is fear of attacks from wild animals. In the Lynngam village is to be seen a high bamboo platform some 20 to 30 ft. from the ground, built in the midst of the village, where the elders sit and gossip in the evening.

 All the villages, Khasi, Wár, Lynngam and Bhoi, swarm with pigs, which run about the villages unchecked. The pigs feed on all kinds of filth, and in addition are fed upon the wort and spent wash of the brewings of country spirit, of rice beer, the latter being carefully collected and poured into wooden troughs. The pigs are of the usual black description seen in India. They thrive greatly in the Khasi villages, and frequently attain extreme obesity.

In the Khasi villages of the high plateaux are often nowadays potato gardens, the latter being carefully protected from the inroads of pigs, calves, and goats by dry dikes surmounted by hedges.

I noticed an interesting custom at a Bhoi village in Nongpoh of barricading the path leading to the village from the forest with bamboo palisading and bamboo *chevaux de frise* to keep out the demon of cholera. In the middle of the barricade there was a wooden door over which was nailed the skull of a monkey which had been sacrificed to this demon, which is, as amongst the Syntengs, called *khlam*.

Furniture and Household Utensils.

As in the case of houses, so with reference to furniture, the influence of civilization shows many changes. The Khasi of the present day who lives in Mawkhar [14] has a comfortable house regularly divided up into rooms in the European style with even some European articles of furniture, but owing probably to the influence of the women, he still possesses several of the articles of furniture which are to be met with in the houses of those who still observe the old style of living. Let us take the furniture of the kitchen to begin with. Above the hearth is slung by ropes of cane a swinging wooden framework blackened with the smoke of years, upon which are spread the faggots of resinous fir-wood used for kindling the fire. Above this again is a wooden framework fixed on to the beams of the house, upon which all sorts of odds and ends are kept. Around the fire are to be seen small wooden stools, upon which the members of the household sit. Up-to-date Khasis have cane chairs, but the women of the family, true to the conservative instincts of the sex, prefer the humble stool to sit upon. Well-to-do Khasis nowadays have, in addition to the ordinary cooking vessels made of iron and earthenware, a number of brass utensils. The writer has seen in a Khasi house in Mawkhar brass drinking vessels of the pattern used in Orissa, of the description used in Manipur, and of the kind which is in vogue in Sylhet. The ordinary cultivator, however, uses a waterpot made from a gourd hollowed out for keeping water and liquor in, and drinks from a bamboo cylinder. Plates, or more properly speaking dishes, are of several kinds in the houses of the rich, the two larger ones being styled *ka pliang kynthei* (female) and *ka pliang shynrang* (male). Needless to say, the first mentioned is a larger utensil than the latter. The ordinary waterpots, *u khiew phiang kynthei* and *u khiew phiang shynrang*, are made of brass, the former being a size larger and having a wider mouth than the latter. The pot for cooking vegetables is made of iron. Another utensil is made of earthenware; this is the ordinary cooking pot used in the houses of the poor. Brass spoons of different sizes are used for stirring the contents of the different cooking utensils, also a wooden spoon.

In the sleeping-rooms of the well-to-do there are wooden beds with mattresses and sheets and pillows, clothes being hung upon clothes-racks, which in one house visited were of the same pattern as the English "towel horse." The ordinary cultivator and his wife sleep on mats made of plaited bamboo, which are spread on the bare boards of the house. There are various kinds of mats to be met with in the Khasi houses made of plaited cane, of a kind of reed, and of plaited bamboo. The best kind of mat is prepared from cane. In all Khasi houses are to be seen *ki knup*, or rain shields, of different sizes and sometimes of somewhat different shapes. The large shield of Cherrapunji is used as a protection from rain. Those of Maharam and Mawiang are each of a peculiar pattern. Smaller shields are used as protections from the sun or merely for show, and there are specially small sizes for children. Then there are the different kinds of baskets (*ki khoh*) which are carried on the back, slung across the forehead by a cane head-strap. These, again, are of different sizes. They are, however, always of the same conical shape, being round and broad-mouthed at the top and gradually tapering to a point at the bottom. A bamboo cover is used to protect the contents of the basket from rain. There is a special kind of basket made of cane or bamboo with a cover, which is used for carrying articles on a journey. These baskets, again, are of different sizes, the largest and best that the writer has seen being manufactured at Rambrai, in the south-western portion of the hills. Paddy is husked in a wooden mortar by means of a heavy wooden pestle. These are to be seen all over the hills. The work of husking paddy is performed by the women. A bamboo sieve is sometimes used for sifting the husked rise, a winnowing fan being applied to separate the husk. The cleaned rice is exposed to the sun in a bamboo tray. Paddy is stored in a separate store-house in large circular bamboo receptacles. These hold sometimes as much as 30 maunds [15] of grain. Large baskets are also used for keeping paddy in. In every Khasi house is to be found the net bag which is made out of pineapple fibre, or of *u stein*, the Assamese *riha* (Boehmeria nivea). These bags are of two sizes, the larger one for keeping cowries id, the cowrie in former days having been used instead of current coin in these hills, the smaller far the ever necessary betel-nut. *Pán* leaves are kept in a bamboo tube, and tobacco leaves in a smaller one. Lime, for eating with betel-nut, is kept in a metal box, sometimes of silver, which is made in two separate parts held together by a chain. The box is called *ka shanam*, and is used all over the hills. This box is also used for divination purposes, one end of it being held in the hand, and the other, by means of the chain, being allowed to swing like a pendulum. An explanation of this method of divination will be found in the paragraph dealing with divination.

There is also a pair of squeezers used by the old and toothless for breaking up betel-nut. In the houses of the well-to-do is to be seen the ordinary hubble-bubble of India. Outside the houses of cultivators are wooden troughs hollowed out of the trunks of trees, which are used either as drinking troughs for cattle or for feeding pigs. A special set of utensils is used for manufacturing liquor. The Synteng and Wár articles of furniture and utensils are the same as those of the Khasis, with different names, a remark which applies also to those of the Bhois and Lynngams. Both the latter, however, use leaves as plates, the Bhoi using the wild plantain and the Lynngam a large leaf called *ka 'la mariong*. The leaves are thrown away after eating, fresh leaves being gathered for each meal. The Lynngams use a quilt (*ka syllar*) made out of the bark of a tree of the same name as a bed covering. This tree is perhaps the same as the Garo *simpak*. In the Bhoi and Lynngam houses the swinging shelf for keeping firewood is not to be seen, nor is the latter to be found amongst the submontane Bodo tribes in Assam.

Musical Instruments.

The Khasis have not many musical instruments, and those that they possess, with one or two exceptions, are of very much the same description as those of the Assamese. There are several kinds of drums, viz. *ka nákrá*, which is a large kettledrum made of wood having the head covered with deerskin; *ka ksing*, which is a cylindrically-shaped drum rather smaller than the Assamese *dhol* (*ka ksing kynthei* takes its name from the fact that this drum is beaten when women, *kynthei*, dance), *ka padiah*, a small drum with a handle made of wood; *katasa*, a small circular drum. Khasi drums are nearly always made of wood, not of metal, like the drums to be seen in the monasteries of Upper Assam, or of earthenware, as in Lower Assam.

Ka duitara is a guitar with *muga* silk strings, which is played with a little wooden key held in the hand. *Ka maryngod* is an instrument much the same as the last, but is played with a bow like a violin. *Ka marynthing* is a kind of guitar with one string, played with the finger.

Ka tángmuri is a wooden pipe, which is played like a flageolet. *Ka kynsháw*, or *shákuriaw*, are cymbals made of bell metal; *ka sháráti*, or *ka shingwiang*, is a kind of flute made of bamboo. This instrument is played at cremation ceremonies, and when the bones and ashes of a clan are collected and placed in the family tomb, or *máwbah*. This flute is not played on ordinary occasions. In the folk-lore portion of the Monograph will be found a tale regarding it. There are other kinds of flutes which are played on ordinary occasions. The Wárs of the twenty-five villages in the Khyrim State make a sort of harp out of reed, which is called *ka 'sing ding phong*. The Khasis also play a Jews' Harp (*ka mieng*), which is made of bamboo.

Agriculture.

The Khasis are industrious cultivators, although they are behindhand in some of their methods of cultivation, (e.g. their failure to adopt the use of the plough in the greater portion of the district); they are thoroughly aware of the uses of manures. Their system of turning the sods, allowing them to dry, then burning them, and raking the ashes over the soil, is much in advance of any system of natural manuring to be seen elsewhere in the Province. The Khasis use the following agricultural implements:—A large hoe (*mokhiw heh*), an axe for felling trees (*u sdie*), a large *da* for felling trees (*ka wait lynngam*), two kinds of bill-hooks (*ka wáit prat* and *ka wáit khmut*), a sickle (*ka ráshi*), a plough in parts of the Jaintia Hills (*ka lyngkor*), also a harrow (*ka iuh moi*). In dealing with agriculture, the lands of the Khasi and Jaintia Hills may be divided into the following classes:—(*a*) Forest land, (*b*) wet paddy land called *háli* or *pynthor*, (*c*) high grass land or *ka ri lúm* or *ka ri phlang*, (d) homestead land (*ka 'dew kypér*). Forest lands are cleared by the process known as *jhuming*, the trees being felled early in the winter and allowed to lie till January or February, when fire is applied, logs of wood being placed at intervals of a few feet to prevent as far as possible the ashes being blown away by the wind. The lands are not hoed, nor treated any further, paddy and millet being sown broadcast, and the seeds of root crops, as well as of maize and Job's tears, being dibbled into the ground by means of small hoes. No manure, beyond the wood ashes above mentioned, is used on this class of land; there is no irrigation, and no other system of watering is resorted to. The seeds are sown generally when the first rain falls. This style of cultivation, or *jhum*, is largely resorted to by the people inhabiting the eastern and southern portions of the Jaintia Hills, e.g. the Bhois and Lalungs, the Lynngams and Garos of the western tracts of the district. Wet paddy land (*hali* or *pynthor*) is, as the name implies, the land where the kind of paddy which requires a great deal of water is grown. The bottoms of valleys are divided up into little compartments by means of fairly high banks corresponding to the Assamese *alis*, and the water is let in at will into these compartments by means of skilfully contrived irrigation channels, sometimes a mile or more in length. The soil is made into a thick paste in the Jaintia Hills by means of the plough, and in the Khasi Hills through the agency of the hoe. Droves of cattle also are driven repeatedly over the paddy-fields until the mud has acquired the right consistency. The seed is then sown broadcast in the wet mud. It is not sown first in a seedling bed and then transplanted, as in Assam and Bengal. When the plants have grown to a height of about four inches, water is let in again; then comes the weeding, which has to be done several times. When the crop is ripe, the ears are cut with a sickle (*ka rashi*) generally, so as to leave almost the entire stalk, and are left is different parts of the field. A peculiarity about the Lynngam and the Khasis and Mikirs of the low hills, or Bhois as they are called, is that they reckon it *sang*, or taboo, to use the sickle. They reap their grain by pulling the ear through the hand. The sheaves, after they are dry, are collected and thrashed out on the spot, either by beating them against a stone (*shoh kba*), or by men and women treading them out (*iuh kba*). Cattle are not used for treading out the grain. The grain is then collected and placed in large bamboo receptacles (*ki thiar*). The paddy-fields are not manured. The Khasis, when cultivating high lands, select a clayey soil if they can. In the early part of the winter the sods are turned over with the hoe, and they are exposed to the action of the atmosphere for a period of about two months. When the sods are dry, they are placed in piles, which are generally in rows in the fields, and by means of ignited bunches of dry grass within the piles a slow fire is kept up, the piles of sods being gradually reduced to ashes. This is the "paring and burning process" used in England. The ashes so obtained are then carefully raked over the field. Sometimes other manure is also applied, but not when paddy is cultivated. The soil is now fit to receive the seed, either high-land paddy, millet, Job's tears, or other crops, as the case may be. The homestead lands are plentifully manured, and consequently, with attention, produce good crops. They are cultivated with the hoe.

The cultivation of oranges in the southern portion of the district ranks equally in importance with that of the potato in the northern. The orange, which is known in Calcutta as the Chhatak or Sylhet orange, comes from the warm southern slopes of the hills in this district, where it is cultivated on an extensive scale. Although oranges do best when there is considerable heat, they have been known to do well as high as 3,000 ft.; but the usual limit of elevation for the growth of oranges in this district is probably about 1,000 to 1,500 ft. The orange of the Khasi Hills has always been famous for its excellence, and Sir George Birdwood, in his introduction to the "First Letter Book of the East India Company," page 36, refers to the orange and lemon of Garhwál, Sikkim, and Khasia as having been carried by Arab traders into Syria, "whence the Crusaders helped to gradually propagate them throughout Southern Europe." Therefore, whereas the potato was imported, the orange would appear to be indigenous in these hills.

Nurseries.—The seeds are collected and dried by being exposed to the sun. In the spring nurseries we prepared, the ground being thoroughly hoed and the soil pulverized as far as possible. The nursery is walled with stones. The seeds are then sown, a thin top layer of earth being applied. The nurseries are regularly watered, and are covered up with layers of leaves to ensure, as far as possible, the retention of the necessary moisture. When the plants are 3 or 4 in. high, they are transplanted to another and larger nursery, the soil of which has been previously well prepared for the reception of the young plants.

An orangery is prepared in the following manner:—

The shrubs, weeds and small trees are cut down, leaving only the big trees for the purpose of shade. The plants from the nurseries are planted from 6 ft. to 9 ft. apart. When they have become young trees, many of the branches of the sheltering trees mentioned above are lopped off, so as to admit the necessary amount of sunlight to the young orange trees. As the orange trees increase in size, the sheltering trees are gradually felled. The orchard requires clearing of jungle once in spring and once in autumn. The Khasis do not manure their orange trees, nor do they dig about and expose the roots. The price of orange plants is from 75 to 100 plants per rupee for plants from 1 to 2 ft. in height, and from fifty to seventy-five plants per rupee for plants from 2 to 5 ft. in height. Orange trees bear fruit when from five to eight years old in ordinary soils. In very fertile soils they sometimes bear after four years. A full-grown tree yields annually as many as 1,000 oranges, but a larger number is not unknown. The larger portion of the produce is exported from the district to the plains, and to fruit markets at the foot of the hills such as Theria, Mawdon, and Phali-Bazar, on the Shella river, whence it finds its way to the Calcutta and Eastern Bengal markets.

Potatoes are raised on all classes of land, except *hali*, or wet paddy land. When the land has been properly levelled and hoed, drains are dug about the field. A cultivator (generally a female), with a basket of seed potatoes on her back and with a small hoe in her right hand, **digs** holes and with the left hand drops two seed-potatoes into each hole. The **holes** are about 6 in. in diameter, 6 in. deep, and from 6 to 9 in. apart from one another. Another woman, with a load of manure in a basket on her back, throws a little manure over the seed in the hole, and then covers both up with earth. After the plants have attained the height of about 6 in., they are earthed up. When the leaves turn yellow, it is a sign that the potatoes are ripe. The different kinds of sweet potatoes grown and the yam and another kind of esculent root—*u sohphlang (femingia vestita Benth.)* will be noticed under the head of "Crops."

The Khasis possess very few agricultural sayings and proverbs, but the following may be quoted as examples:—

(1) *Wat ju ai thung jingthung ne bet symbai ha uba sniew kti.*

Do not allow plants to be planted or seeds to be sown by one who has a bad hand.

As elsewhere, there is a belief amongst the Khasis that some people's touch as regards agriculture is unlucky.

(2) *Thung dieng ne bet symbai haba ngen bnai, ym haba shai u bnai.*

Plant trees or sow seeds not when the moon is waxing, but when it is on the wane.

(3) *Wei la saw bha ka bneng sepngi jan miet phin sa ioh jingrang lashai.*

A red sky in the west in the evening is the sign of fine weather to-morrow.

Cf. our English proverb "a red sky in the morning is a shepherd's warning, a red sky at night is a shepherd's delight."

Crops.

The varieties of rice found in the Khasi Hills are divided into two main classes, one grown as a dry crop on high lands, and the other raised in valleys and hollows which are artificially irrigated from hill streams. The lowland rice is more productive than that grown on high lands, the average per acre of the former, according to the agricultural bulletin, as ascertained from the results of 817 experimental crop cuttings carried out during the fifteen years preceding the year 1898, being 11.7 maunds of paddy per acre, as against an average of 9.4 maunds per acre (resulting from 667 cuttings made during the same period) for the latter. [16] The average out-turn of both kinds is extremely poor, as compared with that of any description of rice grown in the plains. The rice grown in the hills is said by the Agricultural Department to be of inferior quality, the grain when cleaned being of a red colour, and extremely coarse. The cultivation of potatoes is practically confined to the Khasi Hills, there being little or none in the Jaintia Hills. The normal out-turn of the summer crop sown in February and harvested in June is reported by the Agricultural Department to be five times the quantity of seed used, and that of the winter crop, sown in August and September on the land from which the summer crop has been taken, and harvested in December, twice the quantity of seed. The winter crop is raised chiefly for the purpose of obtaining seed for the spring sowings, as it is found difficult to keep potatoes from the summer crop in good condition till the following spring. The usual quantity of seed used to the acre at each sowing is about 9 maunds, so that the gross out-turn of an acre of land cultivated with potatoes during the year may be taken at 63 maunds, and the net out-turn, after deducting the quantity of seed used, at 45 maunds. The above estimate of the Agricultural Department rests chiefly on the statements of the cultivators, and has not been adequately tested by experiment.

Since the appearance of the potato disease in 1885-86 there has been a great decrease in the area under potato cultivation. In 1881-82 the exports of potatoes from the district were as high as 126,981 maunds. From 1886-87 the exports began annually to decrease until in 1895-96 the very low figure of 8,296 maunds was reached. The figures of export for the last nine years are as follows:—

1896-97	16,726 maunds
1897-98	7,805 maunds
1898-99	9,272 maunds
1899-00	5,422 maunds
1900-01	29,142 maunds
1901-02	38,251 maunds
1902-03	36,047 maunds
1903-04	50,990 maunds

It will be seen that in the three years following the earthquake of 1897 the exports fell very low indeed. Since 1901 the trade has been steadily recovering, and the exports of 1904 reached half a lakh of maunds.

It will be observed that there has been some improvement, but the exports are still not half what they were in 1881-82. There are two kinds of sweet potatoes grown in the district, the Garo potato (*u phan Karo*), which appears to have been introduced from the Garo Hills, and *u phan sawlia*, the latter being distinguished from the Garo potato by its having a red skin, the Garo potato possessing a white skin. These kinds of potato are planted on all classes of land except *hali*, they do best on jhumed and homestead lands. The yam proper (*u phan shynreh*) is also largely grown. The small plant with an edible root called by the Khasis *u sohphang (fleminga vestita Benth.)*, is also largely grown. The roots of the plant after being peeled are eaten raw by the Khasis. As far as we know, this esculent is not cultivated in the adjoining hill districts. Job's tears (*coix lachryma-Jobi*) [17] are extensively grown, and are planted frequently with the *sohphlang* mentioned above. This cereal forms a substitute for rice amongst the poorer cultivators. Maize or Indian corn (*u riew hadem*) is grown frequently, thriving best on homestead land, and requires heavy manuring; it is grown in rotation with potatoes. Next in importance to rice comes the millet (*u krai*), as a staple of food amongst the Khasis. There are three varieties of millets generally to be seen in the Khasi Hills:—*u 'rai-soh (setaria Italica), u 'rai-shan (Paspalum sanguinale)*, and *u 'rai-truh (Eleusine coracana)*. U *'rai-shan* is cultivated in rotation with the potato, *u 'rai-soh* and *u 'rai-truh* are generally cultivated on jhumed land, where they thrive well. Millet is sometimes used instead of rice in the manufacture of spirit by the Khasis; *u rymbai-ja (phaseolus calcaratus)*, and *u rymbai ktung (glycine soja)* are beans which are cultivated occasionally: Khasis highly prize the fruit of the plantain, which they give to infants mashed up. The following are the best known varieties:—*Ka kait khún, ka kait siem, ka kait kulbuit, ka kait bamon, ka kait shyieng.*

The most important crop on the southern side of the hills is the orange, which has already been referred to in the paragraph dealing with agriculture.

The oranges are sold by the *spah* or 100, which is not a 100 literally, but somewhat over 3,000 oranges. Different places have different *spahs*. At Phali Hat, on the Bogapani River, the *spah* is computed as follows:—

1 Hali   = 4 oranges.
8 Halis   = 1 Bhar.
100 Bhars = shi spah (one hundred) = 3200 oranges.

At Shella the computation is slightly different, being as follows:—

1 Gai   = 6 oranges.
5 Gais + 2 oranges = 32 oranges.
4 Bhars = 1 hola   = 128 oranges
27 holas + 2 bhars = shi spah (100) = 3,520 oranges.

By another method of calculation the *spah* consists of 3,240 oranges.

The price per *spah* varies from about 10 rupees in good years to Rs. 40, when the orange harvest has been a poor one.

The lime is also cultivated, not separately, but along with the orange. The lime can be grown with success at a higher altitude than the orange. There is extensive betel-nut and *pán* cultivation on the southern slopes of the hills. The betel-nut tree is cultivated in the same manner as in the plains, except that the trees are planted nearer to one another. The trees bear when eight to ten years old. A portion of the crop is sold just after it has been plucked; this is called *u 'wái kháw*, and is for winter consumption. The remainder of the crop is kept in large baskets, which are placed in tanks containing water, the baskets being completely immersed. This kind of betel-nut is called *u 'wái um*. The Khasis, like the Assamese; prefer the fresh betel-nut. They do not relish the dry *supári* so much.

The principal *pán* gardens are on the south side of the hills, *pán* not being grown on the northern slopes, except in the neighbourhood of Jirang. The *pán* creepers are raised from cuttings, the latter being planted close to the trees up which they are to be trained. The creeper is manured with leaf mould. The plant is watered by means of small bamboo aqueducts which are constructed along the hill-sides, the water being conducted along them often considerable distances. As in the plains, the leaves of the *pán* creeper are collected throughout the year.

The bay leaf (*'la tyrpád*, or *tezpát*) is classified in the *Agricultural Bulletin* as *Cinnamomum tamala*, and there is a note in the column of remarks that "this tree, as well as one or two others of the same genus, yields two distinct products, *tezpát* (bay leaf) and cinnamon bark." The bay leaf is gathered for export from the extensive gardens in Maharam, Malaisohmat, Mawsynram, and other Khasi

States. The plants are raised from seed, although there are no regular nurseries, the young seedlings being transplanted from the jungle, where they have germinated, to regular gardens. Bay leaf gardens are cleared of jungle and weeds periodically; otherwise no care is taken of them. The leaf-gathering season is from November to March. The leaves are allowed to dry for a day or two in the sun, and then packed in large baskets for export. The gathering of bay leaf begins when the trees are about four years old.

The following are the other minor crops which are grown in the Khasi and Jaintia Hills:—

Pineapples, turmeric, ginger, pumpkins and gourds, the egg plant, chillies, sesamum, and a little sugar-cane. The arum [18] (*ka shiriw*) is also extensively grown in the hills, and forms one of the principal articles of food amongst the poorer classes; it is generally raised in rotation with potatoes, or is planted along with Job's tears. The stem of the arum is sometimes used as a vegetable, also for feeding pigs.

In the Jowai Sub-Division, notably at Nartiang, there are fairly good mangoes, which are more free from worms than those grown in the plains of Assam.

The Bhois and Lynngams cultivate lac. They plant *arhar dal, u landoo*, in their fields, and rear the lac insect on this plant. Last year the price of lac at Gauhati and Palasbari markets rose as high as Rs. 50 per maund of 82 lbs., it is said, but the price at the outlying markets of Singra and Boko was about Rs. 30. The price of lac has risen a good deal of late years. Formerly the price was about Rs. 15 to Rs. 20 a maund. The lac trade in the Jaintia Hills and in the southern portion of the Khyrim State is a valuable one. The profits, however, go largely to middlemen, who in the Jaintia Hills are Syntengs from Jowai, who give out advances to the Bhoi cultivators on the condition that they will be repaid in lac. The Marwari merchants from the plains attend all the plains markets which are frequented by the hill-men, and buy up the lac and export it to Calcutta. The whole of the lac is of the kind known as stick lac.

Hunting.

The weapons used by the Khasis for hunting are bows and arrows, the latter with barbed iron heads, and spears which are used both for casting and thrusting. Before proceeding on a hunting expedition the hunters break eggs, in order to ascertain whether they will be successful or not, and to which jungle they should proceed. Offerings are also made to certain village deities, e.g. *U. Ryngkew, u Basa*, and *u Basa ki mrád*. A lucky day having been selected and the deities propitiated, the hunters start with a number of dogs trained to the chase, the latter being held on leashes by a party of men called *ki nongai-ksew*. When the dogs have picked up the scent some hunters are placed as "stops" (*ki ktem*), at points of vantage in the jungle, and the drive commences with loud shouts from the hunters, the same being continued until the object of the chase breaks into the open. The man who draws the first blood is called u *nongsiat*, and the second man who scores a hit *u nongban*. These two men get larger shares of the flesh than the others. The *nongsiat* obtains the lower half of the body of the animal, thighs and feet excepted, called *ka tdong*, and the *nongban* one of the forequarters called *ka tabla*. The other hunters obtain a string of flesh each, and each hound gets a string of flesh to itself. These hunting parties pursue deer sometimes for many miles, and are indefatigable in the chase, the latter lasting occasionally more than one day. In the Jaintia Hills, at the end of the chase, the quarry is carried to the house of the *nongsiat*, where a *puja* is performed to some local deity, before the flesh is distributed. At Shangpung, when a tiger or a mithan is killed, the head is cut off, and is carried in triumph to a hill in the neighbourhood where there is a *duwan*, or altar, at the foot of an oak tree (*dieng sning*). The head is displayed on the altar, and worship offered to *u 'lei lyngdoh*, the God of the doloiship.

The Khasis make use of an ingenious species of spring gun for killing game, the spring gun being laid alongside a deer path in the jungle. A string stretched across the path, when touched, releases a bolt and spring, which latter impels a bamboo arrow with great force across the path. This spring gun is called *ka riam siat*. A pit-fall, with bamboo spikes at the bottom, is called *u 'liw lep*, and a trap of the pattern of the ordinary leopard trap is called *ka riam slung*. A noose attached to a long rope laid in a deer run is named *riam syrwiah*.

There is also *ka riam pap*, the principle of which is that an animal is attracted by a bait to walk on to a platform; the platform sinks under the weight of the animal, and a bolt is released which brings down a heavy roof from above weighted with stones, which crush the animal to death.

There are several means employed in snaring birds; one of the most common is to smear pieces of bamboo with the gum of the jack-tree, the former being tied to the branches of some wild fruit tree, upon which, when the fruit is ripe, the birds light and are caught by the bird lime. This is called *ka riam thit*. Another is a kind of spring bow made of bamboo which is laid on the ground in marshy places, such as are frequented by snipe and woodcock. This form of snare is unfortunately most common. A third is a cage into which birds are lured by means of a bait, the cage being hidden in the grass, and the entrance being so contrived that the birds can hop in but not out again. This is called *ka riam sim*.

Fishing.

Although there are some Khasis who fish with rod and line, it may be said that the national method of fishing is to poison the streams. Khasis, except the Wárs and the people of Shella, unlike the Assamese and Bengalis, do not fish with nets, nor do they use the bamboo-work device known by the Assamese as *pala* (pala) and *jakai* (jakaaii). The method of fish-poisoning of the Khasis is the same as that described by Soppitt in his account of the tribes inhabiting North Cachar. The following is a description of how Khasis poison fish in the western portion of the district; it may be taken as a sample of the whole. A large quantity of the bark of the tree *ka mynta* and the creeper *u khariew* is first brought to the river-side to a place on the stream a little above the pool which it is proposed to poison, where it is thoroughly beaten with sticks till the juice exudes and flows into the water, the juice being of a milky white colour. In a few minutes the fish begin to rise and splash about, and, becoming stupefied, allow themselves to be caught in the shallows. If the beating of the bark has been well carried out, many of the fish soon die and after a time float on the surface of the water. A large number of Khasis stand on the banks armed with bamboo scoops shaped like small landing nets, to catch the fish, and fish traps (*ki khowar*) Assamese *khoká* (khookaa) are laid between the stones in the rapids to secure any fish that may escape the fishing party. Another fish poison is the berry *u soh lew*, the juice of which is beaten out in the same manner as described above.

Soppitt says, certain fish do not appear to be susceptible to the poison, and not nearly the destruction takes place that is popularly supposed. The mahseer and the carp family generally do not suffer much, whereas, on the other hand, the river shark, the *bagh mas* of the Bengalis, is killed in large numbers. It is impossible, however, in the opinion of the writer, that the mahseer fry, which abound in these hill rivers in the spring and early summer months, can escape being destroyed in great numbers when the streams are frequently poisoned. In the neighbourhood of lime quarries and other large works where dynamite is used for blasting, this explosive is sometimes employed for killing fish. The practice, however, has been strictly prohibited, and there have been some cases in which the offenders have been punished in the courts. Fish-poisoning is bad enough, but dynamiting is still worse, as with an effective cartridge all the fish within a certain area are killed, none escape. When poisons are used, however, some fish are not affected by them, and others are only stupefied for the time being and afterwards recover.

Food.

The Khasi and Syntengs ordinarily take two meals a day, one in the early morning and the other in the evening, but labourers and others who have to work hard in the open take a midday meal as well, consisting of cold boiled rice wrapped in a leaf (*ka já-song*), cakes (*ki kpu*) and a tuberous root (*u sohphlang*) which is eaten raw. They are fond of all kinds of meat, especially pork and beef, although some of the Syntengs, owing to Hindu influence, abstain from eating the latter. Unlike the neighbouring Naga, Garo and Kuki tribes, the Khasis abstain from the flesh of the dog. Both Bivar and Shadwell say the reason why the Khasis do not eat the flesh of the dog is because he is in a certain sense a sacred animal amongst them. There is a Khasi folk-tale relating how the dog came to be regarded as the friend of man. It is, however, quite possible that the Khasis may never have eaten the flesh of the dog from remote times, and it is nothing extraordinary that the Khasis should differ in a detail of diet from the neighbouring Thibeto-Burman tribes which are so dissimilar to them in many respects. The Khasis, except some of the Christian community and some of the people of the Mawkhar, do not use milk, butter, or ghee as articles of food. In this respect they do not differ from the Kacharis and Rabhas of the plains or the Garos of the hills. The Mongolian race in its millions as a rule does not use milk for food, although the Tibetans and some of the Turcoman tribes are exceptions. Before fowls or animals are killed for food, prayers must be said, and rice sprinkled on the body of the animal. The staple food of the Khasis is rice and dried fish. When rice cannot be obtained or is scarce, millet or Job's tears are used instead. The latter are boiled, and a sort of porridge is obtained, which is eaten either hot or cold according to fancy. Khasis eat the flesh of nearly all wild animals, they also eat field rats and one kind of monkey (*u shrih*). The Syntengs and Lynngams are fond of tadpoles, and the Khasis consider a curry made from a kind of green frog, called *ka japieh*, a *bonne bouche*. They, however, do not eat ordinary frogs (*jakoid*). The Khasis of Mariao, Maharam, Nongstoin and some other Siemships eat the hairy caterpillar, *u'niang phlang*.

A staple food which must not be forgotten is the inner portion of the bark of the sago palm tree, *ka tlái*, which grows wild in the forest and attains a large size. The tree is felled and the outer bark removed, the soft inner part is cut into slices, dried in the sun, pounded in a mortar and then passed through a fine bamboo sieve. A reddish flour is obtained, of sweet taste, which is boiled with rice. This flour is said to make good cakes and puddings.

Although the Khasis are such varied feeders, there are some clans amongst them which are prohibited by the ordinance of *sang*, or taboo, from eating certain articles. The following are some instances:—

The Cherra Siem family cannot eat dried fish (*'khá-piah*); the Siem of Mylliem must not eat the gourd (*u patháw*); a fish called *ka'khá-lani* is taboo to some of the *Siem-lih* class. Some of the Wár people must not eat *ka ktung* (preserved fish), and the clan *'khar-um-núid* in Khyrim is debarred from the pleasure of partaking of pork. The flesh of the sow is *sang* to the *'dkhar* clan, although that of the male pig may be eaten.

Drink.

The Khasis are in the habit of regularly drinking considerable quantities either of a spirit distilled from rice or millet (*ka'iad pudka*), or of rice-beer, which is of two kinds (1) *ka'iad hiar*, (2) *ka'iad um*. Both of these are made from rice and, in some places, from millet, and the root of a plant called *u khawiang*. *Ka'iad hiar* is made by boiling the rice or millet. It is then taken out and spread over a mat, and, when it cools, fragments of the yeast (*u khawiang*) are sprinkled over it. After this it is placed in a basket, which is put in a wooden bowl. The basket is covered tightly with a cloth so as to be air-tight, and it is allowed to remain in this condition for a couple of days, during which time the liquor has oozed out into the bowl. To make *ka'iad um* the material, the rice or millet from which the *ka'iad hiar* was brewed, is made use of. It is placed in a large earthen pot and allowed to remain there for about five days to ferment, after which the liquor is strained off. *Ka'iad hiar* is said to be stronger than *ka'iad um*. The former is used frequently by distillers of country spirit for mixing with the wort so as to set up fermentation. The people of the high plateaux generally prefer rice spirit, and the Wárs of the southern slopes of the Khasi and Jaintia Hills customarily partake of it also. The Khasis of the western hills, e.g. of the Nongstoin Siemship, and the Lynngams, Bhois, Lalungs, and Hadems almost invariably drink rice-beer, but the Syntengs, like the Khasi uplanders, drink rice-spirit. Rice-beer (*ka'iad um*) is a necessary article for practically all Khasi and Synteng religious ceremonies of importance, it being the custom for the officiating priest to pour out libations of liquor from a hollow gourd (*u klong*) to the gods on these occasions. As there is no Excise in the district, except within a five-mile radius of Shillong, liquor of both the above descriptions can be possessed and sold without restriction.

According to some Khasi traditions the Khasis in ancient times used not to drink spirits, but confined themselves to rice-beer. It is only in the last couple of generations that the habit of drinking spirits has crept in, according to them. From Khasi accounts, the use of spirits is on the increase, but there is no means of testing these statements. There can be no doubt, however, that at the present time a very large amount of spirit is manufactured and consumed in the district. The spirit is distilled both for home consumption and for purposes of sale; in some villages, e.g. Mawlai and Marbisu, near Shillong, where there are fifty-nine and forty-nine stills respectively, there being a still almost in every house. Mawlai village supplies a great deal of the spirit which is drunk in Shillong, and from Marbisu spirit is carried for sale to various parts of the hills. Other large distilling centres are Cherrapunji, with forty-seven stills; Jowai, with thirty-one stills; Laitkynsew, with fifty-four stills; Nongwar, thirty-one stills; and Rangthang, thirty-seven stills.

From what has been stated above some idea may be gathered how very large the number of stills in the Khasi and Jaintia Hills is. I am not in a position to state with any degree of accuracy what is the amount of spirit manufactured or consumed in the year, but it is very considerable. The out-turn of a Khasi still has been reckoned at from four to eight bottles per day. From this estimate, and the fact that there are 1,530 stills in the district, it may be roughly calculated what is the consumption annually. Practically the whole of the spirit is consumed within the district. The liquor which is manufactured is far stronger than the spirit distilled in the ordinary out-stills in the plains. It has been stated by an expert analyst that the Khasi spirit contains 60 to 80 per cent. of proof spirit, and that it possesses "an exceptionally nice flavour and taste." The usual price at which it is sold is 4 to 6 annas a quart bottle, a second quality being sometimes sold for 3 annas. It will be seen that the liquor is exceedingly cheap. A Khasi in the villages of the interior can get drunk for 2 annas, [19] or a quarter of an ordinary coolie's daily wage. Drunkenness prevails on every market day at Cherrapunji, Jowai, and other large háts, and on occasions when there are gatherings of the people for various purposes. This cheap but strong spirit is demoralizing the people, and some restriction of its use would be welcomed by many. In the Khasi Welsh Methodist Church abstention from liquor is made a condition of Church membership, but the vast number of stills and the facilities with which liquor can be obtained are a constant source of temptation to the Christian community, and cause many defections.

Games.

The Khasis have many games, but their principal game is archery, this may be said to be the national game, and is a very popular form of recreation amongst them, the sport being indulged in from about the beginning of January to the end of May each year. The following is a description of a Khasi archery meeting, for the details of which I am largely indebted to U Job Solomon. By way of introduction it should be stated that the Khasis opine that arrow-shooting originated at the beginning of creation. The Khasi Eve (*Ka-mei-ka-nong-hukum*) had two sons to whom she taught the toxophilite art, at the same time she warned them never to lose their tempers over the game. At the present day villages have regular archery meetings, the men of one village challenging those of another. There are men on both sides called *nong khan khnam* (lit., he who stops the arrow). This man, by uttering spells, and reciting the shortcomings of the opposite side, is supposed to possess the power of preventing the arrows of the opposing party hitting the mark. These men also, to some extent, may be said to perform the duties of umpires. They may be styled umpires for the sake of convenience in this account. Before the match commences conditions are laid down by the umpires of both sides, such as (*a*) the day on which the contest is to take place; (*b*) the place of the meeting; (*c*) the number of arrows to be shot by each archer; (*d*) the distinguishing marks to be given to the arrows of either side; (*e*) the amounts of the stakes on each side; (*f*) the number of times the competitors are to shoot on the day of the archery meeting, and many other conditions too numerous to mention here. The targets are generally small bundles of grass called "*u skum*," about 1 ft. long by 4 in. in diameter, fastened on a small pole. Sometimes targets are made from the root of a plant called *ka soh pdung*. The distances from the point where the marksmen stand to the targets are some 40 to 50 yards. Each side has its own target, the different targets being placed in a line, and the competitors taking up their positions in a straight line at right angles to the line of fire, and facing the targets; each side in turn then shoots at its own target. Early in the morning of the day fixed for the contest the umpire of each side sits in front of his target with a hollow bamboo full of water in his hand, the bows and arrows being laid on the ground alongside the targets. The umpire then repeats all the conditions of the contest, invokes the aid of the primeval woman (*ka mei ka nong hukum*) aforesaid, goes through certain incantations freely referring to the many faults of the opposite side, and pours water at intervals from the bamboo in front of the target. This business lasts about two hours. Then they exhort the competitors of their respective sides, and the match commences amidst loud shouts. Every time there is a hit there are loud cheers, the competitors leaping high into the air, the umpires muttering their incantations all the while. At the end of each turn the number of hits are counted by representatives of both sides. At the close of the day the side with the greatest number of hits wins the match, the successful party returning home, dancing and shouting. The young women admirers of both sides assemble, and dispense refreshments to the competitors, taking a keen interest in the proceedings withal. Frequently large wagers are made on either side. In the *Khadar Blang* portion of the Nongkrem State as much as Rs. 500 are occasionally wagered on either side. In Jowai the practice is also to bet a lump sum, the amount being raised by subscription from amongst the competitors. More usual bets are, however, about one anna a head. The *nong khang khnam* and the men who prepare the targets receive presents from their respective sides. The Khasi bow carries a considerable distance, an arrow shot over 180 yards being within the personal knowledge of the writer. It is believed that Khasi bows wielded by experts carry up to 200 yards. The average range may be said, however, to be 150 to 180 yards.

Yule mentions peg-top spinning amongst Khasi children as being indigenous and not an importation, but Bivar thinks that the game is of foreign introduction. I am, however, inclined to agree with Yule that peg-top spinning is indigenous, inasmuch as this game could not have been copied from the Sylhetis or the Assamese of the plains, who do not indulge in it. As the British had only recently established themselves in the hills when Yule wrote, they would scarcely have had time or opportunity to introduce an English children's game. Khasi children also play a kind of "hop Scotch" (*khyndat mala shito* and *ia tiet hile*), and Yule writes, "Another of their recreations is an old acquaintance also, which we are surprised to meet with in the Far East. A very tall thick bamboo is planted in the ground, and well oiled. A silver ornament, or a few rupees placed at the top, reward the successful climber." A leg of mutton, or a piece of pork fixed at the top of this pole would render the pastime identical with the "greasy-pole" climbing of English villages. The following are some other Khasi games:—

Wrestling; two persons grasping each other's hands with the fingers interlocked, and then trying to push one another down; tug-of-war with a piece of stick, the two combatants placing their feet one against the other; butting at one another like bulls, and trying to upset each other (*ia tur masi*); long jump; high jump; blind-man's buff; flying kites; pitching cowries into a hole in the ground; a game like marbles, only played with round pebbles, and others.

Manufactures.

The manufactures of the Khasis are few in number, and do not seem to show any tendency to increase. On the contrary, two of the most important industries, the smelting of iron ore and the forging of iron implements therefrom, and the cotton-spinning industries at Mynso and Suhtnga, show signs of dying out. Ploughshares and hoes and bill-hooks can now be obtained more cheaply from the plains than from the forges in the hills, and Manchester piece goods are largely taking the place of cloths of local manufacture. The iron industry in former days was an important one, and there is abundant evidence that the workings were on a considerable scale, e.g. at Nongkrem and Laitlyngkot, in the shape of large granite boulders which have fallen to the ground from the sides of the hills owing to the softer rock which filled the interstices between the boulders having been worked out by the ironworkers, their process being to dig out the softer ferruginous rock, and then extract the iron ore from it by means of washing. The softer rock having been removed, the heavier portions fell by their own weight, and rolled down to the bottom of the slopes, the result being the great number of boulders to be seen near the sites of these workings.

Colonel Lister, writing in 1853, estimated that 20,000 maunds of iron were exported from the hills in the shape of hoes to the Assam Valley, and in lumps of pig iron to the Surma Valley, where it was used by boat-builders for clamps. Nowadays the smelting of iron is carried on in very few places. There are still smelting-houses at Nongkrem and Nongsprung, but these are practically the only places left where smelting of iron ore goes on: there are many forges where rough iron brought from the plains is melted down and forged into billhooks and hoes. Messrs. Yule and Cracroft have described the native process of smelting iron, and it is only necessary to refer to their papers if information is required on the subject. Yule's account is a very full one, and is to be found at page 853, vol. xi. part ii. of the Journal of the Asiatic Society of Bengal. The system pursued, both in the extraction and in the subsequent smelting of the ore, is the same at the present day as that described by Yule. Dr. Oldham, writing in 1863, says, "The quality of this Khasi iron is excellent for all such purposes as Swedish iron is now used for. The impurity of the blooms (or masses of the metal in a molten state), however, as they are sent to market, is a great objection to its use, and the waste consequent thereon renders it expensive. It would also form steel or wootz (Indian steel) of excellent quality. I have no doubt that the manufacture could be greatly improved and possibly extended." Dr. Oldham, however, goes on to remark that the manufacture of iron could not be very much extended, owing to the scanty dissemination of the ore in the rocks, and the consequent high cost of obtaining it. At present the want of any permanent supply of water prevents the natives from working for more than a few days during the year, whilst the rains are heavy, and they can readily obtain sufficient force of water for the washing of the ore from its matrix. The export of iron in any form from the district has now almost died out, only a few hoes being brought down by the Khasis from Laitdom, in Khadsawphra, to the Burdwar and Palasbari markets in the Kamrup District of the Assam Valley. Iron of English manufacture has, of course, much cheapened the market, but probably the fact that the parts of the country in the neighbourhood of the rocks which contain the metal have been denuded completely of timber, charcoal being necessary for smelting, has affected the production almost as much as the presence of cheap iron in the market.

Manufacture of Eri Silk Cloths and Cotton Cloths in the Jaintia Hills.

The number of weavers in the district at the last Census was 533. This number in the Census Report is ascribed to the cotton industry, no mention being made of weavers of silk. The spinning of Eri silk thread, and weaving it into cloths is, however, a fairly considerable industry amongst the Khyrwang and Nongtung villages of the Jaintia Hills. The Nongtungs and Khyrwangs rear their own Eri worms, and spin the silk from the cocoons. The late Mr. Stack, in his admirable note on silk in Assam, says, "Throughout the whole range of the southern hills, from the Mikir country, Eri thread is in great request for weaving those striped cloths, in which the mountaineers delight," but this observation should have been confined to the Jaintia Hills portion of this district, the Khasis not weaving themselves either in silk or cotton. The Khasis obtain their silk cloths from the Assam Valley, and from the Nongtung or Khyrwang villages in Jaintia. The latter villages have given the name to the striped cloth, *ka jáin Khyrwang*, which is almost invariably worn by the Syntengs. Mr. Stack has given in detail a description of the silk industry in Assam, and it is not therefore necessary to go over the same ground here. The Khyrwang cloth is red and white, mauve and white, or chocolate and white, the cloth being worn by both men and women. The Khyrwang cloths vary in price from Rs. 5 to Rs. 25, according to size and texture. These cloths are the handiwork of women alone, and a woman working every day regularly will take six months to manufacture a cloth valued at Rs. 25; but, as a rule, in the leisurely manner in which they work, it takes a year to complete it.

Cotton Cloths.

In the Jaintia Hills at Mynso cotton is spun into thread, and weaving is carried on there, but on a limited scale. The Mynso people weave the small strips of cloth worn by the men to serve the purpose of the Assamese *lengti* or Hindi *languti*. In Suhtnga the people import cotton thread from Mynso and weave the (*ingki*) or sleeveless coat, peculiar to the district; these coats are dyed red and blue. The dark blue or black dye is obtained from the leaf of a plant called *u sybu*, which Mr. Rita has classified as *strobilanthus hoeditolius*, which grows in the gardens round the homesteads. The leaves are dried, then reduced to powder, mixed with hot water, and the skeins of thread are steeped in the liquid. The colour is permanent. The red dye is obtained from the mixture of the dry bark of two shrubs, *ka lapyndong* (*symplocos racemosa*, Roxb.), and *ka 'larnong* (*morinda-tinctoria*, Roxb.), the latter being the same as the Assamese (aacukaa.th) *áchukáth*. The bark is dried, then pounded, and the two sorts are mixed together and made into a paste with hot water. The skeins are steeped in this mixture for twenty-four hours, then taken out and divided, and again steeped for another twenty-four hours. The Lalungs and Bhois and Lynngams all weave cotton cloths, which are generally dyed blue, sometimes striped blue and red. The Wárs weave cotton cloths which are dyed red and yellow, the cloths being woven in checks. Mr. Darrah remarks that the cotton grown in the Jaintia Hills is said to be the best cotton produced in the province. Its thread can be more closely woven than that of other kinds. This statement, however, is not borne out by Mr. Allen, writing in 1858, who says that the cotton is of inferior quality, the staple being short and woolly. The cotton cloths woven by the Bhois are called *spua*.

Pottery.

The Census Report of 1901 gave the number of persons who are supported by the manufacture of pottery at 54 only. Pottery is manufactured at one place only in the Jaintia Hills, Larnai. The Larnai potters make many of the earthen pots to be found in the Khasi houses called *khiew ranei*, or sometimes *khiew Larnai*. Mr. Gait says, "These potters use two kinds of clay mixed; one is of a dark blue colour, *'dew-iong*, and the other of a greyish colour, *'dew khluid*. These clays seem to correspond closely with the *kumár máti* and *hira máti* of the Brahmaputra Valley."

The clay at Larnai is well beaten out upon a hide, or upon a flat disc of wood; the women fashion the pots by hand, they do not use the potter's wheel. The pots are sun-dried and then fired. They are painted black with an infusion of a bark called *sohliya*. The Larnai potters also make flower-pots which are sold in Shillong at from 2 annas to 4 annas each, the price of the ordinary pot or *khiew ranei* varying from 2 pice to 4 annas each. A water-pot (*khiew um*) is also fashioned, which is sometimes used in the manufacture of liquor, price 4 annas to 6 annas each.

CHAPTER III

Laws and Customs

Tribal Organization.

The inhabitants of the Khasi and Jaintia Hills may be said to be divided into the following sections:—Khasi, Synteng or Pnar, Wár, Bhoi, and Lynngam. These divisions represent collections of people inhabiting several tracts of country and speaking dialects which, although often deriving their origin from the Khasi roots, are frequently so dissimilar to the standard language as to be almost unrecognizable. The above sections may be sub-divided as follows:—The Khasis into the inhabitants of the central high plateau, Cherra and Nongstoin, Maharam, Mario, Nongkhlaw, and the neighbouring Siemships. The Syntengs or Pnars may be divided as follows:—Into Syntengs proper, Nongtungs and Kharwangs; the Wárs into War proper, and Wár Pnar; the Bhois into Jinthongs, Mynris, Ryngkhongs, and the Khasi-Bhois, i.e. Khasis who inhabit the low country to the north of the district, which is called generally the "Bhoi." The Lynngams are a separate division. They must not be confused with the Dkos or Hanas who are Garos. It must, however, be remembered that the Jinthong, Mynri, and Ryngkhong Sub-divisions of the Bhoi division are not Khasi, but Mikir, i.e. they belong to the Bodo or Bara group. The Lynngams are half Khasis and half Garos, and the Dkos or Hanas are Garos who observe the Khasi custom of erecting memorial stones. The above tribes and sub-tribes are not strictly endogamous, nor are they strictly exogamous, but they are more endogamous than exogamous; for instance, Syntengs more often marry Syntengs than Khasis, and *vice versâ*, and it would be usually considered derogatory for a Khasi of the Uplands to marry a Bhoi or Wár woman, and a disgrace to marry a Lynngam. These divisions are subdivided into a number of septs, taking Mr. Risley's definition of "sept" as being the largest exogamous division of the tribe. It will, however, be more convenient to speak of these septs as "clans," the word "clan" having been used in other parts of this Monograph and by other writers.

Many of the clans trace their descent from ancestresses or *kiaw* (grandmothers), who are styled *ki Iawbei-Tynrai*, lit. grandmothers of the root (i.e. the root of the tree of the clan). In some of the clans, the name of this ancestress survives; take as instances the Mylliem-ngap and Mylliem-pdah clans of the Khyrim State, the names of the ancestresses of the clans being *ka ngap* (honey, i.e. the sweet one), and *ka pdah* respectively. This tribal ancestress, as will be seen in the paragraph of the monograph dealing with ancestor-worship, is greatly revered, in fact, she may almost be said to be deified. The descendants of one ancestress of the clan, *Ka Iawbei Tynrai*, are called *shi kur* or one clan. We then come to the division of the *kpoh* or sub-clan, all the descendants of one great grandmother (*ka Iawbei Tymmen*), being styled *shi kpoh*. The next division is the *ïing* (lit. house) or family. It is almost invariably the case that the grandmother, her daughters and the daughter's children, live together under one roof, the grandmother during her life-time being the head of the house. The grandmother is styled *ka Iawbei Khynraw*, or the young grandmother, to distinguish her from the other two grandmothers, *ka Iawbei-tynrai* and *ka Iawbei-tymmen* who have been mentioned above. The young grandmother, her daughters and their children are said to belong to *shi iing*, one house, the word *iing* in this instance possessing amongst the Khasis the same significance as the English word *family*.

We will now see how the Khasi clan (*kur* or *jaid*) grew out of the Khasi family (*iing*). Let us take the example of the great Diengdoh clan of Cherra. Disregarding the myth that the Diengdohs are descended from a mermaid, it may be stated that there seems to be a fairly general belief amongst the Diengdohs that their first ancestress or *kiaw* came from the country beyond the Kopili river (some go so far as to say that she came from the Assam Valley), to the Jaintia Hills, where she found a husband. Legend relates that it was one of the peculiarities of this woman that she was able to accommodate herself in an earthen jar or *lalu*, which fact gave rise to the name *Lalu* by which she and her children were called by the Syntengs. The family prospered during the time when a powerful chief of the Malngiang clan held sway in the Jaintia Hills. On the death of this king a civil war arose, and the *Lalu* family, together with many others, beat a retreat across the river Kopili. Here they lived in prosperity for some generations until a plague arose and carried off the whole family except one female, called *Ka Iaw-Iaw*, who became the sole owner of the family wealth. Many desired to marry her for her possessions, and it was owing to their importunities that she fled to Jowai to the house of a *lyngdoh* or priest. The *lyngdoh*, under pressure from his wife, tried to sell Ka Iaw-Iaw as a slave, but no one would offer more than 20 *cowries* for her (*shi-bdi*); this decided the *lyngdoh* to keep her. Out of gratitude for this kindness, Ka Iaw-Iaw brought her wealth from beyond the Kopili to the *lyngdoh's* house, when the son of the *lyngdoh* was given her in marriage. They lived happily for some time, when some adventurers from beyond the Kopili came to Jowai with the intention of carrying off this rich bride. The *lyngdoh*, however, received warning of their intent, arranged for the escape of Ka Iaw-Iaw, and they fled to Sohphohkynrum, a place near Nongkrem in the Khasi Hills, where she established a village. Here Ka Iaw-Iaw was called *Ka Iaw-shibdi*, because she paid every man who was engaged by her in founding a market there 20 cowries (*shi-bdi*) per day for their labours. Here also she is credited with having first introduced the art of smelting iron, and she is said to have made various iron implements which she exported to the plains. She is also said to have kept a huge herd of pigs which she fed in a large trough hollowed out of a *diengdoh* tree; it is to this fact that the Diengdoh clan owes its name. After *Ka Iaw-shibdi* and her children had lived for some years in prosperity at Sohphohkynrum, they were attacked by the Swarga Raja (the Ahom King), U long Raja (probably the Raja of Jaintia), and the Assamese Barphukan. They fled to a place called Lyndiangumthli, near Lyngkyrdem. Finding this place unsuitable as a home, the family split up into four divisions. One division returned to Jowai, where it increased and multiplied and afterwards grew into the Lalu clan, another went to Nongkhlaw and became the Diengdoh Kylla clan; another went to Mawiong and formed what is now known as the Pariong clan; the fourth, after some vicissitudes of fortune, went to Rangjyrteh and Cherra, at which place it established the powerful Diengdohbah clan, and became afterwards one of the chief *mantri* or minister clans of this state. I have quoted the history of the origin of the Diengdoh clan at some length, to show what I consider to be an example of the Khasi conceptions of how the clan was formed, i.e. from a common ancestress, all of the clans having traditions more or less of descent from some particular *Kiaw* or ancestress. This story moreover is remarkable as pointing to a Khasi migration from beyond the Kopili river to their present abode. The clans of the present day are nothing more or less than overgrown families, they are bound together by the religious tie of ancestor-worship in common, and of a common tribal sepulchre, except in cases of clans which have, owing to their size, spit up into several sub-divisions, like the Diengdoh clan; such sub-divisions possessing their own cromlechs. Ancestor-worship in common and tribal sepulchres in common seem to indicate that the original unit was the family and not the tribe, for there would be no reason for the members of a clan to worship the same household gods and to deposit the remains of the clan members in the same tomb unless there was some strong tie, such as that of consanguinity, binding them together. It has been already mentioned that each of these clans is strictly exogamous; this again supports the family origin theory. A Khasi can commit no greater sin than to marry within the tribe. Some of the clans are prohibited moreover from intermarriage with other clans, because of such clans being of common descent. If the titles (see Appendix) are carefully examined, it will be seen that some of them bear the names of animals, such as the *Shrieh* or monkey clan, the *Tham* or crab clan, or of trees, such as the Diengdoh clan (already referred to). The members of these clans do not apparently regard the animals or natural objects, from which they derive their names, as totems, inasmuch as they do not abstain from killing, eating or utilizing them. The names of these objects are connected generally with some story, concerning the history of the clan, but there is no evidence to show that the clans-folk ever regarded the above animals or objects as their tribal totems. If the lists of the Khyrim and Cherra clans are examined, it will be seen what a large number bear the name of *Dkhar* or its abbreviation '*Khar*. The word *dkhar* is that applied by a Khasi to an inhabitant of the plains. We come across names such as '*khar-mukhi, khar sowali*, the first word being an abbreviation of *dkhar*, and *mukhi* being the common Bengali name which occurs in Chandra Mukhi, Surjya Mukhi, &c. Sowali (*chowali*) is the common Assamese word for a girl. The ancestresses of these tribes were plains women, carried off, no doubt, in the raids made by the Khasis over the border into Assam and Sylhet. The word *Jong* in the list of tribes is a Synteng synonym of *kur* or *jaid*, and the Wár word *khong*, which will often be found in the names of the tribes of the twenty-five villages of the Khyrim State, is merely a corruption of *jong* or *iong*, the Synteng word for clan. Let us now see how the State or Khasi Siemship was formed out of a collection of these clans, how these clans obtained political powers, how some clans became more powerful than others, and how a Khasi King or Siem is appointed.

State Organization.

We have studied in the preceding chapter the formation of the clan from the family, and how the former established villages. Let us now turn to the constitution of the Khasi State, which, it will be seen, has been formed, in more than one instance, by the voluntary association of villages, or groups of villages. The head of the Khasi State is the Siem or chief. A Khasi state is a limited monarchy, the Siem's powers being much circumscribed. According to custom, he can perform no act of any importance without first consulting and obtaining the approval of his durbar, upon which the state *mantris* sit. This durbar must not be confused with the electoral durbar which will be referred to later. It is an executive council over which the Siem presides, and also possesses judicial powers (for a description of a judicial durbar, see page 91 of the monograph). The form of summons to appear before this durbar used to be a knotted piece of string or cane, the number of knots denoting the degrees of urgency of the summons, not a piece of pork, as one writer has said. Pork is a luxury which is not usually distributed gratis. The Siem manages the State business through his *mantris*, although it is true that in some States the members of the Siem family have been allowed a considerable share of the State management. This latter arrangement is, however, a departure from the ordinary rule in the Siemships, and is regarded as unconstitutional. In some States there are village headmen, styled Sirdars, who settle cases, collect labour, and assess and receive for the chief the *pynsuk*, which may be literally translated as "gratification." In Nongstoin there is an official styled *lyngskor*, who is the superior of a number of village sirdars, and who acts as the Siem's deputy-governor. In the Khasi Hills there is no land revenue, nor are there any tithes or other imposts levied upon the cultivator's produce. The land, to a great extent, is the property of the different clans and villages, although in some instances there are estates owned by private persons. The chief is entitled to receive the income that arises from what are known as the *raj* or State lands only. All that the Siem usually receives from his people in the way of direct revenue is the State subscription, or *pynsuk*, mentioned above. Even this is supposed to be a voluntary contribution, and it is not demanded in some States. This tax is nominally a collection to meet the expenses of the State ceremonies, but is really a means of increasing the chief's private income. The contribution varies in amount according to the means of the villagers. The Siem's principal source of income, however, in all the Khasi States is the toll (*khrong*), which he takes from those who sell at the markets in his territory. As the Khasis are great traders these tolls are often at the larger markets fairly valuable. The chief raises no excise revenue, the manufacture of both fermented and distilled liquor being subject to no fiscal restrictions whatsoever. In a few States the Siems are commencing to levy registration fees, but the amounts are insignificant. Judicial fines are divided between the chief and the members of the durbar. In some States the Siems' incomes amount to a few hundreds a year only. Generally speaking, the Khasi chiefs are necessarily a very impecunious set of persons, and many of them are indebted to, comparatively speaking, large amounts. The Siem is appointed from the Siem family, there being such a family in each of the fifteen Khasi States. The most important States are Khyrim, Mylliem, Cherra, Nongstoin, and Nongkhlaw. There are a few other petty States presided over by Lyngdohs, Sirdars, or Wahadadars. A fact which is of universal application is, that heirship to the Siemship lies through the female side. The customary line of succession is uniform in all cases, except in Khyrim, save that in some instances cousins rank with brothers, or are preferred to grand-nephews, instead of being postponed to them. The difference between the rule of succession and the rule of inheritance to real property should be noted. In the former case the sons of the eldest uterine sister inherit in order of priority of birth, although it is true that this rule has sometimes been disregarded. In cases of succession to realty, however, the inheritance goes to the youngest daughter of the deceased's mother, and after her to her youngest daughter. In successions to the Siemships, in the absence of male heirs from the eldest sister, the succession passes, by what has been aptly described as the "knight's move," to the male children of the next eldest sister. In Khyrim the custom of succession is peculiar, there being a High Priestess, and heirship being limited to her male relatives. Generally speaking, it would appear that succession was originally controlled by a small electoral body constituted of the heads (*lyngdohs*), of certain priestly clans, who, it is presumed, exercised their authority to reject candidates, when necessary, mainly on religious grounds. There has, however, been a distinct tendency towards the broadening of the elective basic. In the large State of Khyrim the number of the electoral body has been greatly increased by the inclusion of the representative headmen of certain dominant but non-priestly clans (*mantris*). In other States the Council has been widened by the addition to it of village headmen (*sirdars*), or the chief superintendents (*basans*) of the village markets, tolls from which constitute the chief item in the public receipts of these States. A further step towards the recognition of the public will in the nomination of a Siem has been the introduction of popular elections, at which all the adult males vote. Such popular elections were very greatly due to the views held by Colonel Bivar who was Deputy-Commissioner of the Khasi and Jaintia Hills from 1865 to 1877. These elections have been, in many States, an innovation which is hardly in accord with public sentiment, and in many cases the voters have done no more than confirm the selection of a special electoral body. It is, however, clear that the idea of popular elections is not one with which the people are unfamiliar, e.g. in Langrim State, where all the adult males customarily vote at an election of a Siem. Popular election has also customary in the Nobosohpoh and Bhowal States, in cases where a special electoral body has been unable to agree upon a nomination, and also in Nongspung, if a Council of five *lyngdohs*, which has in this State authority to declare who is the rightful heir, but not to disqualify him, cannot come to an unanimous decision. The Siems are appointed by an assembly, or *durbar*, which will be described later. The chiefs, having been thus chosen by the *durbar*, which is supposed by the people to be an institution of

Divine origin, are styled, *ki Siem u blei*, or Siems of God. In most States the Siem is the religious as well as the secular head, e.g. in the Cherra State, where the Siem is also *lyngdoh*. In Khyrim State the Siem has sacerdotal duties to perform at different religious ceremonies, especially at the time of the annual Nongkrem dance. It is the custom for the Siem to consult the auspices with the soothsayers for the good of the State. The Siem in matters judicial acts as a judge, the whole body of the *durbar* being the jury. In olden days the Siem marched to war at the head of his army. It is not customary to recognize an heir-apparent, and the young men of the Siem family pursue the ordinary avocations of a Khasi, not comporting themselves in the least like scions of royalty. In quite recent years there have been instances of Siems having been summoned, like the Roman Cincinnatus, from quite humble positions, to undertake the duties of chief. We will now turn to an examination of the systems in the different Siemships. In the Kyrim or Nongkrem State there is a spiritual head, i.e. a High Priestess, *Ka Siem Sad*, who is responsible for the due performance of the State religious ceremonies, although, as already stated, the Siem also performs some of these duties. The temporal power here is delegated by the High Priestess to a Siem, who is her son or her nephew, or occasionally some more distant male descendant. It is the duty of an official called a *lyngskor*, who is the official spokesman of the Siem's *durbar*, to propose a new Siem to the six *lyngdohs*, or priests, and to the heads of the twenty-four *mantri* clans. The latter then decide in *durbar* whether the proposed Siem should be appointed. In the event of their disapproving of the *lyngskor's* nominations they proceed to elect another Siem. The High Priestess is appointed by the above electors, the order of succession to the post wing as follows:—She is succeeded by her eldest surviving daughter; failing daughters, by the eldest daughter of her eldest daughter; failing daughters of her eldest daughter; by the eldest daughter of her second daughter, and so on. If there are no daughters or grand-daughters, as above, she is succeeded by her eldest sister. In the absence of sisters, she is succeeded by the eldest daughter of her mother's eldest sister, and so on. In this State the tradition runs that the first High Priestess was Ka Pah Syntiew, i.e. the flower-lured one. Ka Pah Syntiew was a beautiful maiden who had as her abode a cave at Marai, near Nongkrem, whence she was enticed by a man of the Mylliem-ngap clan by means of a flower. She was taken by him to be his bride, and she became not only the first High Priestess, but also the mother of the Siems of Nongkrem. [20] In Nongkrem the electors may disqualify the first, or any, heir to the Siemship for sufficient reason according to the Khasi religion and custom, such as bad character, physical disability, change of religion, etc. If the first heir be disqualified, the next in order must be appointed Siem, unless he be disqualified, and so on. In this State there are six divisions, each of which is known as a *raj*. In each *raj* there is a *durbar*, to which are submitted for approval the elections of the heads of the *mantri* clans. These elections are subject to the approval of the Siem. The Siem, sitting with the *durbar* of the *raj* concerned, may dismiss a *lyngdoh*, *lyngskor*, or *mantri*, for bad conduct, or on account of physical disability, in which case another *lyngdoh*, *lyngskor*, or *mantri* would be appointed, as stated above. The Mylliem State originally formed a portion of the Nongkrem State, but owing to a quarrel between one of the Siems and his nephew there was a partition. In this State the electors are the heads of five *mantri* clans, eleven *matabors*, or heads of clans, and certain *basans*, and other heads of clans. A majority of the electors is sufficient for the election of a Siem. A Siem is succeeded by the eldest of his uterine brothers; failing such brothers, by the eldest of his sisters' sons; failing such nephews, by the eldest of the sons of his sisters daughters; failing such grandnephews, by the eldest of the sons of his mother's sisters; and, failing such first cousins, by the eldest of his male cousins on the female side, other than first cousins, those nearest in degree of relationship having prior claim. If there were no heirs male, as above, he would be succeeded by the eldest of his uterine sisters; in the absence of such sisters, by the eldest of his sisters' daughters: failing such nieces, by the eldest of the daughters of his sisters' daughters; failing such grand-nieces, by the eldest of the daughters of his mother's sisters; and failing such first cousins, by the eldest of his female cousins on the female side, other than first cousins, those nearest in degree of relationship having prior claim. A female Siem would be succeeded by her eldest son, and so on. As in the Khyrim State, the first, or any other subsequent heir, may be disqualified by the electors for sufficient reason. An elector is succeeded by the eldest of his brothers; failing brothers, by the eldest of the sons of his sisters, and so on. An elector can be dismissed by the Siem, but only for good cause and with the consent of his *durbar*.

In the Nongstoin State there is a tradition that the first Siem originally came from Simsong [21] Durgapur. The name, Sushong Durgapur, of the place at the foot of the Garo Hills in the Mymensing district, may be a corruption of the former. The Siems are supposed to be descended from a stag, possibly a relic of totemism in this family. In this State there is a large electoral durbar consisting of 2 *mantris*, 31 *lyngdohs*, 25 *sirdars*, 1 *lyngskor*, and 1 *basan*. The *lyndohs* are the heads of the priestly clans, by whom they are chosen. The sirdars of villages are appointed by the Siem in conjunction with the adult males of the different villages. There are two *lyngskors* and two *basans* in the State, but one *lyngskor* and one *basan* only at present are members of the durbar which nominates the Siem. A *lyngskor* is the Siem's agent for the purpose of governing a collection of villages. He is appointed by the Siem with the consent of the adult males of the villages which he is to supervise. The Siem family of Nongkhlaw, or Khadsawphra, is believed to have been founded by a Synteng of the name of U Shajer, who left the Jowai hills with his sister, Ka Shaphlong, because she had failed to obtain her share of the family property in Jaintia. This man is said to have purchased certain lands in Bardwar in Kamrup. Apparently he did not obtain possession of this estate, for he came up into the Khasi Hills, and finding there certain villages without a ruler, he, at the wish of the *lyngdohs* of these villages, consolidated them into a state over which he ruled as a Siem. He was succeeded by his sister's son, U Syntiew who further extended his territories until he obtained possession of other villages. U Syntiew is said to have delegated a portion of his powers to his two sisters, Ka Jem and Ka Sanglar, who ruled at Sohiong and Nongkhlaw respectively. Succeeding rulers further extended the Nongkhlaw territory. In 1829, U Tirut Singh rebelled against the East India Company and carried on for four years a successful guerilla warfare. He was finally captured, and was imprisoned for life by the British Government. According to the statement of Raja Kine Singh, it would seem that formerly the heads of five clans had the right to appoint the Siem, i.e. the heads of 3 *lyngdoh* clans and of the Jaid Dykhar, and Diengdoh clans. In the Cherra State the electors are the male adults of the State, who are represented on the State durbar by the *mantris* of the 12 aristocratic clans, known as the *khadar kur*, and certain representative elders. This State is divided for electoral purposes into the following divisions:—

I. Cherra, or Sohra, consisting of 8 villages, inclusive of Cherra, which is the capital. These villages return the heads of the 12 tribes, as well as 5 elders, as their representativee on the electoral durbar.

II. The "five" villages, or 5 tribes. This division now consists of 17 villages, which return 5 representative elders.

III. The "twelve" villages, comprising now 38 villages, which return 12 representative elders.

IV. The "four" villages, comprising now 5 villages, which return 4 elders.

V. The "sixteen" villages, which return 6 representative elders.

VI. Three villages, which return 3 and 4 sirdars and 2 elders respectively.

In this State it is the custom for a Siem to cremate the body of his predecessor. Unless he performs the cremation ceremony, he is not considered to be Siem according to the Khasi religion. U Hajon Manik Siem failed to cremate the body of his predecessor, U Ram Singh whose remains still repose in a wooden coffin which is kept in the house of the Siem family. The remains of Siems in this state are preserved by a peculiar process of embalming which will be found described elsewhere in this monograph. U Hajan Manik died not long ago, and his body also is awaiting cremation. U Ram Singh's remains, however, have been awaiting the funeral pyre for more than thirty years; but arrangements are being made by the present Siam U Roba Singh for the cremation ceremony. The cremation of Siems in the state is attended by a very great deal of expense, a large amount of money being spent on the feasting which then takes place. The Maharam State was ruled until 1875 by two Siems, called, respectively, the "white" and the "black" Siems. In this State originally there were five *lyngdohs* who appointed the Siems, but as in certain other States the number of the electors has been expanded by the inclusion of *mantris*, *sirdars*, and *basans*. The electors now number seventy-two persons. There is much the same state of things in the Mariaw Siemship as regards the electorate. In Rambrai, on a vacancy occurring in the Siemship, three *lyngdohs* and two *mantris* assemble and decide who is to be Siem. They then summon the sirdars of villages to meet them in *durbar* and obtain the approval of the latter to their nomination. If the sirdars do not approve, the combined durbar than decides who is to become Siem. In Nongspung there is a tradition that two sisters, Ka Jah and Ka Jem, came to the village of Nongspung, which was then ruled by two *lyngdohs*, and that the latter, having ascertained that the two sisters were of royal birth, married them. They then travelled to other villages and obtained the consent of the *lyngdohs* of these villages to the formation of all their villages into a State, of which Nongspung became the capital, and over which U Sngi Shaflong, the son of Ka Jem, was appointed Siem by the five principal *lyngdohs*. After some generations the lyngdoh of Mairang with his villages became subject to the Siem of Nongkhlaw, an event which finds mention in the annals of the Nongkhlaw State as the conquest of the territory of the "Black" Siem of Nongspung. Another *lyngdoh* was appointed in place of the one whose territory had been thus annexed.

In the Mawiong State the ancient custom was that six *basans* appointed the Siem, subject to the approval of the people of the Siemship. In the Nobosohpoh State there are two Siem families, the "Black" and the "White" from either of which it has apparently been the custom for the people to select a Siem, as they wished. In Mawsynram the electors of the Siem are the heads of the four principal clans in the State. On a recent occasion, the electors being equally divided regarding the appointment of a Siem, it was necessary to appeal to the people of the State. In Langrin there are, as in Maharam and Nobosohpoh, two main branches of the Siem family, i.e. the "Black" and the "White" Siems. Here there is no special electoral body; all the adults of the state have the right to vote at the election of a Siem. In Bhawal State Siems are appointed by the heads of eight clans whose decision is apparently final, provided that it is unanimous. In Malai-Sohmat a bare majority of the heads of six clans would be sufficient for the election of a Siem. Presumably both in Bhawal and Malai-Sohmat, if the electors were equally divided, there would be an appeal to the people. Mention has been made above of States over which *lyngdohs* possess temporal as well as spiritual powers. The States of Sobiong, Mawphlang, and Lyniong may be quoted as examples. Here the *lyngdoh* is elected from the *lyngdoh* clan by all the adult males of the state. Some small States, such as Maodon and Pomsanngut, are presided over by Sirdars, a name which has probably been introduced during the British era of supremacy in these hills. The Sirdar is elected by the adult males of the State. In Mawlong there are a Sirdar, a *lyngdoh*, and a *doloi* who govern the State. These two latter officials are elected by the people as in the case of Sirdars. In the Shella Confederacy there are four officials who are styled *Wahadadars*, the name being probably a corruption of the Persian *'uhda-dar*. [22] These officials are elected for periods of three years each by the people.

The Jaintia Hills, which are British territory, are divided up into twenty doloiships, the doloi being an officer elected by the people, the Government reserving the right of approval or the reverse to the doloi's appointment. The dolois, under the rules for the administration of justice in the Khasi and Jaintia Hills, as well as the Sirdars of the British villages in the Khasi Hills, possess certain judicial powers. They are assisted by officials known as *pators, basans*, and *sangots* in the performance of their duties. This administration, on the whole, works well, and its success shows the wisdom of the Government in having made use of the indigenous agency it found to hand when the Jaintia territory was annexed. In the Jaintia Hills there are also three Sirdarships, the office being filled by election as in the case of dolois.

In conclusion it should be stated that it has been attempted here to give but a brief *résumé* of the Khasi political system as it exists at the present time. The above account of the procedure at elections is based on existing usage. The procedure should not, however, be regarded as stereotyped, for it will no doubt be open to such revision as may on occasion be suggested by the legitimate evolution of tribal customs.

Marriage.

It is proposed in this section to consider marriage from its social side, the religious aspect thereof being reserved for another paragraph. The most remarkable feature of the Khasi marriage is that it is usual for the husband to live with his wife in his mother-in-law's house, and not for him to take his bride home, as is the case in other communities. This arrangement amongst the Khasis is no doubt due to the prevalence of the matriarchate. As long as the wife lives in her mother's house, all her earnings go to her mother, who expends them on the maintenance of the family. Amongst the Khasis, after one or two children are born, and if a married couple get on well together, the husband frequently removes his wife and family to a house of his own, and from the time the wife leaves her mother's house she and her husband pool their earnings, which are expended for the support of the family. Amongst the Syntengs, however, and the people of Maoshai, the case is different, for with them the husband does not go and live in his mother-in-law's house, he only visits her there. In Jowai some people admitted to me that the husband came to his mother-in-law's house only after dark, and that he did not eat, smoke, or even partake of betel-nut there, the idea being that because none of his earnings go to support this house, therefore it is not etiquette for him to partake of food or other refreshment there. If a Synteng house is visited, it is unusual to find the husbands of any of the married daughters there, although the sons of the family may be seen in the house when they have returned from work. Generally in the day-time you will find in a Synteng dwelling an old crone, who is the grandmother, or even the great-grandmother, of the family, also grandchildren or great-grandchildren; but the husbands of the married daughters are not there. The Syntengs seem to have more closely preserved the customs of the matriarchate than the Khasis, and the Syntengs claim that their *niam* or religious ceremonies are purer, i.e. that they more closely correspond to what they were in ancient times than those of the Khasis. Amongst the Syntengs, occasionally, a widow is allowed to keep her husband's bones after his death, on condition that she does not remarry; the idea being that as long as the bones remain in the widow's keeping, the spirit of her husband is still with her. On this account many wives who revere their husband's memories, and who do not contemplate remarriage, purposely keep the bones for a long time. If a widow marries, even after the customary taboo period of one year, whilst her deceased husband's bones are still in her keeping, she is generally looked down upon. Her children in such a case perform the ceremony of handing over the bones of their father to his clan in a building specially erected for the purpose. The widow cannot enter therein, or even go near it, whilst the ceremony is proceeding, no matter whether the *jing sang*, or the price for removing the taboo after a husband's death, has been paid to the husband's clan or not. There is no evidence to show that polyandry ever existed amongst the Khasis. Unlike the Thibetans, the Khasi women seem to have contented themselves always with one husband, at any rate with one at a time. Certainly at the present day they are monandrists. Polygamy does not exist amongst the Khasis; such a practice would naturally not be in vogue amongst a people who observe the matriarchate. There are instances, however, of men having wives other than those they have regularly married, and in the Wár country children by such wives enjoy rights to their father's acquired property equally with the children by the legally married wife. As the clans are strictly exogamous, a Khasi cannot take a wife from his own clan; to do this would entail the most disastrous religious, as well as social consequences. For to marry within the clan is the greatest sin a Khasi can commit, and would cause excommunication by his kinsfolk and the refusal of funeral ceremonies at death, and his bones would not be allowed a resting-place in the sepulchre of the clan. To give a list of all the Khasi exogamous clans would perhaps serve no useful purpose, but I have prepared from information, kindly furnished me by the Siems of Khyrim and Cherrapunji, a list of the clans in those States which will be found in Appendices A and B. These will suffice as examples. It will be seen from the Cherra list that the different divisions of the Diengdoh clan, viz. Lalu, Diengdoh-bah, Diengdoh-kylla, are prohibited from intermarriage; this is due to those branches of the clan being descended from a common ancestress. There are other instances of clans being connected with one another, such connection being called by the Khasis *iateh kur*. Whenever such connection exists, intermarriage is strictly prohibited, and is considered to be *sang*. There is no custom of hypergamy. A Khasi cannot marry his maternal uncle's daughter during the lifetime of the maternal uncle. This is probably due to the fact that the maternal uncle, or *kni*, in a Khasi household is regarded more in the light of a father than of an uncle. His children, however, would belong to the clan of his wife, and there would, therefore, in ordinary cases be no bar to the nephew marrying one of them. Marriage with the daughters of a father's sister is not allowed during the lifetime of the father, but after the latter's death there is no religious ban, although such unions are looked upon with disfavour by the Khasis. In the Wár country, however, such marriages are totally prohibited. A Khasi cannot marry two sisters, but he can marry his deceased wife's sister after the expiry of one year from the wife's death, on payment of *jing sang* (price of *sang*, or taboo) to the wife's clan. A Khasi cannot marry the daughter of his father's brother, she is his *para kha* (lit. birth sister). Similarly he cannot marry the daughter of his father's paternal uncle. He can, however, marry the daughter of his mother's brother, provided that the brother is dead. This somewhat paradoxical state of affairs is explained by the fact that the children of the mother's brother belong to a different clan to that of the mother, i.e. to the mother's brother's wife's clan. The Khasi, Synteng, Wár, and Lynngam divisions are not strictly endogamous groups, and there is nothing to prevent intermarriage between them. For instance, it has been the custom in the Nongkhlaw Siem family to obtain husbands for the princesses of the state from the Wár country. There is no custom amongst the Khasis of two men exchanging daughters, i.e. each marrying his son to the other's daughter. Notwithstanding the existence of the matriarchate, and the fact that all ancestral property is vested in the mother, it would be a mistake to suppose that the father is a nobody in the Khasi house. It is true that the *kni*, or mother's elder brother, is the head of the house, but the father is the executive head of the new home, where, after children have been born to him, his wife and children live with him. It is he who faces the dangers of the jungles, and risks his life for wife and children. In his wife's clan he occupies a very high place, he is second to none but *u kni*, the maternal uncle, while in his own family circle a father and husband is nearer to his children and his wife than *u kni*. The Khasi saying is, "*u kpa uba lah ban iai, u kni uba tang ha ka iap ka im*," which may be translated freely as, "the father bears the heat and burden of the day, the maternal uncle only comes when it is a question of life or death." The Khasi father is revered not only when living, but also after death as *U Thawlang*, and special ceremonies are performed to propitiate his shade. Further remarks on the subject of marriage will be found in the Section which deals with religion.

Divorce.

Divorce amongst the Khasis is common, and may occur for a variety of reasons, such as adultery, barrenness, incompatibility of temperament, &c. The rule amongst the Khasis is that both parties must agree, but amongst the Wárs, especially the people of Shella, the party who divorces the other without his or her consent must pay compensation, which is called *ka mynrain*, or *ka thnem*. Amongst the Khasis it is not the custom to enforce restitution of conjugal rights; as a rule, when husband and wife cannot live together amicably, they agree to divorce one another; but occasionally it happens that either the husband or the wife will not agree to a divorce. Usually the husband would be willing to live with his wife; but when the latter consents neither to live with her husband nor to accept a divorce, a difficult situation arises, and it is in the event of such a contingency happening that the necessity of assessing *ka mynrain*, or *ka thnem* (compensation), occurs. The latter is computed by the village elders. Parties who have been divorced cannot afterwards remarry one another, but they are at liberty to marry into other families. A woman cannot be divorced during pregnancy. The following description of the divorce ceremony is taken from U Jeebon Roy's note on the Khasi religion. If the marriage has been celebrated according to the *pynhiar synjat* rite, a *ksiang* (go-between) is necessary on each side, also the *kni*, or maternal uncles of the parties, to witness the divorce. In other cases the presence of the *ksiang* is unnecessary, but some acquaintances and friends as well as the relatives on both sides should witness the ceremony. The husband and the wife each bring five cowries (*sbài*), or, more commonly nowadays, five pice. The wife gives her five cowries or pice to her husband, who places them with his, and then returns the five cowries or coins to his wife, together with his own five. The wife then returns the ten shells or coins to the husband who throws them on the ground. A crier (*u nong pyria shnong*) then goes round the village to proclaim the divorce, using the following words:—"Kaw—hear, oh villagers, that U——, and K—— have become separated in the presence of the elders. Hei: thou, oh, young man, canst go and make love to Ka—— for she is now unmarried (*khynraw*), and thou, oh, spinster, canst make love to U——. Hei! there is no let or hindrance from henceforth." Among the Khasis divorce must be by mutual consent, and the ceremony must take place in the open air. Until the divorce ceremony has been performed as above described, neither husband nor wife can marry again, but after it has taken place, either can remarry, but not within the family of the divorced husband or wife. In the event of a husband or wife being absent for a long period, say ten years, without any communication having been received from either of them, a divorce ceremony is performed by the relatives on his or her behalf. It is stated by U Jeebon Roy [23] that the rule of monogamy is not so strict for the husband as it is for the wife, he can contract an informal alliance with another woman, the only prohibition being that she must not belong to the original wife's village. Such a wife is called *ka tynga tuk*, literally, stolen wife, in contradistinction to the legally married wife (*ka tynga trai*). The children by the unmarried wife are called *ki khum kliar* (children from the top). By children from the top, is understood to mean children from the branches not from the root (*trai*) of the tree. Such children cannot claim ancestral property, except in the Wár country. In the event of a divorce the mother is always allowed the custody of the children. Divorces amongst both Khasis and Syntengs are of common occurrence, the result being that the children in many cases are ignorant of even the names of their fathers. For the mother, on the other hand, the children cherish a very strong affection, all their sympathies and affections binding them closely to the mother's kin. Divorce amongst the Syntengs, though resting on the same principle as that of the Khasis, differs in detail, and must be described separately. It is as follows:—In the first place it is not necessary for both husband and wife to be consenting parties, as is the case with the Khasis. In the Nongkhlih doloiship divorce takes place before the relatives of the parties. The man has to give eight annas as a sign of the divorce, and clothes worth Rs. 3/- or Rs. 5/- to the wife. There is a similar custom in the Suhtnga and Amwi doloiships. In the Jowai doloiship the divorce takes place in the presence of a village official called *U basan*. The husband or the wife gives the *basan* an eight anna piece, the latter gives this either to the wife or to the husband, as the case may be. The *basan's* share of the eight annas is two pice, the remainder being spent on liquor. The *basan* is entitled to a further fee of one anna from the man. If a wife does not agree to accept divorce, she is entitled to receive two pieces of cloth from the husband to the value of Rs. 3/-. This compensation is called *thnem*. The divorce then takes place. If a wife wishes to divorce her husband, and the latter is unwilling, before she can obtain divorce, she must pay *thnem* to the value of the whole amount the husband has spent on her and her children during the marriage. Divorce customs in Nartiang and Nongjinghi doloiships are much the same, only the amounts tendered by the parties and that of compensation differing.

In conclusion it should be stated that the great drawback attaching to divorce in ordinary communities, i.e. the effect that it has on the lives of the children of the marriage, does not apply to the Khasis, for with them the children always live with their mother and their mother's family, which latter would be bound to maintain them in the event of a divorce.

Inheritance.

The Khasi and Synteng laws of inheritance are practically the same, although in some of the doloiships in the Jaintia Hills there are some slight differences. The War law of inheritance differs greatly from that of the Khasis, and the customs of the Bhois or Mikirs, who inhabit the Bhoi doloiship of the Jaintia Hills, are totally different from those of the Khasis, thereby supplying another link in the chain of evidence in support of the conclusion that the Bhois, or, more correctly speaking, the Mikirs, are of Bodo origin, and not Khasi or Mon-Anam. The Lynngams follow the Khasi law of inheritance. It will be convenient to describe the Khasi law first, and then to pass on to the special customs in vogue in the different doloiships in the Jaintia Hills, and, finally, to describe the Wár, Bhoi and Lynngam customs.

The Khasi saying is, "*long jaid na loa kynthei*" (from the woman sprang the clan). The Khasis, when reckoning descent; count from the mother only; they speak of a family of brothers and sisters, who are the great grandchildren of one great grandmother, as *shi kpoh*, which, being literally translated, is one womb; i.e. the issue of one womb. The man is nobody. If he is a brother, *u kur*, a brother being taken to mean an uterine brother, or a cousin-german, he will be lost to the family or clan directly he marries. If he be a husband, he is looked upon merely as a *u shong kha*, a begetter. In some of the War villages a newly married man is spoken of by the bride's family as, "*u khun ki briew*," some one else's son. It is, perhaps, somewhat of a paradox under the circumstances that wives should address their husbands as "*kynrad*," or lord. There is, however, no gainsaying the fact that the husband, at least in theory, is a stranger in his wife's home, and it is certain that he can take no part in the rites and ceremonies of his wife's family, and that his ashes after death can find no place within the wife's family tomb, except, in certain cases, amongst the Syntengs. Further, the ceremonial religion amongst Khasis, especially that of the home, is in the hands of the women. It is, therefore, perhaps not to be wondered at, considering the important status assigned to women by the Khasis, that women should inherit the property and not men. The rule amongst the Khasis is that the youngest daughter "holds" the religion, "*ka bat ka niam*." Her house is called, "*ka iing seng*" and it is here that the members of the family assemble to witness her performance of the family ceremonies. Hers is, therefore, the largest share of the family property, because it is she whose duty it is to perform the family ceremonies, and propitiate the family ancestors. The other daughters, however, on their mother's death are entitled, each of them; to a share of their mother's property, although the youngest daughter gets the lion's share, e.g. the family jewellery, and the family house, and the greater part of what it contains. The youngest daughter cannot dispose of the house without the unanimous consent of her sisters. If the youngest daughter dies, she is succeeded by the next youngest daughter, and so on. All the daughters are bound to repair the house of the youngest daughter free of cost. In the event of the youngest daughter changing her religion, or committing an act of *sang*, or taboo, she loses her position in the family, and is succeeded, by her next youngest sister, as in the case of a death. Failing daughters, inheritance would pass by the "knight's move" to the sister's youngest daughter, who would be succeeded by her youngest daughter, and so on. Failing sister's daughters succession would revert to the mother's sisters and their female descendants. In the Jaintia Hills the inheritance of all real property passes from mother to youngest daughter. No man in the uplands of the Jaintia Hills can possess landed property, unless it is self-acquired property. In the Jaintia Hills, if a man dies and leaves acquired property, his heir will be his mother, if alive, excluding wife, sons, and daughters. If the wife, however, undertakes not to re-marry, she will inherit half of her husband's property, which at her death will descend to her youngest daughter by him.

Amongst Khasis all property which has been acquired by a man before marriage is considered to belong to his mother; indeed it may be said to belong to the man's *kur*, or clan, such property being called by Khasis, "*ka mai iing kur*" (the earnings of the house of the clan). After marriage, if there are children, the case is different, provided that the property has been acquired by the man after marriage. Here the wife and children would inherit the acquired property, the youngest daughter obtaining the largest share of such property on the death of the wife. If there were no daughter, the acquired property would be equally divided amongst the sons.

The following examples of the Synteng law of inheritance are taken from the exhaustive diaries recorded by the late Mr. Heath, who was for some years Sub-Divisional Officer of Jowai. In the Nongkli doloiship ancestral land passes from mother to her youngest daughter; again, if a youngest daughter who has so acquired dies, the next youngest in point of age succeeds. Should such direct female succession fail, the family tree has to be looked up for the nearest branch, in which the youngest female, or her youngest female descendant, succeeds. Thus, respecting ancestral land, the youngest daughter, or youngest female descendant of youngest female heir, is virtually heir to entailed property. If a woman dies leaving acquired property, her youngest daughter or youngest granddaughter of that youngest daughter succeeds to all. In default, next youngest daughter, and so on. In default of daughters, the youngest son inherits. A man can hardly, in any circumstances, possess ancestral land; his property must almost necessarily be self-acquired. If a man dies leaving acquired property, his heir will be his mother, if alive, excluding wife, sons, and daughters. If the wife undertakes, however, not to marry again, she will get half, which will descend to her youngest daughter by her deceased husband. The mother, who thus gets the whole or half of her son's property, leaves it to her youngest daughter, or youngest daughter of that daughter, and so on, as described above in the ease of a woman leaving ancestral or acquired property. If there is no mother, the man's youngest sister stands next heir with the same right as her mother. If there is no mother or sister, then the sister's female descendants stand in the man's mother's place. If there are none of these, then the man's youngest daughter succeeds to all. Ancestral property cannot be alienated without the consent of all the heirs in the entail. A gift of self-acquired property to any amount can be made by a donor during his lifetime. Acquired property cannot, however, be left by will out of the course sanctioned by custom. In the Amwi doloiship a widow who consents to pay the costs of her husband's funeral, provided she agrees not to re-marry, inherits half of her husband's acquired property.

In the Wár country the children inherit both ancestral and acquired property in equal shares, both males and females, with the exception that the youngest daughter is given something in addition to her share, although not such a large share of the property as amongst the Khasis. Amongst the Mikir-Bhois, i.e. the Mikirs who inhabit the Bhoi doloiship of the Jaintia Hills, the law of inheritance is totally different from that of the Khasis, for males succeed to all property, whether ancestral or acquired. Thus, if a man dies, leaving son, mother, wife, and daughters, the son takes all. If there are several sons, they divide. If there are no sons, the property goes to the nearest male heir. If a woman dies, leaving husband and children, the husband takes all. If the husband is dead, and there are sons and daughters, the former inherit. The great difference in the custom of inheritance between Khasis and Bhois is, as I have already pointed out, part of the evidence that these people are of different origin.

The Lynngam law of inheritance is the same as that of the Khasis. The youngest daughter obtains the largest share of the ancestral property, the remainder being divided between the remaining daughters. The sons do not get any share. The rule is also said to apply with regard to acquired property.

Adoption.

Both Khasis and Syntengs observe a custom known as *'rap iing* (an abbreviation for *ia rap iing*, literally, to help the house). This is practically adoption. If in a family the female members have died out, the male members of the family are allowed by custom to call (*khot*) a girl from some other family, to act as *ka'rap iing*, and to perform the family religious ceremonies, and therefore to inherit the family ancestral property. The female so introduced into the family then takes her place as *ka khun khadduh*, or youngest daughter, and becomes the head of the house (*ka trai iing*). The adoption of a female obviates the family dying out (*iap duh*), which to the Khasi is a very serious matter, inasmuch as there will then be no one qualified to place the bones of its members within the family tomb (*ka ba thep shieng mawbah*), and to perform the requisite funeral ceremonies. Amongst the Khasis no particular ceremonies are performed at the time of adoption; but some of the Syntengs observe a religious ceremony which consists largely of a feast to the clans-folk, at which liquor, rice, dried fish, and ginger are partaken of. Before the feast commences, each clansman is provided with a small gourd (*u klong*) filled with liquor, a little of the latter is then thrown on the ground from the gourd, and the following words are uttered:—"Oh, God! oh, Lord! oh, ruling king Biskurom, now the *pynrap üng* ceremony is about to be performed, let the ceremony be propitious, and let males and females (of the clan) increase in numbers, so that the clan may become great, and respected, and that intelligent male members may spring up." No such ceremony is, however, observed, it is understood, in the Nartiang and Raliang doloiships.

In the case of a family being *iap duh* (extinct), the family property, according to Khasi custom, passes to the Siem. Therefore it is to the interest of the members of families to adopt a female, when such necessity arises. As there is no religious ceremony which is compulsory to the Khasis on the occasion of an adoption, perhaps we are almost justified in concluding that in former times the adoption custom did not exist, more especially as the Khasis possess a special word, *iap duh*, for describing a family the females of which have all died out; and it is admittedly the custom for the Siem to succeed to the property of such a family. The Synteng custom of *'rap üng* may have been borrowed from the Hindus, when the Rajas of Jaintia became converts to that religion.

Tenure of Land and Laws Regarding Land.

Land in the Khasi Hills proper, i.e. land in the high plateau, is held somewhat differently from land in the Jaintia Hills and the Wár country; it will be necessary to describe the land tenures and laws regarding land of each of these divisions separately. As land is always jhumed by the Bhois and Lynngams from year to year, customs regarding land with these people are naturally very simple. Taking land in the high plateau of the Khasi Hills first:—The lands are classified under two main divisions, (*a*) public and (*b*) private lands. The following are the different descriptions of lands in the first division:—

Ka ri Raj, or *ka ri Siem*, which are Siem's, or Crown lands. These lands are intended for the support of the Siem family, they cannot be alienated. The Siems are, however, precluded by custom from levying a land tax on persons who cultivate such lands, the relation of landlord and tenant between the latter and their chiefs being unknown.

Ka ri Lyngdoh.—These lands are for the support of the Lyngdohs or priests of the State. In some Siemships, as in Mawiang Siemship, paddy is grown on these lands from which rice is obtained for the State pujas.

Ri shnong, or village lands.—These lands are set apart to provide a supply of firewood, thatching grass, &c., and are the property of the village. The inhabitants of other villages are not allowed to enjoy the produce of such lands. Such lands can be cultivated by ryots of the village, but the latter possess only occupancy rights, and cannot transfer them.

Ki 'lawkyntang.—These are sacred groves, situated generally near the summit of hills, composed of oak and rhododendron trees, which are held sacred (*kyntang*), it being an offence, or *sang*, for any one to cut timber in the grove, except for cremation purposes. These groves are the property of the villages.

(*b*.) Private Lands. These may he subdivided into *ri-kur* or lands which are the property of the clan, and *ri kynti*, family, or acquired landed property. In the Khasi Hills proper a very large proportion, certainly of the high lands, is the property of the clan; for instance, the high lands at Laitkor; which are the property of the Khar kungor and Kur kulang clans, whose ancestors the large memorial stones close to the Laitkor road commemorate, also the lands of the Thang khiew clan, and many others. It has been explained, in a previous paragraph, how the clan grew out of the family. The clan lands originally, when population was sparse, were owned by families, but as the members of the family increased and a clan was formed, the lands became the property of the clan instead of the family. Such clan lands are properly demarcated by stone boundary marks. The manager of the clan lands is the *kni* (maternal uncle of the youngest daughter of the main family, or branch of the clan), whose house "*ka iing khadduh*," or last house, is the place for performing all the religious ceremonies of the clan, and is also called *ka iing seng*. All the members of the clan are, however, entitled to share in the produce of any of the clan lands they may cultivate. No clan lands can be alienated without the consent of a durbar of the whole clan.

Ri kynti are private lands which have been either acquired by a man or woman individually, or, in the case of a woman, inherited from her mother; such lands must he entirely distinguished from the lands of the clan. In portions of the Jaintia Hills, if a man purchases a piece of land, at his death it passes to his mother, to the exclusion of his children; but in the Khasi Hills nowadays a man may leave such lands, provided they were acquired after marriage, either formally by will, or informally, to his children for their support. In land customs as well as other customs the Syntengs seem to preserve more closely than the Khasis what are probably the ancient usages of the race. It must be clearly understood, however, that all land acquired by inheritance must follow the Khasi law of entail, by which property descends from the mother to the youngest daughter, and again from the latter to her youngest daughter. Ancestral landed property must therefore be always owned by women. The male members of the family may cultivate such lands, but they must carry all the produce to the house of their mother, who will divide it amongst the members of the family. Daughters, other than youngest daughters, are entitled to maintenance from the produce of such family lands.

In the Jaintia Hills lands are classified as follows:—

Hali Lands or Irrigated Paddy Lands.

(1) *Raj* lands, which used to be the property of the Raja of Jaintiapur, now the property of Government, which are assessed to land revenue.

(2) Service lands, which are lands given rent free to dolois, pators, and other officers who carry on the administration.

(3) Village puja lands, being land the occupants of which pay rent to the doloi or lyngdoh, which are set apart in each village for purposes of worship. These lands are not assessed to revenue.

(4) Private lands held by individuals and which have been transferred from time to time by mortgage sale or otherwise at the will of the owner. These lands are not assessed to revenue.

High lands are sub-divided into (1) Private lands, held like *hali* private lands. (2) Unclaimed land, or Government Waste.

Up till now the Government has not assessed revenue on the high lands which are its own property. Surveys have been made from time to time of the Government *Raj hali* lands in the Jaintia Hills, but the maps require bringing up to date. The revenue on such lands is assessed at an uniform rate, viz. at 10 annas a bigha, and the leases have been issued so as to expire contemporaneously. A list of service lands of dolois and others, showing the number of plots held by each official and their approximate total area in bighas, is kept in the Deputy Commissioner's Office. Puja lands are plots of lands set apart entirely for the support of the lyngdohs and other persons who perform the pujas of the doloiships. These lands are generally leased out by the dolois, but in some doloiships they are under the management of the lyngdohs. The occupants of the puja lands have either to present annually sacrificial animals or objects, e.g. bulls, goats, fowls, or pigs, rice, liquor, &c., or make a payment in cash. In the War country in the Jaintia Hills, orange, *pán*, and betel-nut gardens, are held as private property except in a few villages where there are some Raj *pán* gardens which have been assessed to land revenue at the same rates as Government *hali* lands. The various gardens are distinguishable by means of boundary stones or stone cairns, by prominent trees on the boundary lines, or by natural boundaries such as streams.

In the Wár country to the West of Cherra, notably the country between the heights of Laitkynsew and the plains, considerable portions of the hill-sides are the property of communities known as *sengs*. A *seng* may be defined as a collection of families sprung from some common ancestress or ancestor. As an instance of these *sengs* I may describe the community known as the *lai seng* which owns land in the neighbourhood of Laitkynsew, the area owned being known as the "*ri lai seng*," or land of the three clans. These clans are descended from three men, U Kynta, U Nabein, and U Tangrai, it being remarkable that in this case descent is traced originally from male ancestors and not from females. The three ancestors are said to have owned a large tract of land, and they had as their abode the village of Laitmawria close to Laitkynsew; but owing to an epidemic, or some such cause, they deserted the village of Laitmawria and went with their families to live in some of the surrounding Wár villages, viz. in Tyrna, Nongkroh, Nongwar, Mastoh, and Mawlong. The descendants of the three men above-mentioned possess a genealogical table, showing their descent from the original three founders of the *sengs*. They claim a large tract of country lying to the south and south-east of the Laitkynsew plateau, containing not only orange gardens, but also valuable lime quarries. There are other *seng* communities also in the neighbourhood, e.g. the *hinriew phew seng*, or sixty *sengs*, who put forward claims to other tracts of land. The boundaries of the *ri lai seng* are identifiable on the ground. The business of the *seng* community is managed by a durbar, an elder or other influential person being chosen as president.

In the country of the Lynngams the crop belongs to the person who cultivates it, but the land belongs to the *kur* or family. The Lynngam villages; like those in the Khasi Siemships, do not pay any rent to the Siem. If outsiders cultivate within the areas set apart for the different Lynngam villages, all of them, including women, have to pay eight annas each to the people of the village in whose circle they cultivate. There is usually a mutual understanding between inhabitants of Lynngam villages, that certain tracts of land belong to the respective villages; sometimes, however, there are disputes regarding those lands between the different villages. Such disputes are settled by the Lynngam Sirdars of villages or by the Sirdars sitting with the two Lyngskors of the Siemship. If the disputes cannot be settled by these officials to the satisfaction of the parties, the latter are taken by the Lyngskors and Sirdars to the Siem of Nongstoin, who tries the case with the aid of the State mantris.

Laws Regarding Other Property.

There is no separate law applying to personal property, as opposed to real property, amongst the Khasis.

Decisions of Disputes.

Khasi Courts of Judicature.

In the first place a complaint is made before the Siem or chief, against a certain party or parties. The facts and circumstances of the ease, are then detailed before the chief and his headmen, the ostensible object being to attempt to bring about a compromise between the parties. If no reconciliation can be effected, a crier (*u nong pyrta shnong*), or in the Jaintia Hills a *sangot*, is sent out to proclaim at the top of his voice the durbar which is to assemble the following evening. He proceeds to cry the durbar in the evening when all the inhabitants have returned to the village from their usual daily pursuits. With a loud premonitory yell the crier makes use of the following formula [24]:—

"*Kaw!* thou, a fellow-villager; thou, a fellow-creature; thou, an old man; thou, who art grown up; thou, who art young; thou, a boy; thou, a child; thou, an infant; thou; who art little; thou, who art great. *Hei!* because there is a contest. *Hei!* for to cause to sit together. *Hei!* for to cause to deliberate. *Hei!* for to give intelligence together. *Hei!* about to assemble in durbar. *Hei!* for to listen attentively. *Hei!* ye are forbidden. *Hei!* ye are stopped to draw water then, not to cut firewood then; *Hei!* to go as coolies then; *Hei!* to go to work then; *Hei!* to go a journey then; *Hei!* to descend to the valley then; *Hei!* he who has a pouch. *Hei!* he who has a bag. *Hei!* now come forth. *Hei!* now appear. *Hei!* the hearing then is to be all in company. *Hei!* the listening attentively then is to be all together. *Hei!* for his own king. *Hei!* for his own lord, lest destruction has come; lest wearing away has overtaken *us*. *Kaw!* come forth now fellow mates."

This proclamation is called *khang shnong*, and by it all are stopped from going anywhere from the village the following day. Anybody who disregards the prohibition is liable to fine. The following day, towards evening, all the grown-up males of the village assemble at the durbar ground, the site of which is marked in some villages by rows of flat stones, arranged in an irregular circle, upon which the durbaris sit. The proceedings are opened by one of the headmen, who makes a long speech; then others follow, touching upon all sorts of irrelevant matters, but throwing out hints, now and then, bearing on the subject of accusation. By degrees the debate waxes warmer, and the parties get nearer the point. Then the complainant and the defendant each of them throw down on the ground a turban, or a bag containing betul and *pán*, lime, &c., in front of the durbar. These are regarded as the pledges of the respective parties and their representatives in the suit; they receive the name of *mamla* (hence the Khasi term *ar liang mamla* for the two contending parties in the suit). There are pleaders on both aides called *'riw said*, who address the durbar in lengthy speeches, the Siem being the judge and the whole body of the durbar the jury. Witnesses are examined by the parties; in former times they were sworn on a pinch of salt placed on a sword. The most sacred and most binding foam of oath, however, is sworn on *u klong* (a hollow gourd containing liquor). As, however, the latter form of oath is regarded by the Khasis as a most serious ordeal, it will be described separately. The durbar sometimes goes on for several days. At length the finding of the durbar is taken, after the Siem has summed up, and sentence is pronounced, which generally consists of a fine in money, almost always accompanied by an order to the losing party to present a pig. The pig is supposed to be sacrificed to a goddess, *Ka 'lei synshar*, i.e. the goddess of the State, but it is invariably eaten by the Siem and the members of the durbar. The Siem then calls out "*kumta mo khynraw*" (is it not so, young people?) The members of the durbar then reply, "*haoid kumta khein khynraw*" (yes, it is so, young ones). Sentences of fine are more often resorted to than other punishments nowadays, probably because very few of the Siems possess jails for the reception of criminals. The condemned one in a criminal case frequently serves his time by working for the Siem as a menial servant. The above description, which is based on the account given by the Rev. W. Lewis, with some modifications, may be taken as the usual form of procedure of the Khasi durbar.

Under the heading of decision of disputes we may perhaps give a short description of some of the punishments which were inflicted by the Siems and their durbars in criminal cases in ancient times. Murder was punishable by beating the culprit to death with clubs (*ki tangon ki lymban*). The killing, however, of a *nong shoh noh*, i.e. a man who seeks for human victims to sacrifice to the monster, *u thlen*, is not considered murder, even now by the Khasis, and the slayer of the *nong shoh noh* only has to inform the Siem and deposit Rs. 5, and one pig in the Siem's court. The slaying of a robber also is dealt with in like manner.

The punishment of adultery was imprisonment for life (*ka sah dain mur*), or a fine of Rs. 1,100, and one pig (*ka khadwei spah wei doh*). Whether such a heavy fine was ever paid is perhaps doubtful, and probably some other form of punishment was substituted for it. A husband finding his wife and a man in *flagrante delicto* could, as under the law of the ancients, kill both adulterer and adulteress without punishment for murder. He was, however, bound to deposit Rs. 5, and the conventional pig in the Siem's durbar. The punishment for rape (*kaba khniot tynga*) was imprisonment for life in the case of the woman being married, and a heavy fine and one pig if the woman was a spinster. Arson was punishable with imprisonment for life, or a heavy fine. The punishment for causing people to be possessed by devils (*ka ba ai-ksuid briew*) was exile (*pyrangkang par*); but if a person so possessed died, the sorcerer was hurled down a precipice (*pynnoh khongpong*). The punishment for robbery and theft was the stocks (*ka pyndait diengsong*), the imposition of fetters, or a punishment known as *kaba s'ang sohmynken*, by which the culprit was compelled to sit on a bamboo platform under which chillies were burnt. The result of such torture can be better imagined than described. Incest, or *sang*, which amongst the Khasis means cohabiting with a member of a man's or woman's own clan, was punishable with exile or a fine of Rs. 550/- and one pig. It is believed by the Khasis that the evils resultant from incestuous connection are very great; the following are some of them: being struck by lightning, being killed by a tiger, dying in childbirth, &c.

Decision of Cases by Ordeal.

Water Ordeal.

In ancient times the Khasis used to decide certain cases by means of water ordeal (*ka ngam um*). Yule, writing in 1844, mentions a water ordeal, and one of my Khasi friends remembers to have seen one during his boyhood. There were two kinds of such ordeals. The first, called *ka ngam ksih*, was as follows:—The two disputants in a case would each of them fix a spear under water in some deep pool. They would then dive and catch hold of the spear. The man who remained longest under water without returning to the surface was adjudged by the Siem and durbar to have won the case. Colonel Maxwell, late Superintendent of the Manipur State, witnessed a similar ordeal in the Manipur State in the year 1903, when two Manipuris dived to the bottom of a river and held on to stones, the result being that one man, who remained under water in the most determined way, was very nearly drowned. Amongst the Khasis sometimes the supporters of the contending parties used to compel the divers to remain under water by holding them down with their spears. Another form of trial was to place two pots, each of them containing a piece of gold and a piece of silver wrapped up in cloths, in shallow water. The two contending parties were then directed to plunge their hands into the water and take up, each of them, one of the packets. The party who brought up a piece of gold was adjudged the victor. If both parties brought up either gold or silver, then the case was amicably settled by the Durbar, and if it was a land case, the land was equally divided between the parties. No instances of trial of cases by such ordeals have come to notice of late years. Yule, referring to water ordeals, says: "I have been told that it was lawful to use the services of practised attorneys in this mode of trial; so that long-winded lawyers have as decided a preference in these regions as they have elsewhere."

Ordeal by U Klong, or by U Klong U Khnam, in the Wár Country.

Of all the ordeals these are the most dreaded by the Khasis. They believe that if a person swears falsely by *u klong* or *u klong u khnam*, he will die or, if he represents his family (i.e. wife and children) or his clan (*kur*), that his family and his clan will die out. Siems, Wahadadars, Lyngdohs, &c., do not order litigants, or even propose to them, to have their cases decided by this ordeal, fearing to incur blame for choosing it, owing to possible evil consequence thereafter to the parties. One of the parties must propose and the other must accept the ordeal, of their own accord and in open Court or Durbar. A gourd (*u klong*) containing fermented rice (*ka sohpoh*) is provided, and a feathered arrow with a barbed iron head is planted in the fermented rice. The following is the procedure:—

The person who wishes to take the oath brings a gourd of fermented rice, or a gourd with an arrow stuck in it, as the case may be, and makes it over to the judge, or a deputy appointed by such judge for this duty. The latter, before returning it to him, invokes the goddess as follows:—

"Come down, and bear witness, thou goddess who reignest above and below, who createst man, who placest him (on earth), who judgest the right and the wrong, who givest him being and stature, (i.e.) life. Thou goddess of the State, thou goddess of the place, who preservest the village, who preservest the State, come down and judge. If this man's cause be unrighteous, then shall he lose his stature (being), he shall lose his age (life), he shall lose his clan, he shall lose his wife and children; only the posts of his house shall remain, only the walls of his house shall remain, only the small posts and the stones of the fireplace shall remain; he shall be afflicted with colic, he shall be racked with excruciating pains, he shall fall on the piercing arrow, he shall fall on the lacerating arrow, his dead body shall be carried off by kites, it shall be carried off by the crows, his family and his clan shall not find it; he shall become a dog, he shall become a cat, he shall creep in dung, he shall creep in urine, and he shall receive punishment at thy hands, oh, goddess, and at the hands of man. If, on the other hand, his cause be righteous (lit. *lada u kren hok*) he shall be well, he shall be prosperous, he shall live long, he shall live to be an elder, he shall rise to be a defender and preserver of his clan, he shall be a master of tens and a master of hundreds (immensely rich), and all the world shall see it. Hear, oh, goddess, thou who judgest." (The whole of this invocation is uttered while a libation is poured out from *u klong*.)

U *klong* is next invoked as follows:—

"Thou, *u klong*, with whose assistance—according to our religion and our custom, a man when he is born into the world is named—hear and judge. If he speaks falsely (his cause be false), his name shall be cut off (by thee) and he shall surely die."

The fermented rice is then invoked as follows:—

"Thou yeast, thou charcoal, thou rice of the plough, thou rice of the yoke, thou, too, hear and judge. If he speaks falsely, eat off his tongue, eat away his mouth."

The arrow is lastly invoked as follows:—

"Thou piercing and lacerating arrow, as thou hast been ordained by the goddess, who creates man, who appoints man to occupy a pre-eminent place in war and in controversy, do thou hear and judge. If he (i.e. the man taking the oath) speaks falsely, let him fall upon thee, let him be cut and be torn, and let him be afflicted with shooting and pricking pains." The man then takes *u klong* or, *u klong u khnam*, and holds it on his head, and while in that posture utters the same invocation. *U klong* is then made over to the judge (the Siem or the Sirdar as the case may be, &c.).

The person who undergoes the above ordeal wins the case, the production of evidence being unnecessary.

War.

Although the Khasis, unlike the Nagas, the Garos, the wild Was of Burma, the Dayaks of Borneo, and other head-hunting tribes, cannot be said to have indulged in head-hunting in ancient times, as far as we know, merely for the sake of collecting heads as trophies, there seems to be some reference to a custom of head-hunting in a description of the worship of the god *u Syngkai Bámon,* one of the principal gods of war amongst the Khasis. This god is described in one of the folk tales (I have obtained it through the kindness of Dr. Roberts, the Welsh missionary at Cherrapunji) as being the deity who gives the heads of the enemy to the successful warriors. To this god, as well as to *Ka Rám Shandi*, they offer a cock. Before sacrifice the warriors dance round an altar, upon which are placed a plume of cock's feathers (*u thuia*), a sword, a shield, a bow, an arrow, a quiver, *pán* leaves, and flowers. After the cock has been sacrificed, they fix its head on the point of a sword and shout three times. The fixing of the cock's head on the point of a sword is said to have been symbolical of the fixing of the human head of an enemy killed in battle, on the top of the *soh-lang* tree. Mr. Shadwell, of Cherrapunji, whose memory carries him back to the time when the British first occupied the Khasi Hills, has a recollection of a Khasi dance at Cherra, round an altar, upon which the heads of some *Dykhars*, or plains people, killed in a frontier raid had been placed. The Khasis used to sacrifice to a number of other gods also for success in battle. An interesting feature of the ancient combats between the people of different Siemships was the challenge. When the respective armies had arrived at a little distance from one another, they used to stop to hear each other shout the *'tien-Blei*, or challenge, to the other side. This custom was called *pyrta 'tien-Blei,* or shouting out the challenge. From the records available of the military operations of the Khasis against the British, the former appear to have relied principally on bows and arrows, ambushes and surprises, when they fought against us at the time of our first occupation of the hills. During the Jaintia rebellion firearms were used, to some extent, by the Syntengs. The military records do not, however, disclose any peculiar battle customs as having been prevalent amongst those hill people then. Both Khasis and Syntengs seem to have fought much in the same manner as other savage hill-men have fought against a foe armed with superior weapons.

Human Sacrifices.

The Thlen Superstition.

There is a superstition among the Khasis concerning *U thlen*, a gigantic snake which requires to be appeased by the sacrifice of human victims, and for whose sake murders have even in fairly recent times been committed. The following account, the substance of which appeared in the *Assam Gazette*, in August, 1882, but to which considerable additions have been made, will illustrate this interesting superstition:—"The tradition is that there was once in a cave near

Cherrapunji, [25] a gigantic snake, or *thlen*, who committed great havoc among men and animals. At last, one man, bolder than his fellows, took with him a herd of goats, and set himself down by the cave, and offered them one by one to the *thlen*. By degrees the monster became friendly, and learnt to open his mouth at a word from the man, to receive the lump of flesh which was then thrown in. When confidence was thoroughly established, the man, acting under the advice of a god called U *Suid-noh*, [26] (who has as his abode a grove near Sohrarim), having heated a lump of iron red hot in a furnace, induced the snake, at the usual signal, to open his mouth, and then threw in the red-hot lump, and so killed him. He proceeded to cut up the body, and sent pieces in every direction, with orders that the people were to eat them. Wherever the order was obeyed, the country became free of the *thlen*, but one small piece remained which no one would eat, and from this sprang a multitude of *thlens*, which infest the residents of Cherra and its neighbourhood. When a *thlen* takes up its abode in a family there is no means of getting rid of it, though it occasionally leaves of its own accord, and often follows family property that is given away or sold. The *thlen* attaches itself to property, and brings prosperity and wealth to the owners, but on the condition that it is supplied with blood. Its craving comes on at uncertain intervals, and manifests itself by sickness, by misadventure, or by increasing poverty befalling the family that owns the property. It can only be appeased by the murder of a human being." The murderer cuts off the tips of the hair of the victim with silver scissors, also the finger nails, and extracts from the nostril a little blood caught in a bamboo tube, and offers these to the *thlen*. The murderer, who is called *u nongshohnoh*, literally, "the beater," before he sets out on his unholy mission, drinks a special kind of liquor called, *ka 'iad tang-shi-snem*. (literally, liquor which has been kept for a year). This liquor, it is thought, gives the murderer courage, and the power of selecting suitable victims for the *thlen*. The *nongshohnoh* then sets out armed with a short club, with which to slay the victim, hence his name *nongshohnoh*, i.e. one who beats; for it is forbidden to kill a victim on these occasions with any weapon made of iron, inasmuch as iron was the metal which proved fatal to the *thlen*. He also takes the pair of silver scissors above mentioned, a silver lancet to pierce the inside of the nostrils of the deceased, and a small bamboo or cylinder to receive the blood drawn therefrom. The *nongshohnoh* also provides himself with rice called "*u 'khaw tyndep*," i.e. rice mixed with turmeric after certain incantations have taken place. The murderer throws a little of this rice over his intended victim, the effect of which is to stupefy the latter, who then falls an easy prey to the *nongshohnoh*. It is not, however, always possible to kill the victim outright for various reasons, and then the *nongshohnoh* resorts to the following subterfuge:—He cuts off a little of the hair, or the hem of the garment, of a victim, and offers these up to the *thlen*. The effect of cutting off the hair or the hem of the garment of a person by a *nongshohnoh*, to offer up to the *thlen*, is disastrous to the unfortunate victim, who soon falls ill, and gradually wastes away and dies. The *nongshohnoh* also sometimes contents himself with merely throwing stones at the victim, or with knocking at the door of his house at night, and then returns home, and, after invoking the *thlen*, informs the master that he has tried his best to secure him a prey, but has been unsuccessful. This is thought to appease the *thlen* for a time, but the demon does not remain inactive long, and soon manifests his displeasure for the failure of his keeper to supply him with human blood, by causing one of the latter's family to fall sick. The *thlen* has the power of reducing himself to the size of a thread, which renders it convenient for the *nong-ri thlen*, or *thlen* keeper, to place him for safety in an earthen pot, or in a basket which is kept in some secure place in the house. When the time for making an offering to the *thlen* comes, an hour is selected, generally at dead of night, costly cloths are spread on the floor of the house of the *thlen* keeper, all the doors are opened, and a brass plate is laid on the ground in which is deposited the blood, or the hair, or a piece of the cloth of the victim. All the family then gathers round, and an elderly member commences to beat a small drum, and invokes the *thlen*, saying, "*ko kni ko kpa* (oh, maternal uncle, father), come out, here is some food for you; we have done everything we could to satisfy you, and now we have been successful; give us thy blessing, that we may attain health and prosperity." The *thlen* then crawls out from its hiding-place and commences to expand, and when it has attained its full serpent shape, it comes near the plate and remains expectant. The spirit of the victim then appears, and stands on the plate, laughing. The *thlen* begins to swallow the figure, commencing at its feet, the victim laughing the while. By degrees the whole figure is disposed of by the boa constrictor. If the spirit be that of a person from whom the hair, or a piece of his or her cloth, has been cut, directly the *thlen* has swallowed the spirit, the person expires. Many families in these hills are known, or suspected, to be keepers of a *thlen*, and are dreaded or avoided in consequence. This superstition is deep-rooted amongst these people, and even nowadays, in places like Shillong or Cherrapunji, Khasis are afraid to walk alone after dark, for fear of being attacked by a *nongshohnoh*. In order to drive away the *thlen* from a house or family all the money, ornaments, and property of that house or family must be thrown away, as is the case with persons possessed by the demon *Ka Taroh*, in the Jaintia Hills. None dare touch any of the property, for fear that the *thlen* should follow it. It is believed that a *thlen* can never enter the Siem's or chief's clan, or the Siem's house; it follows, therefore, that the property of the *thlen* keeper can be appropriated by the Siem. A Mohammedan servant, not long ago in Shillong, fell a victim to the charms of a Khasi girl, and went to live with her. He told the following story to one of his fellow-servants, which may be set down here to show that the *thlen* superstition is by no means dying out. In the course of his married life he came to know that the mother of his Khasi wife kept in the house what he called a *bhut* (devil). He asked his wife many, many times to allow him to see the *bhut*, but she was obdurate; however, after a long time, and after extracting many promises from him not to tell, she confided to him the secret, and took him to the corner of the house, and showed him a little box in which was coiled a tiny snake, like the hair spring of a watch. She passed her hands over it, and it grew in size, till at last it became a huge cobra, with hood erected. The husband, terrified, begged his wife to lay the spirit. She passed her hands down its body, and it gradually shrank within its box.

It may be stated that the greater number of the Khasis, especially in certain Siemships, viz. Cherra, Nongkrem, and Mylliem, still regard the *thlen*, and the persons who are thought to keep *thlens*, with the very greatest awe, and that they will not utter even the names of the latter for fear some ill may befall them. The superstition is probably of very ancient origin, and it is possible that the Khasi sacrifices to the *thlen* demon may be connected with the primæval serpent-worship which characterized the Cambodians, which Forbes says was "undoubtedly the earliest religion of the Mons." But it must be remembered that snake-worship is of very ancient origin, not only in Further India, but also in the nearer peninsula, where the serpent race or Nagas, who may have given their name to the town of Nagpur, were long held in superstitious reverence. Mr. Gait, in the Journal of the Asiatic Society of Bengal, vol. i. of 1898, gives some account of the human sacrifices of the Jaintias or Syntengs. He writes as follows:—

"It appears that human sacrifices were offered annually on the *Sandhi* day in the month of Ashwin (Sukla paksha) at the sacred *pitha*, in the Faljur pargana. They were also occasionally offered at the shrine of Jainteswari, at Nijpat, i.e. at Jaintiapur, the capital of the country. As stated in the *Haft Iqlim* to have been the case in Koch Behar, so also in Jaintia, persons frequently voluntarily came forward as victims. This they generally did by appearing before the Raja on the last day of Shravan, and declaring that the goddess had called them. After due inquiry, if the would-be victim, or *Bhoge khaora*, were deemed suitable, it was customary for the Raja to present him with a golden anklet, and to give him permission to live as he chose, and to do whatever be pleased, compensation for any damage done by him being paid from the royal treasury. But this enjoyment of these privileges was very short. On the Navami day of the Durga Puja, the *Bhoge khaora*, after bathing and purifying himself, was dressed in new attire, daubed with red sandal-wood and vermilion, and bedecked with garlands. Thus arrayed, the victim sat on a raised dais in front of the goddess, and spent some time in meditation (*japa*), and in uttering mantras. Having done this, he made a sign with his finger, and the executioner, after uttering the usual sacrificial mantras, cut off his head, which was placed before the goddess on a golden plate. The lungs were cooked and eaten by such *Kandra Yogis* as were present, and it is said that the royal family partook of a small quantity of rice cooked in the blood of the victim. The ceremony was usually witnessed by large crowds of spectators from all parts of the Jaintia pardganas.

"Sometimes the supply of voluntary victims fell short, or victims were needed for some special sacrifice promised in the event of some desired occurrence, such as the birth of a son, coming to pass. On such occasions, emissaries were sent to kidnap strangers from outside the Jaintia Raj, and it was this practice that eventually led to the annexation of the country by the British. In 1821, an attempt was made to kidnap a native of Sylhet proper, and while the agents employed were punished, the Raja was warned not to allow such an atrocity to occur again. Eleven years later, however, four British subjects were kidnapped in the Nowgong district, and taken to Jaintia. Three of them were actually sacrificed, but the fourth escaped, and reported the matter to the authorities. The Raja of Jaintia was called on to deliver up the culprits, but he failed to do so, and his dominions were in consequence annexed in 1835."

There seems to be an idea generally prevalent that the Raja of Jaintia, owing to his conversion to Hinduism, and especially owing to his having become a devotee of the goddess Kali, took to sacrificing human victims; but I find that human victims were formerly sacrificed by the Jaintias to the Kopili River, which the Jaintias worshipped as a goddess. Two persons were sacrificed every year to the Kopili in the months U' *naiwing* and U' *nai prah* (November and December). They were first taken to the *hat* Mawahai or Shang-pung market, where they were allowed to take any eatables they wished. Then they were conducted to Sumer, and thence to Ka Ieu Ksih, where a stone on the bank of a small river which falls into the Kopili is pointed out as having been the place where the victims were sacrificed to the Kopili river goddess. Others say that the sacrificial stone was situated on the bank of the Kopili River itself. A special clan in the Raliang doloiship used to carry out the executions. It seems probable that the practice of sacrificing human victims in Jaintia was of long standing, and was originally unconnected with Hinduism, although when the Royal family became converts to Hinduism, the goddess Kali may easily have taken the place of the Kopili River goddess. Many of the Syntengs regard the River Kopili to this day with superstitions reverence. Some of these people will not cross the river at all, others can do so after having performed a sacrifice with goats and fowls. Any traveller who wishes to cross the river must leave behind him the rice which he has taken for the journey, and any other food supplies he may have brought with him. This superstition often results in serious inconvenience to travellers between the Jaintia Hills and North Cachar, unless they have arranged for another batch of coolies to meet them on the Cachar side of the River Kopili, for the Synteng coolies throw down their loads at the river side, and nothing will induce them to cross the river. The Kopili is propitiated by pujas in many parts of the Jaintia Hills, and at Nartiang a tank where sacrifices are regularly performed is called Ka Umkoi Kopili.

CHAPTER IV

Religion

General Character of Popular Beliefs.

The Khasis have a vague belief in a God the Creator, U *Blei Nong-thaw*, although this deity, owing, no doubt, to the influences of the matriarchate, is frequently given the attribute of the feminine gender, cf., *Ka lei Synshar*. The Khasis cannot, however, be said to worship the Supreme God, although it is true that they sometimes invoke him when sacrificing and in times of trouble. The religion of the Khasis may be described as animism or spirit-worship, or rather, the propitiation of spirits both good and evil on certain occasions, principally in times of trouble. The propitiation of these spirits is carried out either by priests (*lyngdohs*), or by old men well versed in the arts of necromancy, and as the *lyngdoh* or wise man deals with good as well as evil spirits, and, as often as not, with the good spirits of ancestors, the propitiation of these spirits may be said to partake of the nature of Shamanism. A very prominent feature of the Khasi beliefs is the propitiation of ancestors; but this will be described separately. There is a vague belief amongst the Khasi of a future state. It is believed that the spirits of the dead, whose funeral ceremonies have been duly performed, go to the house or garden of God, where there are groves of betel-nut trees; hence the expression for the departed, *uba bam kwai ha iing u blei* (he who is eating betel-nut in God's house), the idea of supreme happiness to the Khasi being to eat betel-nut uninterruptedly. The spirits of those whose funeral ceremonies have not been duly performed are believed to take the forms of animals, birds, or insects, and to roam on this earth; but this idea of transmigration of souls has been probably borrowed from the Hindus. Bivar writes that although the ideas of a Godhead are not clearly grasped, yet a supreme creator is acknowledged, and that the following is the tradition relating to the creation of man. "God in the beginning having created man, placed him on the earth, but on returning to look at him, found he had been destroyed by the evil spirit. This happened a second time, whereupon the Deity created first a dog, then a man; and the dog, who kept watch, prevented the devil from destroying the man, and the work of the Deity was thus preserved." The Khasis, apparently, do not believe in punishment after death, at least there is no idea of hell, although the spirits of those who have died under the ban of *sang* remain uneasy, being obliged to wander about the earth in different forms, as noted above. The spirits worshipped by the Khasis are many in number; those of the Syntengs being specially numerous. The particular spirit to be propitiated is ascertained; by egg-breaking. The offering acceptable to the spirit is similarly ascertained and is then made. If the particular sacrifice does not produce the result desired, a fowl is sacrificed; the entrails being then examined, an augury is drawn, and the sacrifice begins afresh. As the process of egg-breaking is believed to be peculiar [27] to the Khasis amongst the Assam hill tribes, a separate description of it is given in the Appendix. It should be remarked that the Khasis never symbolise their gods by means of images, their worship being offered to the spirit only. The following are some of the principal spirits worshipped by the Khasis and Syntengs, omitting the spirits of deceased ancestors such as *Ka Iawobi, u Thawlang* and *u Suidnia*, which will be described under the heading of ancestor-worship.

U'lei muluk—the god of the State, who is propitiated yearly by the sacrifice of a goat and a cock.

U'lei umtong—the god of water, used for drinking and cooking purposes. This god is similarly propitiated once a year so that the water supply may remain pure.

U lei longspah—the god of wealth. This god is propitiated with a view to obtaining increased prosperity.

U Ryngkew, or *u Basa shnong*, is the tutelary deity of the village. This godling is propitiated by sacrifices whenever they are thought to be necessary.

U Phan u kyrpad is a similar godling to the above.

Then follows a list of minor deities, or, rather, evil spirits, e.g. *Ka Rih*, the malarial fever devil; *ka Khlam*, the demon of cholera; *ka Duba*, the fever devil which is said to haunt the neighbourhood of Theriaghat.

Bivar says "the Khasi religion may be thus briefly defined as forms used to cure diseases and to avert misfortunes, by ascertaining the name of the demon, as the author of the evil, and the kind of sacrifice necessary to appease it." We may accept this description as substantially correct. In the Jaintia Hills there is a peculiar superstition regarding a she devil, called "*ka Taroh*" which is supposed to cause delirium in cases of fever. When such cases occur, it is believed that "*ka Taroh*" has caused them, and inquiries are made by means of breaking eggs to find out in whose person the demon has obtained a lodgment; or sometimes the sick person is asked to reveal this. When in either of these ways the name of the person possessed by "*ka Taroh*" is known, the sick person is taken to the house of the possessed, and ashes and bits of broken pots are cast into the enclosure, after which, if the sick person recovers, the party indicated is denounced as possessed by the demon; but if the patient dies, it is concluded that the person possessed has not been properly ascertained. If people are satisfied that some one is really possessed, they denounce the person, who is then out-casted. The only way for him to regain his position is to exorcise the demon by divesting himself of all his property. He pulls down his house, burns the materials, his clothes, and all his other worldly goods. Lands, flocks, and herds are sold, the money realized by the sale being thrown away. No one dares touch this money, for fear he should become possessed by *ka Taroh*, it will be observed that, as in the case of the *thlen*, the demon is believed to follow the property.

Mr. Jenkins, in his interesting little work on "Life and Work in Khasia," gives a slightly different account of the superstition, in that he states that it is the sick person who is possessed by *ka Taroh*. The above belief is perhaps a Synteng development of the Khasi *thlen* superstition. In the Jaintia Hills "the small-pox" is believed to be a goddess, and is reverenced accordingly. Syntengs regard it as an honour to have had small-pox, calling the marks left by the disease the "kiss of the goddess"; the more violent the attack and the deeper the marks, the more highly honoured is the person affected. Mr. Jenkins says, "When the goddess has entered a house, and smitten any person or persons with this disease, a trough of clean water is placed outside the door, in order that every one before entering may wash their feet therein, the house being considered sacred." Mr. Rita mentions cases of women washing their hair in water used by a small-pox patient, in order that they may contract the disease, and women have been known actually to bring their little children into the house of a small-pox patient, in order that they may become infested and thus receive the kiss of the goddess. It is possible that the Syntengs, who were for some time under Hindu influences; may in their ignorance have adopted this degraded form of worship of the Hindu goddess, "Sitala Devi," who is adored as a divine mother under different names by Hindus all over India, cf., her name *mari-amman*, or mother of death, in the South of India, and the name Ai, mother, of the Assamese.

In the Khasi Hills the god of small-pox is known under the name of *u Siem ñiang thylliew*. He is not, however, appeased in any way, the people calling on two other spirits, *Thynrei* and *Sapa*, to whom a fowl or a goat is offered. This section cannot be closed without some reference to the household gods of the Syntengs. The legend is that in ancient times there came a woman "from the end of heaven to the borders of the country of *u Truh*" (the country of the plains people at a distance from the foot of the Khasi and Jaintia Hills). The name of the woman was Ka Taben, and she was accompanied by her children. She offered herself to *u Dkhar*, the plains man, as a household goddess, but he rejected her. She then went to the Khasis; who were ploughing their fields, and offered to help them with their cultivation. The Khasis also refused her, saying they were capable of managing their own cultivation, and at the same time told her to go to the country of the Bhois and Syntengs, i.e. the Jaintia Hills. Acting on this advice, she went to the village of Nongphyllud in the Jaintia Hills, where the people again turned a deaf ear to her. She proceeded to Mulagula village in Jaintia, at the foot of the Jaintia Hills, and ascended from thence to Rymbai, where she met a man who conducted her to the house of the Siem, who consented that she and her children should live with him. Ka Taben then apportioned to her children various duties in the house of the Siem as follows:—Ka Rasong was to look after the young unmarried folk, and was to supervise their daily labour and to prosper their trading operations at the markets. Next Ka Rasong was given a place at the foot of the king post, *trai rishot*, and her duty was to befriend young men in battle. Then came *Ka Longkhuinruid*, alias *ka Thab-bulong*, who said, "There are no more rooms in the house for my occupation, so I will go and live in the forest, and him who turns not his coat when I meet him I will make mad." Finally came U *Lamsymphud*, who elected to live with his youngest sister inside the house.

There are special sacrifices offered to these household deities. The leaves of the *sning*, or Khasi oak, are wrapped round the post of the house, and, a fowl is sacrificed and other formalities are observed which it would be tedious to describe in detail. The legend of the arrival of Ka Taben with her children in the

Synteng country from a distant clime is interesting in that it perhaps indicates the possibility of the migration of these people, i.e. the Syntengs, in ancient times from some distant place to their present abode.

Ancestor-worship.

The Khasis not only revere the memories of deceased ancestors, but they adore them by means of offerings, which are sometimes periodical, and sometimes made when thought necessary, as in times of trouble. These offerings take the shape of articles of food which are theoretically partaken of by the shades of the deceased ancestors, the idea of making such offerings being very similar to that of the Hindus when they offer the "*pinda*," or cake, to nine generations of ancestors, i.e. to propitiate the shades of the departed, and to obtain their help thereby. U Hormu Rai Diengdoh writes that, "the real religious demand" amongst the Khasis is the *ai bam*, or giving of food to the spirits of deceased ancestors, in order that the latter may aid the living members of the clan with their help; and bless them. To honour dead ancestors is the duty of every Khasi, and he who wilfully neglects this duty it is believed, will neither receive their help, nor be defended from the influence of the numerous spirits of evil in which the Khasis believe. Amongst the Syntengs, a few days after depositing the bones in the ancestral tomb, the ceremony of feeding the spirits of the dead is performed: At this ceremony there are some families which give two pigs for each person of the family who is dead, and there are some who give one. The pigs are taken to the *iing-seng*, or puja house of the clan. Presumably, pigs are usually offered to the shades only of those members of the family whose remains have been recently deposited in the clan cromlech. In the chapter dealing with memorial stones the reader will notice how many of them are erected to the memory of deceased ancestors, and how they bear the names of such ancestors, e.g. *Ka Iawbei* (the first grandmother), *U Suidnia*, or *U kni rangbah* (the first maternal uncle). It was the custom in former days to make offerings of food upon the flat table-stones to the spirits of the deceased ancestors, and this is still the case in places in the interior of the district. This practice, however, may be said to be largely dying out, it being now commonly the custom to make the offerings in the house, either annually, or at times when it is thought necessary to invoke the aid of the departed. Such acts of devotion may well be said to partake of the nature of worship. As has been the case in other countries, and amongst other people, it is possible that the Khasi gods of today are merely the spirits of glorified deceased ancestors transfigured, as has happened with some of the gods of the Shinto Pantheon of Japan. It may be interesting to note that the ancient Shinto cult of Japan possesses some features in common with the ancestor-worship of the Khasis. Take the funeral ceremonies. With both people we find the dead laid out in the house, food placed before the corpse; and the funeral ceremonies taking place, accompanied by music and dancing. Mr. Lafcadio Hearn, in an interesting book on Japan, writes "that in ancient times the Japanese performed ceremonies at regular intervals at the tombs of deceased members of the family, and food and drink were then served to the spirits;" this is exactly what the Khasis used to do at their *cenotaphs. This, apparently, was the practice in Japan before the "spirit tablet" had been introduced from China, when the worship of the ancestors was transferred from the tomb to the home. We have an exactly similar instance of evolution amongst the Khasis of the present day, i.e. the transfer of the ancestor cult from the flat table-stones erected in honour of deceased ancestors to the home. Last, but not least, is the idea common to both people, that no family or clan can prosper which does not duly perform the worship of deceased ancestors; this, as Hearn puts it, is "the fundamental idea underlying every persistent ancestor-worship; i.e. that the welfare of the living depends upon the welfare of the dead." The "Khasi Mynta," in an interesting article, notes some further points of resemblance between the methods of ancestor-worship adopted by the two people. The following instances may be quoted. Amongst the Japanese the spirits of those who fall in battle are said to help their fellow-warriors who are still fighting. The "Khasi Mynta" quotes a similar belief as having existed amongst the Khasis in former days. The remains of Japanese warriors who die in battle are said to be reverently taken to the warrior's home at the first opportunity. The Khasis do likewise, the clothing in default of the ashes of Khasi transport coolies, who were employed on military expeditions on the North-Eastern Frontier, having been carried home by the survivors to present to the dead men's relations, who then performed the ceremonies prescribed by custom for those who have died violent or unnatural deaths. Of all deceased ancestors the Khasis revere *Ka Iawbei* the most, the word *Iawbei* being made up of *'iaw*, short for *kiaw* (grandmother), and *bei*, mother. *Ka Iawbei* is the primeval ancestress of the clan. She is to the Khasis what the "tribal mother" was to old Celtic and Teutonic genealogists, and we have an interesting parallel to the reverence of the Khasis for *Ka Iawbei* in the Celtic goddess Brigit, the tribal mother of the Brigantes. Later on, like *Ka Iawbei*, she was canonized, and became St. Bridget. [28]

The greater number of the flat table-stones we see in front of the standing monoliths in these hills are erected in honour of *Ka Iawbei*. In former times, it was the custom to offer food to her on these stones. In cases of family quarrels, or dissensions amongst the members of the same clan, which it is desired to bring to a peaceful settlement, it is customary to perform a sacrifice to the first mother, "*Ka Iawbei.*" They first of all take an augury by breaking eggs, and if it appears from the broken egg-shells that *Ka Iawbei* is offended, they offer to her a cotton cloth, and sacrifice a hen. On these occasions incantations are muttered, and a small drum, called, "*Ka 'sing ding dong*," is beaten. It is not likely that the Khasi household deities, *Ka lei iing* and *Ka ksaw ka jirngam*, to whom pujas are offered for the welfare of the house, are also *Ka Iawbei* in disguise. Notwithstanding the strong influence of the matriarchate, we find that *U Thawlang*, the first father and the husband of *Ka Iawbei*, is also revered. To him on occasions of domestic trouble a cock is sacrificed, and a *jymphong*, or sleeveless coat is offered. This puja is called *kaba tap Thawlang*, i.e. covering the grandfather. The following incantation to *U Thawlang* is then chanted:—"Oh, father Thawlang, who hast enabled me to be born, who hast given me my stature and my life, I have wronged thee, oh father, be not offended, for I have given thee a pledge and a sign, i.e. a red and white sleeveless coat. Do not deliver me into the power of (the goddess of) illness, I have offered thee the propitiatory cock that thou mayest carry me in thine arms, and that I may be aware of thee, my father, Thawlang." We see clearly from the above prayer that the Khasi idea is that the spirit of the deceased male ancestor is capable of being in a position to help his descendant in times of trouble. The same thought underlies the extreme reverence with which *Ka Iawbei* is regarded. Thus we see a striking point of resemblance between the Khasi ancestor-worship and the ancient Shinto cult of Japan, as described by Mr. Lafcadio Hearn. *U Suid-Nia*, or *u Kni Rangbah*, the first maternal uncle, i.e. the elder brother of *Ka Iawbei*, is also much revered. It will also be noticed under the heading of memorial stones that the great central upright monolith of the *máwbynna*, or memorial stones, is erected in his honour. The influence of the *kni*, or mother's elder brother, in the Khasi family is very great, for it is he who is the manager on behalf of the mother, his position in the Khasi family being very similar to that of the *karta* in the Hindu joint family. It is on this account that he is so much revered, and is honoured with a stone which is larger than the other up-right memorial stones after death. It will be seen in the article dealing with "the disposal of the dead," that at Cherra, on the occasion of the bestowal of the ashes in the cinerarium of the clan, a part of the attendant ceremonies consists of the preparation of two effigies called *Ka Puron* and *U Tyngshop*, intended to represent *Ka Iawbei* (the first mother) and U Suid-Nia (the first maternal uncle). The Wárs of Nongjri have a custom peculiar to themselves. They erect small thatched houses in their compounds, which they call *iing ksuid*. When they worship their ancestors they deposit offerings of food in these houses, the idea being that the ancestors will feed on the offerings. These Wárs do not erect memorial stones, nor do they collect the ashes of the clan in a common sepulchre; they deposit the ashes in circular cineraria, each family, or *iing*, possessing one. It should further be noted with reference to the Khasi custom of *ai bam*, or giving food to the spirits of deceased ancestors, that Dr. Frazer, in his "Golden Bough," has mentioned numerous instances of firstfruits being offered to the spirits of deceased ancestors by the tribes inhabiting the Malay Archipelago. (See pages 462-463 of the "Golden Bough.") Some other points of similarity in customs have already been noticed between the Khasis and certain Malay tribes.

Worship of Natural Forces and of Deities.

In the Khasi Hills, especially on the southern side, there are numerous rivers, sometimes of considerable size, which find their way to the Sylhet plains through very deep valleys, the rivers flowing through narrow channels flanked by beetling cliffs which rise to considerable altitudes. The scenery in the neighbourhood of these beautiful rivers is of the most romantic description, and the traveller might imagine himself in Switzerland were it not for the absence of the snowy ranges. Of such a description is the scenery on the banks of the river Kenchiyong, the Jádukátá [29] or Punatit of the plains. It is in the bed of the river, a few miles below Rilang, that there is the curiously-arched cavity in the rock which resembles an upturned boat, which the Khasis call *Ka lieng blei* (the god's boat), and the plains people Basbanya's ship. Near to this, on the opposite side of the river, there is a rock bearing a Persian inscription, but so defaced by the action of the water as to be impossible to decipher. Like other inhabitants of mountainous countries, the Khasis reverence the spirits of fell and fall, and propitiate them with offerings at stated times. A brief description of the ceremonies which are performed at Rilang, on the occasion when the annual fishing in the river Punatit takes place, may be of interest. The three Siems of Nongstoin, Langrin, and Nobosohpoh each sacrifice a goat to *Ka blei sam um* (the goddess of the river) before the boatmen can cast in their nets. In former times they say the passage up the river was obstructed by the goddess, who took the form of an immense crocodile; but she was propitiated by the gift of a goat, and the boatmen were then allowed to pass up the river in their boats. Hence it became necessary for the owners of the fishery to sacrifice annually a goat each to the goddess. At the time of my visit each Siem's party erected an altar in the bed of the river, in the midst of which a bough of the Khasi oak (*dieng sning*) was planted. The goats were then decapitated, it being considered an essential that the head should be severed with one blow. As soon as the head was cut off there was a rush on the part of the sacrificers to see in which direction the head faced. If the head faced towards the north or west, it was considered an evil omen; if it faced towards the south or east, a good omen. The east is a lucky quarter amongst the Assamese also. The people ended up the proceedings by giving a long-drawn-out, deep-toned chant, or *kynhoi*. Immediately after the ceremony was concluded hundreds of boats shot out from the numerous creeks, where they had been lying, and fished the river all night, the result being an immense haul, to the delight of the Lynngams, who were seen next morning roasting the fish whole on bamboo stakes, after which they consumed them, the entrails being eaten with great gusto. Such is the worship of the goddess of the Punatit.

Similar pujas take place among the people of Wár-ding (the valley of fire) before they fish in the Khai-mara river and elsewhere in the Khasi Hills. In the Jaintia Hills there is the Synteng-worship of the Kopili river, which used to be accompanied by human sacrifices, as has been mentioned above, pp. 102-104. The Myntang river, a tributary of the Kopili, must also be annually appeased by the sacrifice of a he-goat. Numerous hills also are worshipped, or rather the spirits which are said to inhabit them. One of the best known hill godlings is the deity who is thought to inhabit the little wood close to the summit of the Shillong Peak. This deity is said to have been discovered by a man named "U Shillong" who gave his name to the Shillong Peak, and indirectly to our beautiful hill station. The Siems of Mylliem and Nongkrem reverence *U'lei Shillong*, and there are certain clans who perform periodical sacrifices to this god. Probably the origin of the superstitious reverence with which U'lei Shillong is held by the Siems of Nongkrem and Mylliem is that their fabled ancestress "Ka Pah Syntiew," of whom an account will be found in the folk-lore section, took her origin from a rock not far from the Shillong Peak in the Nongkrem direction.

Rableng Hill, which is within full view of the Shillong Peak in an easterly direction, is also said to be the abode of a minor god who is periodically propitiated by the members of the Máwthoh clan of the Khyrim State with a he-goat and a cock. Apparently no special puja is performed to U Kyllang (the Kyllang Rock) nowadays.

The picturesque hill of Symper, which rises abruptly from the plain in the Siemship of Maharam, is visible for many miles. It is in shape not unlike the Kyllang. Symper is said to be the abode of a god called "U Symper." There is a folk-tale that Kyllang and Symper fought a great battle, and that the numerous holes in the rocks at the base of the Symper hill are evidences of their strife. At the base of Symper there is a great cave, where many cattle find shelter in rainy weather. The people of Mawsynram propitiate the god of Symper in cases of sickness by sacrificing a he-goat or a bull. Symper, like *U'lei Shillong*, is one of the minor deities of the Khasis.

Close to Shangpung, in the Jaintia Hills, there is a small hill called "*u lúm pyddieng blai lyngdoh*," where sacrifices are offered on an altar at seed time, and when the corn comes into ear. This altar used to be overshadowed by a large oak tree. The tree is now dead.

The Wárs of Nongjri worship "*u'lei lyngdoh*" the tutelary deity of the village, under the spreading roots of a large rubber tree which gives its name to this village Nongjri. This village worhsip is performed by a village priest (*lyngdoh*) at stated intervals, or whenever it is considered necessary. There are numerous other instances of hills and rivers being regarded as the abode of godlings, but those quoted above are sufficient for purposes of illustration.

Religious Rites and Sacrifices, Divination.

The Khasis, as has been explained already, worship numerous gods and goddesses. These gods and goddesses are supposed to exercise good or evil influence over human beings according to whether they are propitiated with sacrifice or not. They are even supposed to possess the power of life and death, over men and women, subject to the control of *u Blei Nongtháw*, God the Creator. Thus illness, for example, is thought to be caused by one or more of the spirits on account of some act or omission and health can only be restored by the due propitiation of the offended spirits. In order to ascertain which is the offended spirit, a system of divination by means of cowries, breaking eggs, or examining the entrails of animals and birds, was instituted. The Khasi method of obtaining auguries by examining the viscera of animals and birds may be compared with that of the Roman *haruspex*. Some description of these modes of divination has been given at the end of this chapter. The Khasi religion has been described by Bivar as "demon worship, or a jumble of enchantments muttered by priests who are sorcerers." But even a religion which is thus unflatteringly described is based on the cardinal doctrines of sin and sacrifice for sin. Tradition amongst the Khasis states that in the beginning (*mynnyngkong ka sngi*) there was no sin, heaven and earth were near each other, and man had direct intercourse with God. How man fell into sin is not stated, but it is certain that he did fall. Experts at "egg healing" never forget to repeat the formula "*nga briéw nga la pop*"

(I man have sinned). The cock then appears as a mediator between God and man. The cook is styled, "*u khún ka blei uba kit ryndang ba shah ryndang na ka bynta jong nga u briéw*," i.e. the son of god who lays down his neck (life) for me man. The use of the feminine *ka blei* is no doubt due to matriarchal influences. There is another prayer in which the Khasis say, "*ap jutang me u blei ieng rangbah me u briéw*" (oh god do not forget the covenant arise oh man). The idea is that man has fallen into sins of omission and commission (*ka pop, ka lain ka let*) but that God is nevertheless expected to spare him, and to accept a substitute for him according to the covenant (*jutang*). By this covenant God is supposed to have accepted in exchange the cock as a substitute for man. How the cock came to occupy such an important position, tradition is vague and self-conflicting. The fact remains that the covenant of the cock is the foundation of the Khasi religion. It is of interest to mention that amongst the Ahoms the tradition is that Khunlung and Khunlái brought down from heaven the *kái-chán-mung*, [30] or pair of heavenly fowls, and that to this day the sacrifice of the fowl is considered by the Deodhais, or priest-soothsayers of the Ahoms, a most important feature of the ancient Ahom ritual. But amongst the Ahoms there is the difference that auguries are obtained, not from the entrails, but by examining the legs of the fowls. The Ahoms are Shans belonging to the Tai branch, another great division of the Indo-Chinese group of the human race.

The covenant of the cock as thus explained shows the importance of this sacrifice to the Khasis. The large intestine of a fowl has two pea-like protuberances, one close to the other. One is symbolically called *u blei* or god, and the other is styled *u briéw* or man, they are connected by a thin membrane. Directly the bird has been disembowelled the sacrificer throws a few grains of rice on the entrails and then watches their convulsive movements. If the portion of the entrail called *u blei* moves towards that portion which represents man, it is considered proof positive that the god has heard the prayer of the sacrificer, but if the movement proceeds in the opposite direction, then the reverse is the case and the omen is bad. If the entrails are full and healthy, having no spots (*brai*), or blood marks (*thung*), and if the membrane between the two protuberances has not been fractured, these are favourable signs. If the intestines are empty, wrinkled, or spotted, and the membrane mentioned above is fractured, these are bad signs. Auguries also are drawn by examining the livers, the lungs and spleens and gall bladders of pigs, goats and cattle. If the liver of a pig is healthy and without spot, the augury is good; if the reverse, it is bad. The spleen must not be unduly distended, otherwise the omen is unfavourable and the gall bladder must not be over full. Invocations to deduce omens from the appearance of the entrails are quoted on page 11 of Col. Bivar's Report. From the first invocation quoted by him it appears that the method of drawing the augury from the fowl differs slightly in detail from that which has been described to me by certain Khasis, but both descriptions agree in the main, and the slight dissimilarity in detail may be due to the methods of obtaining auguries varying slightly in different localities. Divination by breaking eggs and by other means, although not strictly sacrifice with the Khasis, partakes of the nature of a religious ceremony. Such divinations are of almost every-day occurrence in a Khasi house, and always precede sacrifices. The Khasis, moreover, do nothing of what they consider to be of even the least importance without breaking eggs. When a Khasi builds a new house, or before he proceeds on a journey, he always breaks eggs to see whether the building or the journey will be lucky or not. The description of egg-breaking given by Shadwell in his account of the Khasis is not altogether correct. A detailed description of this method of divination will be found in Appendix C. The description can be depended upon, as it is the result of my personal observations of egg-breaking on several occasions. A board of the shape shown in the diagram (Appendix C) is placed on the ground, the egg-breakers' position being that indicated in the diagram. After the egg has been smeared with red earth, it is thrown violently down and the contents and the fragments of egg-shell fall on the board. Auguries are drawn from the positions of the fragments of shell on the board, and from the fact of their lying with the inner sides facing upwards or downwards. Another method of egg-breaking is for the diviner to wrap up the egg in a plantain leaf with the point uppermost, or merely to hold the egg in his hand in this position without wrapping it up, and then to press another egg down upon it. If the end of the egg so pressed breaks at once, this is a good sign, but if it remains unbroken, the egg has a god in it, and the omen is bad.

A common method of divination is by means of the *shanam*, or lime-case. The diviner holds the lime-case by the end of its chain, and addresses the god. He then asks the lime-case a question, and if it swings, this is supposed to be an answer in the affirmative; if it does not move, this is a negative reply. This seems to be a very simple trick, for the diviner can impart movement to the lime-case by means of the hand. A similar way of consulting the oracle is by the bow, which is held in the hand by the middle of the string. A simple method of divining is by means of cowries or grains of rice. The diviner plunges his hand into a bag or basket after asking the god a question. If the number of cowries or grains of rice comes out odd, the omen is good; if it comes out even, the reverse is the case. The Khasi word for consulting the omens is khan, and a diviner is called a *nongkhan*. Another method of obtaining omens is by dropping two leaves into a pool of water or on a stone, the position of the leaves as they fall, either right side uppermost or upside down, signifying good or evil as the case may be; this is called *khan-sla*.

Priesthood.

The Khasi priest is usually called *Lyngdoh*, or *langdoh*; he is always appointed from the lyngdoh clan. The etymology of the word *lyngdoh* is said by certain lyngdohs of the Khyrim State to be *lang* = together and *doh* = flesh. A *lyngdoh*, or *langdoh*, is one who collects sacrificial victims, i.e. flesh for the purpose of sacrificing. It must be confessed, however, that this definition is doubtful, owing to the absence in the word *lyngdoh* of the prefix *nong* which is the sign of the agent in Khasi. Besides *lyngdohs* there are persons called *soh-blei* or *soh-sla*, who may also be said to be priests. The Khasis, unlike the Hindus, have no *purohit* or priest to perform the family ceremonies. Such duties fall to the lot of the head of the family or clan, who carries them out generally through the agency of the *kni*, or maternal uncle. Old Khasis are frequently well versed in the details of sacrifices, and in the art of obtaining auguries by examining the viscera of sacrificial victims. Apart from family and clan sacrifices, there are the sacrifices for the good of the State or community at large; it is these sacrifices that it is the duty of the *lyngdoh* to perform. He may be said to be the priest of the communal religion, although he has certain duties in connection with offences committed against the social law of marriage, and with regard to the casting out of evil spirits from houses which may be thought to be infested with them. The *lyngdohs* of the Khasis may be likened to the Roman *pontifices*. In the different Khasi States there is, as a rule, more than one *lyngdoh*; sometimes there is quite a number of such priests, as in Nongkrem where there is a *lyngdoh* for each *raj* or division of the state. There are a few Khasi States where the priest altogether takes the place of the Siem, and rules the community with the help of his elders in addition to performing the usual spiritual offices. The duties of *lyngdohs*, their methods of sacrificing, and the gods to whom they sacrifice, vary in the different Siemships, but there is one point in which we find agreement everywhere, i.e. that the *lyngdoh* must be assisted at the time of performing sacrifices by a female priestess, called *ka soh-blei, ka soh-sla*, or simply *ka lyngdoh*. This female collects all the *puja* articles and places them ready to the *lyngdoh's* hand at the time of sacrifice. He merely acts as her deputy when sacrificing. The female *soh-blei* is without doubt a survival of the time when, under the matriarchate, the priestess was the agent for the performance of all religious ceremonies. Another such survival is the High Priestess of Nongkrem, who still has many religious duties to perform; not only so, but she is the actual head of the State in this Siemship, although she delegates her temporal powers to one of her sons or nephews, who thus becomes Siem. A similar survival of the ancient matriarchal religious system is the *Siem sad*, or priestess, at Mawsynram, who, on the appointment of a new Siem or chief, has to assist at certain sacrifices. Here we may compare Karl Pearson's remark, when dealing with matriarchal customs, that "according to the evidence of Roman historians, not only the seers but the sacrificers among the early Teutons were women." The duties of the *lyngdohs*, as regards communal worship, consist chiefly of sacrificing at times of epidemics of cholera, and such-like visitations of sickness (*jing iap khlam*). In the Khyrim State there is a goddess of each *raj*, or division, of the state, to whom sacrifices are offered on such occasions. To the goddess are sacrificed a goat and hen, powdered rice (*u kpu*), and a gourd of fermented liquor; the leaves of the *dieng sning*, or Khasi oak, are also used at this ceremony. The *lyngdoh* is assisted by a priestess called *ka soh-sla*, who is his mother, or his sister, or niece, or some other maternal relation. It is the duty of the priestess to prepare all the sacrificial articles, and without her assistance the sacrifice cannot take place. Sacrifices are also performed by the *lyngdoh* to *u Lei Lyngdoh*, alias *u Ryngkew*. This used to be the tutelary deity in times of war, but in less troublous times the Khasi *lyngdoh* sacrifices to him for success in tribal or State litigation. A pig and a cock, with the usual accessories, are sacrificed by the *lyngdoh* to this god. As in the case of sacrifices to *Ka lei Raj*, the services of a priestess are indispensable.

A *lyngdoh* is a *lyngdoh* for life. When a *lyngdoh* dies and his successor is appointed, certain rather elaborate ceremonies are observed in the Nongkrem *raj* of the Khyrim State. The funeral ceremonies of the old *lyngdoh* having been completed, the *lyngdoh* clan appoints his successor. The latter then, after performing his ablutions, proceeds, accompanied by the assembled members of the *lyngdoh* clan, to the top of the Shillong Peak. The *lyngdoh* and his clansmen advance along the road dancing, this dancing being carried on all the way from the *lyngdoh's* house to the Shillong Peak. All are clad in the distinctive Khasi dancing dress. Having reached the Peak, they pick the leaves of a tree called *ka 'la phiah*, which they spread on the ground. A goat and a cock are then sacrificed, the new *lyngdoh* acting as the sacrificer. There are the usual accessories, including branches of the Khasi *sning* or oak. Nine portions (*dykhot*) are cut from different parts of the victims and are offered to the god of the Shillong Peak, *U lei Shillong*. The *lyngdoh* and his companions then perform obeisance three times to the god, and the *lyngdoh* walks backwards some paces. The puja is then over, and they return dancing to the *lyngdoh's* house. On another day the *lyngdoh* performs a puja to *u lei Lyngdoh*, alias *u Ramjah*. Undoubtedly the most interesting feature of the ceremonies on these occasions is the dancing. This dancing is carried out by the *lyngdoh* and his companions armed with sword and shield, a fly-flap made of goat's hair (*symphiah*) being also sometimes held in one hand, a quiver of arrows being slung on the back, and a plume of black and white cocks' feathers (*u thuya*) fixed in the turban. The dance is executed in a regular figure, the dancers advancing and retiring in an orderly and methodical manner, and finally clashing their swords together in mock combat. The dance of the present day is not unlikely the survival of a war dance of ancient times. The *lyngdohs* say they dance in honour of *U lei Lyngdoh*, to whom such dances are thought to be pleasing. The dance of the *lyngdohs* on these occasions may be compared with that of the Roman *salii*, who, in the month of March, performed a war dance in honour of Mars.

The above and other similar sacrifices to the gods of the State or divisions of the State may be said to be the communal religious duties of the *lyngdohs*. The duties of *lyngdohs* with reference to private persons may now be mentioned. When it is found that any two people have made an incestuous marriage, that is to say a marriage within the exogamous group of the *kur*, or clan, the parties at fault are taken before the *lyngdoh* by their clansmen, who request him to sacrifice in order to ward off the injurious effects of the *sang*, or taboo, of such a connection from the kinsfolk. On this occasion a pig is sacrificed to *u'lei lyngdoh* and a goat to *ka lei long raj*. The parties at fault are then outcasted. As mentioned in another place, the sin of incest admits of no expiation for the offenders themselves. In the Khyrim State, it is said by the *lyngdohs* themselves, although not by the Siem or the myntries, that they are the reversionary legatees of all the persons who die without leaving female heirs (*iap duh*). In other Siemships such property passes to the Siem. The *lyngdoh* of Nongkrem can also take possession of the property of persons who have been found to harbour an evil spirit (*jingbih*) in their houses. It appears that in such cases the house and furniture are burnt, as in the case of the *Taroh* superstition in the Jaintia Hills, the *lyngdoh*, however, taking possession of jewellery or anything else of value. The only practical service the *lyngdoh* renders in return is to build the afflicted person a new house; unless, indeed, we take into account the casting forth of the devil by the *lyngdoh*. Mr. Jenkins, of Shangpung, in the Jaintia Hills, writes: "Such is the belief of the people in the evil spirits, that they are completely under the influence of the priests and spend large sums of money in order to secure their favour. They live in constant dread lest by the least transgression or omission they should offend these avaricious men and so bring upon themselves the wrath of the demons." The influence of the *lyngdohs* over the people in the Jaintia Hills seems to be stronger than in the Khasi Hills. For instance, it came to my notice in Raliang that crops cannot be cut until the *lyngdoh* has seem them, in other words, until the *lyngdoh* has claimed and obtained his share of the produce. In many places, however, in the Khasi Hills the *lyngdoh* is much discredited, owing, no doubt, to the advance of Christianity and education.

Ceremonies and Customs Attending Birth and Naming of Children.

The Khasi birth ceremonies and customs are as follows:—When a child is born the umbilical cord is cut by a sharp splinter of bamboo; no knife can be used on this occasion. The Mundas of Chota Nagpur similarly taboo a metal instrument for this purpose. The child is then bathed in hot water from a red earthen pot. The placenta is carefully preserved in an earthen vessel in the house till after the naming ceremony has taken place. When the umbilical cord, after being tied, falls off, a puja is performed with eggs to certain water deities (*ka blei sam-um* and *ka niangriang*), [31] also to a forest spirit (*u'suid bri* or *u'suid khláw*). The naming ceremony of the child is performed the next morning after the birth. Certain females are invited to come and pound rice in a mortar into flour. The flour when ready is placed on a bamboo winnower (*u prah*). Fermented rice is mixed with water and is placed in a gourd. Some powdered turmeric is also provided, and is kept ready in a plantain leaf, also five pieces of *'kha piah*, or dried fish. The earthen pot containing the placenta is then placed in the *nongpei*, or centre room of the house, If the child is a male, they place near him a bow and three arrows (the implements of a Khasi warrior); if a female, a *da* and *u star*, or cane head-strap for carrying burdens. An elderly man, who knows how to perform the naming puja, which is called by the Khasis "*kaba jer khun*," places a plantain-leaf on the floor and sprinkles some water on it. He takes the gourd in his hand and calls a god to witness. The people assembled then mention a number of names for the child, and ask the man who is performing the puja to repeat them. This he does, and at the same time pours a little liquor from the gourd on to the ground. As he goes on pouring, the liquor by degrees becomes exhausted, and finally only a few drops remain. The name at the repeating of which the hot drop of liquor remains adhering to the spout of the gourd is the name selected for the child. Then the puja performer invokes the god to grant good luck to the child. The father takes the pot containing the placenta, after having previously placed rice flour and fermented rice therein, and waves it three times over the child, and then walks out with it through the main entrance of the house and hangs up the pot to a tree outside the village. When he returns from this duty, before he re-enters the house, another throws water over the father's feet. The father, being thus cleansed, enters, and holds the rice flour to his mouth three times. Two people then, holding the dried fish by their two ends, break them in two. The powdered turmeric mixed with rice flour and water is applied to the right foot of the father, the mother and the child receiving the same treatment. The friends and relations are then anointed, the turmeric being applied, however, to their left feet. The bow, arrows, *da*, and *u star* are carefully placed inside the inner surface of the thatch on the roof, and the ceremony is over. Rice flour is then distributed to all who are present, and the male adults are given liquor to drink. After two or three months the ears of the child are bored and ear-rings are inserted. These ear-rings are called, *ki shashkor iawbei* (i.e. the ear-rings of the great-grandmother). Mr. Jenkins mentions that the naming ceremony amongst the Syntengs is performed by the "eldest aunt," presumably on the mother's side. A basket of eggs is placed in the centre of the room, and before the ceremony begins one egg has to be broken. Then the aunt of the child takes two sticks, and, raising them to her shoulder, lets them fall to the ground. Before they fall she shouts, "What name do you give the child?" The name is mentioned, and if, on falling upon the ground, one stick crosses the other, it is a proof that the name has won the approval of the spirit. If the sticks do not fall in this position, another egg is broken and another name is chosen, and the sticks are dropped as before until they fall in the required position, when it is understood by the performers that the name is a good one. Mr. Jenkins was informed by a young man "who had renounced heathenism" that some of the more cunning women cross the sticks before lifting them, and that when they do this they invariably fall crossed to the ground. "They thus save their eggs, save time and trouble, get the name they desire for the child. . . ." It is noteworthy that the Khasis consider it necessary to preserve the placenta until the ceremony of naming the child is over, and that the pot containing the placenta is waved over the head of the child before it is removed and hung up in a tree.

Dr. Fraser, at page 53 *et seq.* of the "Golden Bough," when dealing with the subject of sympathetic magic, refers to the navel string and the placenta as parts which are commonly believed amongst certain people to remain in sympathetic union with the body after the physical connection has been severed, and it is interesting to note that in the Babar Archipelago, between New Guinea and Celebes, the placenta is mixed with ashes and put in a small basket, which seven women, each of them armed with a sword, hang up on a tree of a peculiar kind (*citrus hystrix*). The women carry the swords for the purpose of frightening the evil spirits, otherwise the latter might get hold of the placenta and make the child sick. Mr. C. M. Pleyte, Lecturer on Indonesian Ethnology, at the Gymnasium William III at Batavia, who has most courteously furnished me with some interesting information on this subject, states that it is especially in the Southern Moluccas that the placenta is mixed with ashes and hung in a tree. Wider spread is the custom of placing the after-birth on a small bamboo raft in a river "in order that it may be caught by crocodiles, incarnations of the ancestors, who will guard it till the person to whom it has belonged dies. Then the soul of the placenta is once more united with that of the dead man, and together they go to the realms of the dead. During lifetime the connection between men and their placentas is never withdrawn." The Khasis, although they cannot explain the meaning of the presence of the placenta at the naming ceremony, and the care with which they remove it and hang it up in a tree, are probably really actuated by the same sentiments as the inhabitants of the Southern Moluccas, i.e. they believe that there is, as Dr. Fraser puts it, a sympathetic union with the body after the physical connection with the child has been severed. There is no fixed period of *sang*, or taboo, after a birth, but the parents of the child are prohibited by custom from crossing a stream or washing their clothes until the navel-string falls off, for fear that the child should be attacked by the demons of the hills and the vales.

The Wár birth customs are substantially the same as those of the Khasis, but there is the difference that a Wár family after a birth is *sang*, or, taboo, for seven days, whereas amongst the Khasis the only prohibition is that the parents must not cross a stream or wash their clothes until they have propitiated the spirits. A twin birth is *sang*, or taboo. The Khasis argue that as there is but one *Ka Iawbei* (first ancestress), and one U *Tháwlang* (first ancestor), so one child, either male or female, should be born at a time. A twin birth is accordingly regarded as a visitation from God for some *sang*, or transgression, committed by some member of the clan. When the twins are of opposite sexes the *sang* is considered to be extremely serious, the Khasi idea being that defilement has taken place within the womb. The case is treated as one of *shong kur*, or marriage within the clan, and the bones of the twins cannot be placed in the sepulchre of the clan. There are no special birth customs amongst the Lynngams.

There is no trace of the *couvade* amongst the Khasis.

Marriage.

We now come to consider marriage amongst the Khasis from a religious point of view. Shadwell has said that marriage amongst the Khasis "is purely a civil contract." This statement is not correct, for there is an elaborate religious ceremony at which God the creator, *U'lei thaw briew man briew*, the god or goddess of the State, U or *ka'lei Synshar*, and, what is probably more important, the ancestress and ancestor of the clan, *Ka Iawbei-tymmen* and U *Thawlang*, are invoked. There are three marriage ceremonies prevalent amongst the Khasis, which are (*a*) *Pynhiarsynjat*, (*b*) *Lamdoh* and (*c*) *Iadih-kiad*, respectively. The first and second forms above mentioned are considered the more respectable; the last-named is resorted to by the very poor who cannot afford the greater expense entailed by the first two ceremonies.

Preliminaries.—A young man of marriageable age, say between seventeen or eighteen years of age and twenty-five, fixes upon a girl of, say between thirteen and eighteen years, as likely to become a fitting partner; probably he has been acquainted with the young woman for some time before, and is on more or less easy terms of intimacy with her. He mentions the name of the girl to his parents, and uncles and aunts in the house, and they agree or disagree, as the case may be. Sometimes marriages are arranged by the parents of the young people themselves. Having agreed regarding the fitness of the bride, the young man's parents send a male representative of the family, or in some cases a man unconnected with the family, to arrange matters with the parents of the bride. The latter then ascertain their daughter's wishes. According to the late U Jeeban Roy, the daughters nearly always agree, it is very seldom that it is necessary to bring any pressure to bear. The parents then investigate whether there is any *sang*, or taboo, such as clan relationship, between the young woman and her intended, in the way of the marriage. If there is found to be no such hindrance, they fix a date for finally arranging the marriage (*ban ia kut ktien*.) On the day appointed the bride's family consult the auspices by breaking eggs and examining fowls' entrails. If the omens are favourable, well and good. Should they be unfavourable, they abandon the marriage project. There is a strong prejudice against a marriage taking place under unfavourable auspices, the belief being that such an union will be childless, that the bride will die an untimely death, or that poverty will ensue. Given favourable auspices, the parents fix a day for the marriage. It was formerly the custom for the bridegroom to provide himself beforehand with a ring, usually of silver, but, amongst the rich, of gold, which is called *ka synjat* (hence the name of the marriage ceremony *pynhiar-synjat*), and for the bride to provide herself with a similar ring. The bridegroom used to place his ring upon the bride's finger, and the bride used to place her ring upon the bridegroom's finger; it is however believed that this custom is rare nowadays. On the marriage day a man is selected from the party of the bridegroom called *u ksiang*, or go-between. The bridegroom then sets out with this man and a number of followers, clothed in clean garments and wearing either white or red pagris (a black pagri not being considered a fitting head-dress on this occasion), to the house of the bride, where a feast has been prepared, and fermented rice-beer (*ka-kiad-hiar*) in gourds (*klong*) placed ready. The bride, her female attendants, and her mother and aunts have collected in the meantime, dressed in their best, wearing their jewellery, and with their heads uncovered, for it is not thought proper for the females to cover their heads on the marriage day. On the side of the bride, also, a *ksiang* (go-between) has been appointed, and it is his duty to manage all the business of the marriage on behalf of her family. Some young men of the bride's party go to meet the bridegroom's contingent by way of doing them honour. When they have reached the bride's house, the *ksiang* of the bridegroom enters first, followed by the bridegroom, and after him the bridegroom's party. The *ksiang* then hands over the bridegroom to the maternal uncle (*kni*) of the bride, or to the bride's father. Either of the latter then provides the bridegroom with a seat next the bride. The bride and bridegroom exchange bags of betel-nut, and where the custom of investiture of the ring is in vogue, these tokens are interchanged. The *ksiangs* of the bridegroom and bride recite the marriage contract in lengthy formulae, which may be found on pages 6, 7, 8 of the late U Jeebon Roy's interesting notes on the Khasi religion. The two *ksiangs* then take up, each of them, a gourd containing fermented liquor from the gourd provided by the contracting party, and give them to an old man who is versed in sacrificial lore, who solemnly mixes the contents together. Three dried fish are produced, and are placed on the floor of the house. The priest thus appointed then solemnly adjures the gods in the following words:—

Hei, oh god from above; oh god from below; oh *'lei synshar*; oh god who hast created man; as thou hast ordained this marriage, the ring has been given this day; thou wilt know; thou wilt hear; from the clear firmament above that . . . . have been married this day. Thou wilt bless them; thou wilt grant them prosperity; thou wilt show them the way; thou wilt show them the road, that they may be well, that they may obtain dwellings and houses, that they may prosper, that they may obtain rice and fish, that they may possess hundreds and thousands; thus, oh god." The priest then pours liquor on the ground three times from the gourd, counting "one, two, three." He then continues the invocation thus, "*Hei*, thou, oh mother; oh grandmother; oh maternal uncle; oh father: oh *Suid-nia*; oh younger grandmother; oh elder grandmother; oh younger grandfather; oh elder grandfather. As the flesh has fallen (on the floor, i.e. the feast has been prepared), the ring has been put on, the three strips of flesh are ready (alluding to the three dried fish already mentioned), you will all of you (ancestors) give ear, you will continue giving strength and spirit (i.e. to the married pair) that they may be well" (and so on, as written in the first invocation). He then pours out the liquor three times as before. He then adjures the Siem, the elders, and all the people who do not belong to either of the two clans, and pours out liquor three times as before. The three pieces of dried fish are first placed on the *tympan*, the high rack above the fire-place, then removed and tied to the ridge-pole of the house, amidst shouts of *Ho, hoi, hoi, hoi*. The poor then sacrifice a fowl, and the rich a pig without blemish (*uba tlem*), to *u Suid nia* and *ka Iaw-bei* (the spirits of deceased ancestors of the family), and present them with *dykhot*, or pieces of flesh. Two or three days afterwards, the bride, accompanied by her female relatives, pays a visit to the bridegroom at his house, and after this they go and come as they like to one another's houses. After two or three children have been born, they take down the pieces of dried fish from the roof and sacrifice two pigs, one on behalf of the husband and another on behalf of the wife. Then they say there can be no possible *sang*, and husband and wife use each other's things and pool their earnings, and if the husband has a house of his own, the wife can go and live with him; this, however, is not the custom amongst many of the Syntengs, who more strictly observe the principles of the matriarchate. The cost of the marriage ceremonies amongst Khasis, Syntengs and Wárs, may be put down at between Rs. 50 and Rs. 200 according to the position of the parties.

Lamdoh Ceremony.

This ceremony is identical with that of *Pynhiar synjat*, except that the bride and bridegroom do not interchange rings, and that there is no sacrifice of the pig. The parties merely buy some pig's flesh and perform a puja with a small portion of the flesh of the legs of the animal. Amongst the poor, fish sometimes takes the place of pork at the *Iadih-kiad* ceremony. The latter consists of a drinking bout mingled with muttered sentences by a *nongkinia* (sacrificer), the invocations and prayers being the same as at the *Pynhiar synjat*. The *Lamdoh* and *Iadih-kiad* ceremonies take the place of the more elaborate *Pynhiar synjat* in most places now-a-days.

Lynngam Marriages.

The ritual observed at these marriages is described as under:—First of all a proposal is made in the following manner. A *ksiang*, or go-between, is sent, with the brother of the girl for whom a husband is required, to the house of the father of the young man (not to the house of the mother as is the case with the Khasis). If the proposal is accepted, the father of the young man kills a pig, and gives a feast to the people of the village of his father-in-law elect; also to the go-between and the *borang* (brother of the bride). The father of the bride then gives a similar feast. A sum of Rs. 1 each is given as a present to the go-between by the fathers of the bride and bridegroom, and the father of the bride pays from Rs. 5 to Rs. 15 to the father of the bridegroom. Further feasting ensues at the house of the father of the bride. The go-betweens then sacrifice a pig and two fowls at the house of the bridegroom, and afterwards perform the same sacrifice at the house of the bride. At the house of the bride, after the fowls and the pig have been sacrificed, the go-between, after drinking liquor himself, pours out some on the floor of the house and then gives some to the bride and bridegroom to drink. The killing of the fowls, the sacrifice of the pig, and the libation of liquor are essentials at a Lynngam marriage. The sacrifice of the fowls is also an essential feature of a Garo marriage. The Lynngams, unlike the Garos, do not observe which way the beaks of the fowls turn when they are thrown on the ground after being sacrificed. The Lynngams, like the Khasis, take auguries from the entrails of the fowls and the pig. After these ceremonies are over, the Lynngam pair are allowed to cohabit. The cost of an ordinary Lynngam marriage is from Rs. 30 to Rs. 40. The marriage system in vogue among the Lynngams may be described as a mixture of the Khasi and Garo customs. As has already been stated, the Lynngams are a mongrel breed of Khasis and Garos.

Ceremonies Attending Death.

The death customs of the Khasis are not only very elaborate, but possess a significance of their own, it is; therefore, necessary to describe them in detail; they are as follows:—

A member of the family bends down towards the ear of the apparently deceased person and calls him or her by name three times, to make sure that death has occurred. If no answer comes, the family laments, for it is then concluded that the person is really dead. The body is then bathed in warm water from three earthen pots and is reverently laid on a mat (*japung*), where it is dressed in white cloth, a peculiar feature of the dressing being that the waist-cloth and turban are folded from left to right, and not from right to left, as in the case of the living. An egg called *u'leng kpoh* is placed on the stomach of the deceased, and nine fried grains, of *riw hadem*, or Indian corn, are tied round the head with a string. The rich place ear-rings in the ears and other jewellery on the body of the deceased, it being necessary that this jewellery should be specially made for the occasion, and they deck the corpse with valuable cloths. A cock, *u'iar krad lynti* (literally the cock that scratches the way), is sacrificed, the idea being that a cock will scratch a path for the spirit to the next world. A sacrifice of a bull, or of a cow in case the deceased is a woman, (*u* or *ka masi pynsum,*) follows. Portions of the left leg of the fowl and the lower part of the jaw of the bull or cow are kept, to be placed afterwards in the *mawshieng,* or bone, receptacle. A small basket (*ka shang*) is hung up over the head of the corpse, the basket containing pieces (*dykhot*) of the sacrificed animals. A dish containing eatables, and betel-nut, and a jar of water are placed near the head of the corpse by way of offering refreshment to the spirit of the departed. The food is given each morning and evening that the corpse remains in the house; this is called *ái ja miet ja step*. Each night the corpse remains in the house guns are fired, drums are beaten and flutes (*sháráti*) are played. It is a noteworthy custom that the body is not retained in the house for an even number of nights, the usual time being three nights. If it is intended to burn the body on a masonry pyre (*jingthang*), a bull (*u masi kynroh*) is sacrificed. If the body is placed in a coffin (*ka shyngoid*), a pig named *u'niang shyngoid* is sacrificed, and if it is intended to adorn the pyre with flags, a fowl called a *u'iar kait* is sacrificed. On the day of the funeral procession pigs are sacrificed by the relatives and friends of the deceased; those who cannot afford pigs bring liquor (*ka'iad rong*), a small portion of which they pour on the funeral pyre. The coffin is laid on a bamboo bier (*ka krong.*), money being placed close to the corpse, so that the spirit of the deceased may possess the wherewithal to buy food on its journey. Cotton, or, in the case of the rich, silk cloths are tied cross-ways over the bier, if the deceased is a male, and in the form of a parallelogram, if it is a female. Before lifting the bier a handful of rice and water from a jar are thrown outside, and a goat (*u'lang sait ksuid*) is sacrificed. These are purificatory ceremonies. The funeral procession then forms up and slowly passes along the way to the plaintive music of flutes (*sharati*) and the beating of drums. At intervals, in the case of the rich, salutes from guns are fired. Copper coins are also scattered along the route. On nearing the pyre the dead body is exposed to view, and the pieces of flesh of the sacrificial animals, which are with the corpse, are thrown away. They make ready three baked loaves (*ki kpu*), an egg, the lower jar-bones of the animals which have been sacrificed, the left leg of the fowl (*u'iar krad lynti*), a jar of water, eatables in a dish, and a bow and three arrows. A goat is then sacrificed, *u'lang mawkjat*. The corpse is laid on the pyre, inside the coffin, if one is used, with the head to the west and the feet to the east. Logs of wood are placed around the body, and the egg, "*u'leng kpeh,*" is broken, not over the stomach of the deceased, as has been sometimes supposed, but by being thrown on the pyre in the direction of the feet of the corpse. Fire in applied to the pyre, first by the *kur,* or members of the clan, and then by the children, if any, of the deceased. Another fowl, "*u'iar padat,*" is sacrificed, its blood being smeared round the pyre three times, and across the corpse three times. The bier is then broken to pieces, the cloths having been removed from it previously. The eatables and the jaw-bones of the sacrificial animals are then placed at the head of the pyre. After the fowl (*u'iar padat*) has been sacrificed, the three arrows already mentioned are shot from the bow, one to the north, another to the south, and the third to the east. These arrows are called *ki'nam tympem*. It is, perhaps, significant that the arrows which are shot at death despond in numbers with those which are used at the time of the birth ceremony. When the fire has blazed up, another goat, "*u'lang dholia*," is sacrificed. In some cases all the clothes of the deceased are burnt with the body, in others the clothes are merely held over the fire and then taken away, after which they can be used (this is only in the case of poor persons). Before leaving the burning-place the relatives and friends of the deceased place betel-nuts on the pyre and bid farewell to the deceased, saying "*Khublei khie leit bam kwai sha iing u Blei ho*" (good-bye, go and eat betel-nut in the house of god). When the body has been thoroughly burnt, the fire is extinguished with water, and the uncalcined bones are collected by the relatives in three trips. The collectors ace not allowed to turn back and pick up a bone which has been forgotten in any one of these trips. The bones thus collected are carefully wrapped in a piece of white cloth by the female relatives, and an old member of the family throws on the ground some powdered rice from a leaf, at the same time adjuring the spirit of the deceased not to trouble the *kur*, or the family, as the funeral ceremonies have been duly performed. The party then sets out to the bone repository, or *mawshieng*. In front walks one who strews along the line of route leaves of the tree known by the Khasis as *diang shit* (the berries of which are need for fishing with), and grains of rice, all the way from the pyre to the cairn. If any stream has to be crossed, a rough bridge is made of branches and grass. This trail of leaves and the bridges are intended to guide the spirit of the deceased to the cairn. The person who carries the bones is not allowed to turn round, or to the right, or to the left, but must proceed straight to the cairn. On reaching it, a *nongknia*, or sacrificer, washes the bones three times and then places them in an earthen pot, tying up the mouth with a white cloth. Then, having taken three pieces of the hard yolk of an egg, three loaves of bread, the leg of the fowl, "*u'iar krad lynti*," and the lower jaw-bones of the animals which have been sacrificed, he places them inside the cairn and shuts the door. Eatables and betel-nut are then placed on the top of the cairn. Early next morning the relatives and friends go to the cairn with fresh food and water, and look about for new foot-prints, the idea being that from these foot-prints they can foretell future events. This they do until the third night after the cremation. During these three nights the front door of the house formerly occupied by the deceased is never closed, it being thought that the spirit may wish to return and visit its earthly abode. The whole family is moreover *sang*, or taboo, during this period, and no manner of work can be done. When the three nights are over, it is called the *lait ia*, i.e. the days (of mourning) are passed, and three eggs are broken to ascertain what was the cause of the death. After this the family goes to bathe, and the clothes and mats in the house are washed. When this has been done, the taboo is removed and the family can go to work. After a month a pig or a fowl is sacrificed, the ceremony being called "*ai bam lait bnai*." It will be observed that three seems to be the lucky number throughout these funeral ceremonies. The number seems to bear a similar significance in other matters of Khasi ritual, e.g. the pouring out of libations, which is always done three times.

It is *sang* or taboo for a Khasi widow to re-marry within one year from the death of her husband, there is a similar prohibition for a husband re-marrying; but such *sang* can be got over by the payment of a fine to the clan of the deceased. After the expiration of one year the fine is reduced in amount. Khasi widows do not as a rule re-marry, according to U Jeebon Roy, unless they have no female children, in which case the clan urges them to re-marry, so that the chain of inheritance may not be broken, inheritance amongst the Khasis always passing in the female line.

Customs in Connection with Deaths by Violence or Accident.

These customs are interesting enough to deserve a separate description; they are as follows:—

If a man dies by the sword, before his body can be burnt, a sacrifice of a black hen must be offered to *Ka Tyrut*, the goddess of death. The bones are then placed in a stone cairn. Again they are removed, and, after eggs have been broken, are taken to a river bank and there washed. If there is no river at hand, a tank is dug for the purpose, which is called *umkoi*. There are various such *umkois* in different parts of the district, e.g. near Raliang and Nartiang. A sacrifice of a goat is offered to the god *U Syngkai Bamon*, and a sow to *Ka Ramshandi*, both of whom are evil deities. Another sow is sacrificed to *Ka Tyrut*. After this the bones are placed in another newly-built cairn. The ceremony of placing the bones in one and then removing them to another cairn is usually performed three times; but unless the auspices, as deduced from the eggs, are favourable, the relatives must go on sacrificing and removing the bones until they are so. These ceremonies having been completed, they erect a flat table-stone, or *mawkynthei*, for the ghost of the departed to sit upon, and return home, where they propitiate their ancestors with offerings of food. In the case of the murdered victims of the *thlen* superstition the same ceremonies are observed. For people who have died by drowning, or been killed by wild animals, and for women who have died in childbirth, similar pujas are offered, except that a sacrifice to *U Syngkai Bamon* does not take place. In the case of one who has died at a distance from his home, e.g. in a foreign country, whose body has not been burnt in accordance with custom, and whose bones have not been collected, the members of his clan, or his children, take three or five seeds or cowries (*sbai*) to a place where three roads meet. Here they summon the spirit of the departed in a loud voice, and throw up the seeds or cowries into the air, and when they fall to the ground they say, "*to alle noh ba ngin sa lum sa kynshew noh ia phi,*" come now we will collect you (the idea being that the seeds represent the bones of the deceased). Having collected the seeds, they place them on a bier and perform the service for the dead just in the same way as if a real dead body were to hand. If possible a portion of the dead person's clothes should be burnt with the seeds in the bier, and it is with this view that the coats or cloths of Khasi coolies, who die when employed as porters on military expeditions at a distance from their homes, are brought back by their friends to give to the relatives. If a person, dies of cholera, small-pox, or other such infectious or contagious disease, the body is buried, but is dug up again and burnt with all the customary rites when fear of infection or contagion is over. In parts of the district upright stones called *maw-umkoi* are erected along the line of route when the remains of a person who has met with an accidental death are brought home. This is stated to be the case in the Rambrai Siemship.

Miscellaneous Customs in Connection with Death.

In Nongjri, a large village in the Wár Country, the dead body is placed on a bier near the door of the house, a turban being tied about the head, the face being left bare and turned towards the door. In some of the Shella villages a second cremation is performed, in which a bamboo frame-work represents the corpse. This second cremation takes place when the body has been disposed of without the requisite ceremonies. The bones and ashes of the dead in Shella are in some cases kept in a cavity hollowed out of a post erected for the purpose. The bones and ashes find a temporary resting-place here, but are afterwards removed to a cromlech.

At Nartiang, in the Jaintia Hills, the head of the corpse is shaved, but a tuft of hair in the middle of the head is left; this is called (*u'niuh Iawbei*), the great grandmother's lock. At Nartiang betel-nut, which has been chewed by one of the mourners is put into the mouth of the corpse, also cooked rice. There is a similar custom prevalent amongst the Khyrwangs. The Nongtungs, in the Jaintia Hills, keep dead bodies sometimes as long as a month, until the *phur* or ceremonial dance has been performed. Hence they are called Nong-tung, or "stinkers." Amongst the Lynngams the dead body is kept for sometimes three or four months, or up to the time when a bull can be procured for a feast to the villagers. This feast is an essential, and, cattle being scarce in the Lynngam country, there is often great delay in disposing of the body. Lynngam villages at such a time are best avoided. The Lynngams of Nongsohbar bury the unburnt bones of the deceased within the village, and in front of the house occupied by the deceased when alive; the bones being placed in a hole in the ground, over which is laid a stone, a bamboo mat being nailed over the stone. A bamboo fence three or four feet high is erected round the grave. Other Lynngams bury the uncalcined bones and ashes in a gourd in the jungle near the burning-place. On their way home, the members of the clan of the deceased who have come from other villages to witness the funeral obsequies, put up a stone on the path in honour of the deceased, a turban being tied round the top of the stone. The Garos or Dkos, who live at the foot of the hills on the Kamrup border, and are called by the Assamese *Hana* (spear-men), erect memorial stones in honour of the deceased, the lower jaw-bones of sacrificial animals and other articles being hung on the stones. The stones are also swathed in cloths, and turbans are tied round the tops. The death customs of the Lynngams, and, indeed, other customs also, are partly Khasi and partly Garo, it being difficult to say that the Lynngams are more Khasi than Garo, or more Garo than Khasi in this respect; their language, however; has been found by Dr. Grierson to be a corruption of

Khasi. In Nongstoin, Mawlih, and Mariaw villages, the inhabitants of which profess to be Khasis, the bones and ashes of the deceased are not collected and placed in repositories, as at Cherrapunji. At Mariaw and Nongstoin a large wooden coffin is used, painted white, with ornamentations on the outside, and standing on four legs. This coffin is not burnt on the funeral pyre. In the family of the chiefs of Cherra, the body of a deceased Siem is subjected to the following process:—It is wrapped in a cloth and placed in the hollowed-out trunk of a tree, *ka-shyngoid*, there being a small hole with a plug at the bottom of this receptacle. Spirit is then poured into the *shyngoid* until the whole body is immersed, the liquor being allowed to stand for three days. After the body has been thus steeped, the liquor is allowed to run out, and the body is washed with warm water, after which it is allowed to dry for a day. Then a quantity of lime-juice is poured in, the latter being obtained from the fresh fruit of the lime (*u soh jew*). The body is thus exposed to a process of pickling, which continues until the whole is thoroughly dry and becomes like that of a mummy. It is then placed in a coffin, which is kept in the house of the Siem family until it is time to perform the funeral obsequies. These ceremonies entail a very large amount of expense, and it sometimes happens that they cannot be completed for some years after the death of a Siem. The body of a deceased Siem according to the Cherra custom should be burnt by his successor otherwise the latter is not Siem according to the Khasi religion. The last Siem of Cherra, U Hajon Manik, did not perform the funeral obsequies of his predecessor U Ram Singh, and it is stated that many of his subjects did not regard him as Siem, according to the Khasi religion, in consequence. There are at the present time the corpses of two Siems of Cherra which have been preserved in the manner described above, awaiting cremation. The first Siem, U Ram Singh, died as far back as 1875, and the second, U Hajon Manik, died in 1901.

Sir Joseph Hooker and other authorities have stated that the bodies of deceased Siems of Cherra used to be embalmed in honey, and an amusing story is told regarding the necessity of exercising caution in purchasing honey from Cherra (honey being plentiful in this neighbourhood), except in the comb, for fear of honey which has been used for embalming purposes being passed off on the unwary purchaser. But the members of the Siem family and the old residents deny that honey is used for this purpose nowadays, possibly in the interests of the trade. It is, however, not unlikely that honey was so utilized in days gone by, as it is a well-known agent for embalming. The bodies of priests in Burmah are said to be embalmed in honey, *vide* Yule's "Embassy to Ava."

The Disposal of the Dead.

The collection of the uncalcined bones and ashes of the deceased members of the clan and their bestowal in the *mawbah*, or great *cinerarium* of the clan, is without doubt the most important religious ceremony that the Khasis perform. That this ceremony is now but seldom celebrated, is due partly to the difficulty that exists in obtaining general agreement amongst the members of the clans, and partly to the considerable expense it entails. The information I have obtained regarding the ceremony, although differing to some extent in detail from that recorded by the late U Jeebon Roy, agrees with the latter's account as regards the main facts. The information may now be set down as follows. By way of premise it may be stated that the bones and ashes of the deceased are kept after cremation in small stone cairns, or *mawshieng*. From these small cairns the bones and ashes are removed to larger bone repositories called *mawphew*, each branch of a clan possessing a repository of its own. The ceremony attending the removal of the bones and ashes from the small cairns to the larger repository, or *mawphew*, and the ceremony attached to the removal of these remains from the *mawphew* to the sepulchre of the clan are practically the same, except that when the bones are removed to the *mawphew*, no female dancing takes place. First of all, the members of the various branches of the clan collect the bones from the different subsidiary repositories, when a ceremony called "*khot ia u lor u kap*," which it is not necessary to describe here, is performed. The bones of the deceased males and females are kept separately, and preparations are made to bring them to the sepulchre of the clan. Before, however, anything further can be done, it must be ascertained that the members of the clan are at peace with one another and no differences exist. If all differences are settled, a sacrificer offers up a prayer that the sins of the clans-folk may be forgiven, and then breaks eggs and sacrifices a cock to ascertain which will be a propitious day for depositing the bones in the sepulchre. A lucky day having been thus ascertained, the bones and ashes are brought to the *iing seng*, or clan puja-house, the bones of males and females being kept in separate bundles wrapped in white cloth, two women of the clan reverently carrying them in their arms, bidding the bundles of bones to their breasts. One female carries the bones of the males and the other those of the females. In front of these women walks an old man who scatters along the way leaves of the *dieng-shit* tree and grains of rice, and when it is necessary to cross any stream or river, he ties a thread from one side of the bank to the other, this is for the spirit of the departed to cross the water. Sometimes *u'nam tohrih*, a kind of long grass, is used instead of thread for the above purpose. On arrival at the clan puja-house, the bones of the males are laid on one bed and those of the females on another, the beds being bedecked with rich hangings. A cock, *u'iar kradlynti* (lit.: "the cock which scratches the way"), is sacrificed, this sacrifice being considered by the Khasis to be of peculiar significance. A pig, a cock, and a bull are then sacrificed, and portions of the above are offered to the spirits of the deceased. These offerings are known by the name of ai-bam, and are placed in a basket which is hung up in the house, together with the left thigh of the fowl and the lower jaw-bone of the bullock. A dance is performed that night, first in the house by two women, one belonging to the clan and the other an outsider, and afterwards in a specially prepared place outside the house called "*lympung*." The *sharati*, or flute, which is played at funerals is sounded, drums are beaten, and bombs are exploded. This dancing lasts from one to nine days, the limit being always an uneven number of days. At Cherra two effigies called *Ka Puron* and *U Tyngshop* are prepared and dressed up; the former is intended to represent *Ka Iawbei*, the first ancestress, and the other *U Suidnia*, the first maternal uncle of the clan. These effigies are held in the hands of the dancers. In the meantime two lines of upright stones consisting of three each, with a table-stone in front of each line, have been set up. These are called *mawkjat* or *mawlynti*, and are intended to serve as resting-places for the spirits of the dead on their way to the tomb of the clan. These stones are generally not more than three feet in height, and must not be confounded with the larger stones or *mawbynna*. On the night before it is proposed to deposit the bones, a ceremony called "*Beh-tympew*" is performed, which consists of driving out the devils from the house, so that they may not interfere with the peace of the spirits of the departed whilst they rest in the house, and on their journey to the tomb. All the men after they have performed this ceremony are given a drink of rice-beer known as *'iad nonglieh*. Another cock is sacrificed, and a small bamboo ladder of three rungs is prepared for the use of the spirits when climbing into the tomb. Rice is then thrown outside the door. The next morning they perform further sacrifices, which need not be detailed here, and let loose a bull whose horns have been cased in silver. They dig two shallow tanks called *umkoi*, into which is poured water supposed to possess the virtue of purifying the bones of any deceased clansmen who have died violent or unnatural deaths, or at places far away from their homes, where it was not possible to perform their funeral ceremonies according to custom. Three vertical stones are also erected, called *maw umkoi*. A bamboo with a white flag, and a plantain tree are set up; to the bamboo are attached three bamboo rings (*kyrwoh*), which are supposed to act as summonses to the spirits of the departed who have not received the benefits of a proper funeral ceremony. It may be explained that this ring of bamboo or cane is the form of summons used by the Khasi chiefs to their subjects when they wish to call them before them. Then a cock, *u'iar umkoi*, is sacrificed as a vicarious victim to bear the sins of the departed. When the procession reaches the *mawkjat* or *mawlynti* (the upright stones which have been erected), a goat called *u'lang mawlynti* is sacrificed. Then a bamboo is fixed to the centre one of the three upright stones, to which is attached the lower jaw-bone of one of the cattle sacrificed in the puja-house; this is called *u masi mawlynti*. A special ceremony called *ka-lyngka-pongrei* is then performed for those of the clan who have died childless. We now come to the actual ceremony of placing the bones in the tomb of the clan. Having arrived at the tomb, the bones are washed three times in a dish (this is a Cherra custom). In Mawshai, the bones are exposed to the heat of a fire kindled on a small *jingthang*, or burning-platform. The stone door of the *cinerarium* is then opened, and the bones of the females are placed in an earthen pot inside the tomb close to the wall which is farthest away from the door, the bones of the males being deposited in a pot inside the tomb nearest the door. Some clans keep the pot containing the bones of the males on the right, and the vessel containing those of the females on the left hand. Then offerings of food and libations of liquor are offered to the ancestors on a stone in front of the tomb. The males them perform a ceremonial dance with swords and shields, three times, and the door of the sepulchre is closed, a flag being fixed to the tomb. All the clansfolk then depart except three men. One of these sacrifices a cock (*iar-tanding*) in front of the tomb, a second sits behind the sacrificer, holding three firebrands, and a third sits behind the tomb. The man with the firebrands shakes them about, and then crows like a cock three times. The man behind the tomb listens attentively for any fancied noise within it, the superstition being that if the ceremonies detailed above have not been properly performed, the whole tomb will quake. If the three watchers are satisfied that there is no commotion within the tomb, then all is well, and they return and report the result to the clanspeople. This ceremony is called *tanding*, or the fire test. Next morning the woman who is the head of the *iing-seng*, or puja-house, distributes to all those who have taken part in these sacrifices the hinder portions of the sacrificial animals. She then blesses one by one the assembled clansfolk. The latter are not permitted by custom to go to work until after three days from the time of the ceremony; the third day being called *ka sngi lait ia*. The ceremony described above is a symbolical one. The massive stone sepulchre is regarded as a symbol of a secure place of rest for the departed spirits. If the spirits of the dead are not, however, appeased by the due performance of the ceremonies attending the bestowal of the remains in the clan *cinerarium*, it is believed that they roam about and haunt their relations on earth, and plague them with various misfortunes. It may be interesting to note here, that Mr. Moberly, the Superintendent of Ethnography in Bengal, reports that the ashes of deceased Hos, after being sprinkled with water by means of peepul branches, we collected, dried, and placed in a new earthen pot, and kept in the house until the day of burial, which may take place, as with the Khasis, long afterwards. The bones are buried in the village under a large slab of stone (cf. the Khasi stone *cinerarium*), and a monolith is erected outside the village to commemorate the deceased.

Khasi Memorial Stones.

Probably one of the first objects which strikes the eye of a visitor to the Khasi Hills is the very large number of monoliths, table-stones, and cromlechs that are to be met with almost everywhere in that country. Yule, Dalton, and other writers have incidentally referred to them, but, as far as is known at present, no attempt has been made to explain in any detail what is the peculiar significance of these objects to the Khasis. These stones are rightly styled memorial stones; *kynmaw*, literally, "to mark with a stone," is the word in the Khasi language for "to remember" The memorial stone, in the ordinary sense of the word, is a memorial to the dead; but we have such names of places in these hills as *Maomluh*, the salt stone (the eating of salt off the blade of a sword being one of the Khasi forms of oath), *Maosmai*, the oath stone, *Maophlang*, the grassy stone, and others. To commemorate with a stone an important event has been a constant custom amongst many people in many places, and the erection of grave-stones, to mark the spot where the remains of the dead are buried, is an almost universal practice amongst the Western nations, as indeed amongst some of the Eastern also. But the Khasi menhirs are no more gravestones, in the sense of marking the place where the remains of the dead lie, than some of the memorials of Westminster Abbey and other fanes; the Khasi stones are cenotaphs, the remains of the dead being carefully preserved in stone sepulchres, which are often some distance apart from the memorial stones. It is proposed to treat this subject under the following heading:—

(1) A general description of the memorial stones in the Khasi Hills, showing, that they are very similar in shape to monoliths, table-stones, or cromlechs in other parts of the world and of India.

(2) A comparison between Khasi memorial stones and those of the Ho-Mundas, the stones near Belgaum, those of the Mikirs, the monoliths at Willong in the Manipur Hills, and the Dimapur monoliths.

(3) The meaning of the stones.

(4) The method of their erection.

With regard to the first heading, the stones may be divided, into (*a*) menhirs, or vertical stones; (*b*) table-stones, or dolmens, and (*c*) stone cromlechs, or cairns, which serve the purpose of cineraria. Taking the different stones in order, the menhirs are large upright stones varying in height from 2 or 3 ft. to 12 or 14 ft., but in exceptional instances rising to a more considerable elevation, the great monolith at Nartiang, in the Jaintia Hills, being 27 ft. high, and 2 1/2 ft. thick. A photograph of this stone has been included. These menhirs are erected all in one line which nearly always consists of an uneven number of stones. Three is the commonest number of menhirs, but five together are frequently to be found, and there are some instances of seven stones; at Laitkor nine stones are standing, an illustration of which will be found in this book. The stones are of hewn gneiss granite, or sandstone, to be met with in many places in these hills. They are rough hewn, and generally taper gradually to their tops, which are sometimes neatly rounded off. The tallest stone is usually in the middle, and is occasionally ornamented with a small stone, through the middle of which a hole has beam drilled so that it may fit on the top of the other. At Nongkrem there is a centre stone with a regularly carved top, evidently intended to represent the head of a man. At Umstow, some two miles from Cherrapunji by the cart road, stood two rows of fine monoliths, each row five in number, and standing on either side of the old bridle road. All of these stones except one were thrown down by the earthquake shock of June, 1897. The centre stone, or *mawkni*, of one of these rows was surmounted by a carved stone covering shaped like a hat, but having a rim with indented edges, the intention being evidently to represent a crown. This stone crown was riveted to the top of the large centre stone. All the stones, including the *mawkynthei*, or dolmen, have been very neatly hewn. They appear to be of granite. Stones with top coverings or carved heads are however rare. In front of the line of menhirs is a large flat table-stone resting on stone supports, the top of the uppermost plane being some 2 to 2 1/2 ft. from the ground; this flat stone is sometimes as much as a foot or more thick. The largest table-stones are to be seen at Nartiang, in the Jaintia Hills, and Laitlyngkot in the Khasi Hills. The Laitlyngkot stone measures 28 1/2 by 13 3/4 ft., and that at Nartiang 16 1/2 by 14 3/4 ft. The Laitlyngkot stone is 1 ft. 8 in. thick. Sometimes two table-stones are found parallel to one another. The table-stones are always placed towards the centre of the group, generally in front of the great central menhir. These groups of stones are usually situated alongside roads, or close to well-known lines of route, where they readily attract the attention of passers-by. They do not necessarily face in any particular direction, but are to be found fronting all points of the compass. There is nothing therefore to show that they were erected so as to face the direction of the sunrise, or of any particular planet's. We will now pass on to the numerous stone cromlechs which are to be found, frequently in proximity to the menhirs and table-stones. These stone cromlechs contain the bones of the dead, and the menhirs and table-stones are intimately connected with them, inasmuch as memorial stones to deceased ancestors are erected when the ceremony of depositing bones in the *cineraria* has been completed. The *cineraria* are built of blocks of stone, sometimes on stone platforms, and sometimes resting on the ground. They are frequently of considerable size. The cromlech is opened by removing one of the heavy stone slabs in front. There are no windows such as are to be seen in some of the illustrations of dolmens or cromlechs in France and Circassia in Waring's book of "Stone Monuments, Tumuli, and Ornaments of Remote Ages," probably because the Khasi idea was to confine the spirits and not allow them to escape from the tomb and haunt the living. The cromlechs are generally square or oblong, but are sometimes circular in shape also. Let us now compare the Khasi menhirs with some to be found in other parts of the world. In Lord Avebury's "Prehistoric Times" Fergusson's work, and Waring's collection of plates of stone monuments, there are numerous illustrations of menhirs and dolmens to be found in other parts of the world, which may be said to resemble those of the Khasis in appearance, but this is by no means a matter for surprise, for, given like conditions, amongst primitive peoples, totally unconnected with one another as regards race, and living in countries far remote from one another, the results, i.e. the erection of stones as memorials of important persons, or events, are probably the same all the world over. Waring in his book gives an illustration of several lines of stone monuments with two table-stones, either in front or in rear according to the position of the photographer or draftsman in taking the picture, which would appear to be very similar to the lines of menhirs we find in the Khasi Hills. In plate XLII, fig. 6, of Waring's book, are the lines of stones to which I refer. They may be said to be almost exactly similar to the lines of Khasi memorial stones, except that the stones depicted by Waring have circles or ovals painted on them, which are said to signify that certain sacrifices of animals have been performed. Now the Khasis perform such sacrifices; but they do not mark their performance thus on the stones. Fergusson on page 447 of his "Rude Stone Monuments" apparently refers to these stones, which are near Belgaum in the Bombay Presidency, and he is of opinion that "they were dedicated or vowed to the spirits of deceased ancestors"; further it is stated that these stones are always in uneven numbers, a striking point of similarity to the Khasi stones. We know, for a fact, that the Khasi memorial stones were dedicated to the same objects as those of the Belgaum stones, i.e. to the worship of ancestors; so that we have not only similarity in appearance, in confirmation, and invariable unevenness of number, but identity of purpose, if Fergusson's conclusion is correct. It is, however, a far cry from Shillong to Belgaum, and it may, perhaps, be thought more reasonable if we look for stones nearer at hand. Bradley Birt in his interesting book on Chota Nagpur has given a photograph of certain Ho memorial stones, which would appear to resemble greatly the Khasi menhirs, and if his photograph is carefully examined, it will be seen that there are in rear of the stones what would seem to be stone cairns, very similar in appearance to the Khasi *cineraria*. The funeral ceremonies of the Hos as described by Bradley Birt, viz. the cremation of the body, the collection of the ashes, their consignment to a grave, and the offering of food to the spirit of the deceased, are similar to those of the Khasis. Although not wishing to lay too much stress on what may be merely a coincidence, I think that the above similarity in death customs is well worth considering with regard to the view, based on linguistic affinity, that the Khasis and the Ho-Mundas were originally descended from a common stock, i.e. the Mon-Khmêr or Mon-Anam family, as has been postulated by Logan.

But there are other tribes in Assam which erect memorial stones, e.g. the Mikirs and certain Naga tribes. The Mikirs erect memorial stones in a line, the taller stone being sometimes in the centre, as in the case of the Khasi memorial stones. Such stones are set up by the Mikirs only in memory of important personages, such as *mauzadars* or leading *gaonburas* (village headmen). Besides the standing stones (*long-chong*), a flat stone (*long pak*) is also erected in honour of the deceased. I understand that the Mikir stones, like the Khasi, are mere cenotaphs, the ashes of deceased Mikirs being left at the burning places which are generally by the sides of rivers, and the memorial stones not being necessarily anywhere near the burning grounds. Unlike the Khasis, the Mikirs do not collect and carefully keep the bones in stone cairns. Before erecting memorial stones, they dig a small tank, cf. the Khasi custom of digging similar tanks (*um-koi*), before erecting memorial stones (*maw umkoi*), to those of the clan who have died unnatural deaths. As with the Khasis, feasts and entertainments are given when the stones of the Mikirs are erected: but they need not necessarily consist of uneven numbers, it appears. It is possible that the Mikirs may have obtained the custom of erecting memorial stones from their near neighbours, the Khasis.

Then there is the interesting collection of stones at Willong in the Manipur Naga Hills, for a description of which I am indebted to the kindness of Colonel Maxwell, the late Political Agent and Superintendent of the State. It is said that about 300 or 400 years ago these stones were erected by the rich men of the village as memorials (probably to deceased ancestors). It is the custom of the Willong village that any person who wishes to erect such a stone should, with the members of his family, abstain from food; but liquor and ginger are allowed to them. Having chosen what he thinks is a suitable stone, the Naga cuts off a flake of it, returns home, and sleeps on it with a view to dreaming of the stone. If his dreams are favourable, he brings it in, otherwise not. From the day of the selection of the stone, until it is brought in and erected, he must fast. Women are taboo to him for the space of one year from the date of its erection. The custom of erecting memorial stones is not therefore peculiar to the Khasis amongst the hill tribes in Assam. An incidental reference should, I think, be made to the interesting carved monoliths at Dimapur, regarding the meaning of which there has been so much doubt. These Dimapur stones are remarkably similar in shape to the carved wooden *kima* posts of the Garos, another hill tribe speaking a language which is undoubtedly connected with the great Boro group of languages in North Eastern India. The Garo *kima* posts, like the Khasi stones, are erected to commemorate deceased ancestors. Some of the other Naga tribes, besides the Willong Nagas, are in the habit of erecting what are called *genna* stones, a description of which will, we hope, be given in a subsequent Naga monograph. The object of the erection of such stones is certainly to show reverence to the memories of deceased ancestors amongst the Khasis, and Garos, and not improbably among the Nagas also.

It is only with the very greatest difficulty that it has been possible to obtain any intelligible information regarding the Khasi monoliths. Whether through feelings of delicacy in revealing the secrets of their religious system to a foreigner, or through ignorance or apathy (there being but few Khasis nowadays who observe the ancient ritual), it has been no easy task to extract information from people about these stones. As far as my information goes at present, I am inclined to classify the stones as follows:—

(*a*) *Mawlynti*, or *mawkjat*, the stones which are erected to serve as seats for the spirits of departed clansfolk on their way to the tomb of the clan, i.e. when their remains are carried by their relations to the clan cromlech (see the section entitled "The Disposal of the Dead").

(*b*) *Mawbynna*, or *mawnam*, which are stones erected to commemorate a parent or some other near relation.

(*c*) *Maw-umkoi*, which are put up to mark the position of tanks or *umkoi*, the water of which is supposed to cleanse the ashes and bones of those who have died unnatural deaths.

(*d*) *Maw-shongthait*, or flat table-stones, often accompanied by vertical stones, which are placed in the market places and by the side of roads to serve as seats for weary travellers. Taking the above main divisions seriatim, *mawlynti*, or *mawkjat*, may be described as follows. These generally consist of three upright stones, the tallest being in the centre, and a flat table-stone being placed in front. There are, however, some clans which erect more than three upright stones, as *mawlynti*, or *mawkjat*. As already stated, the clansfolk used to erect these stones, *mawlynti* (the stone of the way), or *mawkjat* (the stone of the leg), at each place at which they halted for the night on their way to deposit the bones of their deceased maternal relations in the clan sepulchre, or *mawbah*. The stones are called *mawkjat*, or stones of the leg, because it is supposed that the spirits of the departed sit and rest their limbs on the flat table-stones. The upright stones are not as a rule more than 3 or 4 ft high, and are not massive like the great *mawbynna*, or memorial stones. They are to be found in great numbers all along the roads or paths which lead to the clan cromlechs. These stones, unlike the *mawbynna*, have no names.

(*b*) *Mawbynna*, or *mawnam*, are erected to commemorate deceased parents or deceased ancestors, and consist of 3, 5, 7, 9, or even, in an exceptional case, 11, upright stones with flat table-stones in front. The upright stones are called *maw-shynrang*, or male stones, and the flat table-stones *maw-kynthei*, or female stones. Turning to the plate of the Laitkor stones, it will be observed that there are nine upright stones, and one large flat table-stone in front. Counting from right to left, stone No. 5 is called u maw *kni*, or the maternal uncle's stone; and the stones to the right and left of it, *ki maw pyrsa ki para*, i.e. the stones of the maternal brothers and nephews. The table-stone is called *ka Iawbei tynrai*, or *ka Iawbei tymmen*, literally the grandmother of the root, or the old grandmother, in contradistinction to *ka Iawbei khynraw*, or *ka Iawbei kpoh* (the grandmother of the family, or branch of the family). It frequently happens that there are two flat table-stones in front of the upright stones, the one on the left being *ka Iawbei tynrai*, or the first ancestress, and the one on the right *ka Iawbei longkpoh*, the grandmother of the branch of the clan to, which the memorialists belong, or *ka Iawbei khynraw*, the young grandmother, i.e. the grandmother of the actual family to which the memorialists belong. In olden days it used to be the custom for the clanspeople to place offerings of food on the flat table-stones for the shades of the departed ancestors, and this is sometimes the case still; but now it is more frequently the custom to make these offerings in the *iing-seng*, or clan puja-house. The flat table-stones are some 2 to 2 1/2 ft. from the ground, and it is difficult to resist the impression that they were originally sacrificial stones, i.e. that animals or even human beings were actually sacrificed upon them. In connection with this theory I would refer to the interesting folk-tale about the Kopili river. It is here related that in olden days human victims were sacrificed to the Kopili goddess on the flat table-stone (*maw-kynthei*) at a place called *Iew Ksih*, close to the Kopili river. A careful search has been made for this stone, with the result that a flat table-stone has been found near the above village, where goats are still annually sacrificed to the Kopili. The *doloi* reports that this is an ancient custom. None can remember, however, having heard that human victims were ever sacrificed there. Yet I do not think it at all unlikely that this is the stone, locally called *Mynlep*, which is referred to in the folk-tale. At Jaintiapur and Nartiang, both of which places were the headquarters of the kings of Jaintia, there are very large table-stones. We know for a fact that human sacrifices used to take place at Jaintiapur. Is it possible that human beings were immolated on these table-stones? It would be unsafe to base any conclusion on the solitary folk-tale about the *Iew Ksih* table-stone; but the tale certainly furnishes food for reflection. The Khasis borrowed their religious customs largely from the Synteng inhabitants of Jaintia, and it is possible that they may have obtained the custom of erecting the table-stones from the Syntengs also, and that the latter were originally used by both of them for sacrificing human victims. Sometimes, immediately on either side of the *mawkni*, or large central stone, there are two much smaller stones called *mawksing*, or the stone of the drum, and *mawkait*, the stone of the plantain; the drum being used in all religious ceremonies by the Khasis, and the plantain relating to their custom of feeding young children on plantains. The *mawnan* must be described separately from the *mawbynna*, because they differ from them in an important particular, i.e. that the former may be erected to commemorate the father, while the latter are set up to perpetuate the memory of the ancestors on the female side of the family. *Mawnam* consist of three upright stones and one flat table-stone in front. The large central stone is called *u maw thawlang*, or the stone of the father, and the upright stones on either side are meant to represent the father's brothers or nephews. The flat table-stone is *ka Iawbei*, i.e. the grandmother of the father, not the first grandmother of the clan, as in the case of the *mawbynna*.

(*c*) The *maw umkoi* have already been described. They use erected to mark the sites of purificatory tanks, which have been dug so that the remains of deceased persons may be cleansed from the impurities attending an unnatural death, and to counteract the adverse influence upon the clan of *Ka Tyrut*, or the goddess of death. These stones are sometimes called *mawtyrut*.

(*d*) *Maw-shongthait*, or stones upon which weary travellers sit, are to be found alongside all the principal lines of communication in the district. It may serve as an example of these stones to describe the very interesting collection of stones at Nartiang *hát*, or market. A reference is invited to the plate which gives a representation of some of the Nartinga stones. The great height of the upright stone will at once be seen; it is 27 ft. in height and 2 1/2 ft. thick. This stone is the largest erect stone in the Khasi and Jaintia Hills at the present day, and is a very fine specimen. The upright stones and the flat table-stones at Nartiang are called "*ki maw jong Siem*." There is no separate designation for each of them. These stones are popularly supposed to have been erected long ago by two men, U Lah Laskor and U Mar Phalyngki, to commemorate the establishment of Nartiang market, which is called Iew Mawlong. "Laskor" is the Synteng equivalent of the Khasi *lyngskor*, or prime minister. "Mar" is a Synteng word meaning a giant, the idea amongst the people being that in the olden days there were giants in the land who performed marvellous feats of strength, e.g. the erection of the megalithic remains at Nartiang and elsewhere. A puja is performed upon a great flat stone by the *doloi* and his officers in honour of the founders of the market, but no animals are sacrificed, rice and *rynsi* (balls of rice) only being offered. In the days of the Jaintia kings only the Raja could sit upon the great flat stone; hence the name *maw jong Siem* (or Siem's stone). The great upright stone is said to have been brought by U Lah Laskor and a great number of people from Suriang, a place near Nartiang. With reference to the Nartiang stones I would refer to my theory, formulated above, that they were originally connected with human sacrifices. It may be mentioned that at Nartiang there is a bridge constructed out of a single stone, which is also said to have been set in position by U Lah Laskor. Near Suhtnga there is a group of stones, said to have been originally thirty in number, together with *maw shongthait*, or stones to seat the weary, which were erected to the memory of a woman, Ka Kampatwat, who in generations past is alleged to have had no less than *thirty* husbands. The lady is not supposed to have been polyandrous, nor nine-lived, but to have divorced one husband after another. As she probably established a record for divorce, her descendants afterwards commemorated her in the manner described. There is another very large atone at Nongkeeh, which unfortunately fell to the ground in the great earthquake shock of 1897. This stone must have stood over 20 ft. above the ground. It is called *u mawkni Siem*, the stone of the Siem's maternal uncle, and it used to form the central stone, or *mawkni*, of a line of stones. These stones belong to the clan of the *basans* of Nongkseh, which furnishes the *sohblei*, or head sacrificer, of the Siems of Khyrim. The stones at Mawsmai; which in ancient days used to be the headquarters of a Siem, are some of the best carved in the hills. At Mawrongjong, in the Jaintia sub-division, is a stone upon which a figure, evidently of a Hindu god, has been carved, without doubt after the erection of the stone. Here we have a striking parallel case to the painted and carved menhir near Tregastel in Brittany, upon which has been carved the representation of a crucifix. There are also some carved stones near Nartiang (said to represent two women) called *mawthawdur briew*.

The Khasis say that these great stones were brought sometimes from considerable distances. After being hewn, the stones were laid on a large, wooden trolley and dragged across country by means of ropes of cane, of which plenty can be bad from the War country on the southern side of the district, and then placed in position by means of ropes and levers. It seems little short of marvellous that these stones, which sometimes weighed many tons, were placed in position by such primitive means, especially when we consider the great trouble there was to re-erect one of the fallen stones at Stonehenge lately. Nowadays only comparatively small stones are erected, which are generally hewn and erected on the spot, so that there is no necessity for any conveyance.

In conclusion, it may be remarked that the subject of the Khasi monoliths is in reality a large one, on which a great deal could be written, but owing to considerations of space it has been found necessary to compress the account within its present limits.

Festivities, Domestic and Tribal.

Dancing forms the principal part of all the Khasi festivities, and is an important adjunct of some of their religious ceremonies. One of the greatest festivals in the Khasi Hills is the Nongkrem dance; it may be said to be as important an event to the Khasis as the *Beh dieng-khlam* festivities are to the Syntengs.

The Nongkrem dance is really part of what is known as the *pom-blang*, or goat-killing ceremony, performed by the Siem of Khyrim (or Nongkrem)) with the aid of his *soh-blei* (high priest) and the various *lyngdohs* (or priests) to Ka Blei Synshar (the ruling goddess), that the crops may prosper and that there may be a successful era in store for the people of the State. The goddess on this occasion may be regarded as a Khasi Demeter, although no mysteries form part of her services as at the Grecian Eleusis. The Nongkrem ceremony and dance (now held at Smit) take place in the late spring, generally in the month of May. A lucky day having been fixed; the Siem sends a ring of cane (*kynwoh*) by way of a summons to the people of every village in the State, at the same time informing them of the date of the puja and requesting them to attend with their offerings, consisting of goats and different articles of food. In the meantime various pujas have been taking place in the house of *Ka Siem Sad*, the Siem priestess, which it would be tedious to describe in detail. The more interesting points only will be mentioned. A fortnight before the puja and dance at Smit the *soh-blei*, or high priest, pours out libations of liquor in the *kyram-blang*, or place where the sacrificial goats are kept, and in front of the great post (of *dieng sning*, or Khasi oak), in the house of the Siem priestess. Dancing then takes place in front of the post. Later on the Siem, with the high priest and other attendant priests, walks with extremely slow gait to a small hill where a stone altar has been prepared, and sacrifices a cock in honour of *u'lei Shillong*, or the god of the Shillong Peak. A silver dish with powdered rice, liquor in a gourd, (*ka'iad um*), betel-nut, and some leaves of the Khasi oak (*dieng sning*), are also necessary adjuncts of the puja. A goat is then sacrificed, and the sacrifice is followed by a dance of twenty two men armed with swords and shields and chowries (fly-flaps). Having danced before the altar, the party returns to the house of the Siem priestess and executes another dance in the great courtyard. The Siem and certain selected persons dance in front of the *rishot blei*, or holy post of Khasi oak inside the house of the Siam priestess, the dancers being entertained with dried fish and ginger. Then follows the great dance of girls and men in front of her house. The girls dance in the centre, taking such tiny steps, that the lifting of their feet from the ground is hardly perceptible, the arms held down to the sides and the eyes demurely downcast. It is on this occasion that they wear the peculiar silver (and sometimes gold) crowns illustrated in the plate. The hair is worn tied in a knot behind the head, but with a long tail hanging down the back. Rich silk cloths are worn by the girls, who present the appearance of being, if anything, over-clothed, or, as Yule aptly puts it, of "perfect parallelograms." They wear a profusion of gold and coral bead necklaces, silver and gold chains, bracelets, ear-rings of gold, and any other jewellery they can lay hands on. Not only is the whole of the family jewellery, requisitioned by the fair *débutante* (it is only the unmarried who dance), but she borrows from her friends. The men dance round the outside of the circle, waving fly-flaps, and prancing (often nowadays, wearing huge boots) with ungainly strides. The music necessary for the dance consists of *tangmuri* (pipes), drums, and cymbals. This is *ka shad kynthei*, or the dance of the women. Then there *is ka shad mastieh*, or the dance of the men, who are gaily dressed, wearing plumes of black and white cock's feathers (*u thuiyah*) and hold swords and shields. After gyrating for some time, two men at a time rapidly approach one another and clash their swords together in mock combat. They then retire, and, after again revolving for a period, repeat the process; then other couples follow and take their place. This goes on, until the dancers get tired or are told to stop.

    The above description, may be taken as applicable to all the Khasi dances. Dancing forms part of the ceremony of placing the ashes in the sepulchre of the clan. Dancing also forms a part of certain ceremonies performed at market for the prosperity of the State and for the good of trade.

    When I was at Mawsynram, at the time of the appointment of a Siem, I witnessed a very pretty dance called *ka shad lymmoh*, performed by men who held the leafy branches of trees in their hands. This is most effective. Then followed a dance of some forty young girls, very well dressed, covered with the usual gold and coral beads and silver chains, and wearing the silver crown, or *pansngiat*. The young women danced with great spirit, and with an absence of all shyness, but still with the greatest decorum. Many of the women, spectators as well as dancers, were observed to be without the usual *tap moh khlih*, or head-cloth, the absence of which is always a sign amongst the Khasi women of merry-making. There were women from the Wár country, wearing their picturesque dress amongst whom was the wife of the Siem of Bohwal with her little daughter. The dance was a pretty sight, and I have seldom seen such evidence of unaffected happiness as was exhibited by the people on this occasion. Dancing may be described as one of the characteristic features of Khasi life.

The Synteng *Beh-diang-khlam* festival takes place annually at Jowai and elsewhere in the Jaintia Hills in the deep water moon month (*u Jyllieu*, or June). *Khlam* is the Khasi word for plague or pestilence and *beh-dieng* signifies to drive away with sticks. The festival may be described as follows:—The males rise betimes on the day fixed and beat the roof with sticks, calling upon the plague-demon to leave the house. Having done this, later on in the day they go down to the stream where the goddess "Aitan" dwells. Then poles of great length, which have been newly cut, are held across the stream. The people jump on the poles and try to break them; when they succeed in doing so, a great shout is given. After all these poles have been broken, a very large pole is fixed across the stream. The people then divide themselves into two parties, and contend for the possession of the tree. The contest, however, is a good-humoured one, and although many buffets are given and received, these are not regarded seriously, and there are seldom any fights. Col. Bivar says the contending villagers in their excitement, sometimes relapse into a state of almost complete nudity. The party which succeeds in obtaining possession of the post is supposed to gain health and prosperity during the coming year. Col. Bivar remarks that the origin of this so-called ceremony is said to be that the god of thunder, "*u'lei pyrthat*," and Ka Aitan, the goddess of the stream, enjoined its performance. Many innovations, however, have crept in. People disguise themselves as giants and wild beasts, they also parade images of serpents, elephants, tigers, peacocks, &c. Dancing is carried on with enthusiasm by the males, the girls, clad in their best attire, remaining on-lookers. Before the meeting breaks up the males play a sort of game of hockey with wooden balls.

Genna

The word *genna* is one in common use amongst the Naga tribes. It seems to be a matter of doubt whether the word belongs to any of the numerous languages or dialects spoken by these tribes; but for our purposes it may be taken to mean taboo. The Khasi word *sang*, which implies an interdiction either religious or social from doing any particular thing, might have been employed; but as the word *genna* is so commonly used when speaking of taboos amongst the hill tribes of this province, I have thought fit to employ it here. The word *genna*, or taboo, may be held to include the Khasi *sang*. Taboos amongst the Khasis, Wars and Lynngams may be divided into two sections; (*a*) general, and (*b*) special. Instances of general taboo have not been found amongst the Khasis, but the following taboo called *Ka sang kla* amongst the Wár villages of Sohbar and Nongjri is peculiar, and therefore worthy of description. Its chief peculiarity is that during the time the *sang kla* continues, the inhabitants of these two villages are not allowed to associate with foreigners. This *genna* takes place twice a year, in the months of June and November, and lasts for a month each time. During the *genna* foreigners are not allowed to stay the night in these two villages, and the villagers must not sleep the night outside their villages. If they do not return home for the night, they are subjected to a fine. There is a prohibition against eating, smoking, or chewing betel-nut with foreigners during the period. The above is the only instance of general taboo that I have been able to find amongst the Wárs, but in the Lynngam villages there is a taboo on all outsiders at the time of the village pujas. Such a taboo amongst the Lynngams is not to be wondered at, as they have probably imbibed the notion from their Garo mothers, intermarriages between Lynngams and Garos being common. The Garos, like other Thibeto-Burmans, have numerous taboos. There are numerous instances of special taboos among the Khasis. *Kaba shong sang*, or marrying within the *kur* or clan, is the most important taboo of all, and is regarded as the most serious offence a Khasi can commit. It admits of no expiation, and the bones and ashes of the offender cannot be placed in the family tomb. There are special taboos for certain clans, of which the following are some examples. The clan Nongtathiang cannot eat the lemon, the Kharumnuid clan must abstain from pork, the Cherra Siem family cannot eat dried fish, and the Siem family of Mylliem taboo the pumpkin. Possibly these taboos may be relics of totemism amongst these communities. The following are some of the other taboos, although some of them are but lightly regarded now-a-days.

(i.) To build a house with stone walls on all four sides.
(ii.) To use nails in building a house.
(iii.) To use more than one kind of timber in building the hearth.
(iv.) To build a house with resinous timber. Only the Siem family can use such timber.
(v.) To cut trees from a sacred forest.
(vi.) To take or give anything with the left hand.
(vii.) To step over any one's body.
(viii.) To kill any animal or bird without first throwing rice over its body...
(ix.) To drink the milk of a cow or goat.
(x.) To talk with any one, except with one of a man's or woman's fellow-workers, when the thrashing of paddy is going on.

There are the following special taboos for pregnant women.
(*a*) To Accompany a funeral procession.
(*b*) To finish any sewing she may have commenced before she became *enceinte*. There is a similar prohibition regarding the finishing of the plaiting of wicker baskets.
(*c*) It is *sang* for the husband of a pregnant woman to thatch the ridge of the house at such a time, or to fix a handle to an axe or a *dao*.

CHAPTER V

Folk-Tales, Traditions and Superstitions

Folk-Tales.

The Khasis possess a considerable amount of folk-lore. The tales which will be found reproduced in the original Khasi have been obtained from a collection which was in the possession of the Rev. Dr. Roberts, of Cherrapunji, who very kindly placed it at my disposal. The translations are by U Nissor Singh, Sub-Inspector of Schools, and the author of a Khasi English Dictionary as well as certain other educational works in that language. Dr. Roberts's collections would fill a book; so I have selected only a few of what I consider typical tales. At the instance of Sir Charles Lyall, I have given the Khasi and English side by side. The stories will speak for themselves, but I add a few explanatory notes. The water-fall of Ka Likai is a magnificent cascade in the rainy season; it can best be viewed from the heights of Laitkynsew. The water-fall is situated close to the village of Nongriat, which is approached by a succession of stone steps from the village of Tyrna, just below the Charrapunji Laitkynsew bridle-path. "Dingiei," which is mentioned in the second tale, is the high hill to be seen on the right-hand side of the Shillong-Cherrapunji road soon after leaving Shillong. The highest point of the range is over 6,000 ft. The third tale contains the well-known story of Ka Pah Syntiew, the fabled ancestress of the Khyrim and Mylliem Siem families. The cave where Ka Pah Syntiew is said to have made her abode is still to be seen in the neighbourhood of Nongkrem. The story of the origin of the Siems of Suhtnga, who afterwards became the Rajas of Jaintiapur, is a well-known tale in the Jaintia Hills. A description of the wonderful mass of granite known by the name of the Kyllang Rock will be found in the section of the monograph which deals with geographical distribution. I have also added a photograph of the rock. The Syntengs have a story that when the strong west wind blows in the spring this is due to the advent of *U Kyllang,* who comes to visit his wife, the river *Umngot,* at that season: amongst the Khasis hills are all of them masculine, but to rivers is usually attributed the feminine gender. U Symper is another isolated rocky eminence rising from the Maharam plain close to the village of K'mawan. The best view of the hill is obtainable from Laitmawsiang on the path to Mawsynram. The village of Mawsmai every traveller from Therria to Cherrapunji knows. It is chiefly remarkable for a fairly large limestone cave, and its fine memorial stones. The Khasi theory to explain how the moon got its spots is, I believe, original, but is no more extraordinary than our own nursery tale about the "man in the moon." The *Sohpet Byneng* hill is the first hill of any size that the traveller sees on the Gauhati road when journeying to Shillong. It is close to Umsning Dak Bungalow. There are caves in the hill which are tenanted by bears. Strange to say, according to Khasi ideas, this is one of the highest points in the hills; in reality *Sophet Byneng* is some 2,000 ft. lower than the Shillong Peak. As mentioned elsewhere, the Khasis are very fond of dogs; so I have given their version of how the dog came to live with man. The well-known *thlen* superstition will be found fully described under the heading of "Human sacrifices." I have, however, thought the tale of sufficient interest to reproduce at length here. The story of the river Rupatylli is a pretty tale, and is just such a one as would appeal to the imagination of mountaineers like the Khasis. The Kopili story is important, in that it indicates the origin of human sacrifices in the Jaintia Hills; it also throws, perhaps, some light on the question of the use to which the flat table memorial stones were put in years gone by. The superstition about the crossing of the Kopili can be vouched for by many, who have taken the journey from the Jaintia Hills to North Cachar by the Kopili route. Mawpunkyrtiang is a small village close to Cherrapunji. The weird tale about the Siem of Malyniang is the pride of the Maskut people, for in olden days their King, i.e. the Siem of Malyniang, is supposed to have been a very powerful monarch amongst the Khasis. The story of Manick Raitong is interesting, in that it explains the origin of the use of the *sharati*, a bamboo flute of special make which is played only at funerals. The pool of water, which was formed after U Manick and the erring queen were burnt, may be connected with the *Umkoi*, or tank, which is dug to cleanse the souls of those who have died violent deaths. The idea of the bamboo, which bore leaves that grew upside-down, springing up from the buried flute, is also to be found in the Synteng tale regarding U Loh Ryndi's fishing rod. Owing to considerations of space, I have had to curtail largely the folk-lore section. I have, however, kept the materials by me, and if at any future time there is reason to believe that the reproduction of more Khasi folk-lore is called for, I shall be glad to try to arrange that some of the other folk-tales be printed.

The Water-Fall of Ka Likai.

The water-fall of Ka Likai is one of the most beautiful water-falls in the Khasi Hills. Its stream flows from a certain river from the village of Rangjirteh and passes by the village of Nongriat. The fall can be seen distinctly from the village of Laitkynsew. What a beautiful fall it is when viewed in the autumn. It is also a very high fall. There was in olden days in the village of Rangjirteh a woman called Ka Likai. She was a poor woman who had a husband. When she had given birth to a child, the husband died. Whilst the child was yet a baby, she experienced much trouble in taking care of it on account of her poverty. After the child was able to walk, what a pleasure it was to her to see it growing, and able to play with other children. Then that woman married another man; but he did not love the little child, and many a time he got angry because she could not take care of him more, on account of that child.

One day when she went to carry iron ore, her husband took the child and killed it. When he had cut up the body into pieces, he prepared curry with it and placed the curry where the mother would come and eat it. When he had finished doing so, he threw the head and the bones of the child far away, but he forgot to throw away the fingers, which he had placed in a basket where the betel-nut was kept. When the mother returned from her journey, she inquired "Where is the child?" "She has just gone somewhere, I don't know where," he said. She remained silent awhile; then she said, "Is there any rice and curry?" He said "Yes, it is ready," and went out at the same time. When she ate, she found the curry very tasty, and she thought that he had got the flesh of a young pig from some one who had performed a sacrifice. When she had finished eating, she took up the betel-nut basket, but found the fingers of her child there. She shrieked and threw herself down, and then ran to the precipice and cast herself down it. All the villagers wondered, but no one ventured to prevent her as she held a *da* in her hand. From that time the waterfall was called the "Fall of Ka Likai."

Ka Kshaid Ka Likai.

Ka ksháid-ka-Likai ka long kawei ka ksháid ha ri Khasi kaba itynnad shibún eh. Ka wan tuid na kawei ka wah ha ka shnong Rangjirteh kaba wan hap ha ka shnong Nongriat. Ia kane ka ksháid lah ban ioh-i bha na ka shnong Laitkynsew. Katno ka long kaba i-tynnad lada khmih ia ka ha ka por synrái. Ka long ruh kaba jrong shibun eh. La don kawei ka briew ha ka shnong Rangjirteh hyndái kaba kyrteng ka Likai. Kane ka briew ka long kaba duk bad ka la don u tnga, te ynda la kha iwei i khun kynthei uta i tnga u la iap noh. Hamar ka por ha dang lung ita I khun ka la shitom shibún ban sumar ha ka jinglong duk jong ka. Te ynda i la nangiaid katno, ka la sngewbhá ban ioh-i ia la i khun ba i la sháit, bad ba i la nang ba'n leh kái bad ki para khynnah. Te kane ka briew ka la shongkurim bad uwei pat u briew; hynrei uta u'm ieit ia ita i khún, bad katno ba u la jiw sngew bitár ba ka'm lah ban khreh ba'n sumar ia u na ka bynta ita i khún.

Te ha kawei ka sngi ba ka leit kit nongnar, utá u tnga u la shim ia ita i khún bad u la pyniap noh. Bad haba u la ot u la shet jintah ia ka doh jong i, u la buh ruh ha ka jaka ba ka'n wan bam ka kmie; bad ynda u la dep kumta baroh u la leit bred noh ia ka khlih bad ki shyieng sha jngái, hynrei ia ki shimpriahti ba u la buh ha ka shang kwái u'm kynmáw shuh ban leit bred. Haba la wan ka kmie na kata ka jingleit ka la kylli, "hangno ka khun"? "Tip ei, u ong, shano ka leit kái myntan." Ka shu sngap noh bad ka ong "La don ja don jintah ne em" u ong, "la don," bad hamar kata ka por u leit kái noh. Te haba ka la bam ja, ka sngew bang shibun, bad ka la tharai ba u ioh doh khún sniang na kino-kino kiba kñia, bad haba ka la lah bám ja ka la shim ka shang kwái ba'n bam kwái, ka shem pynban da ki shimpriahti ita i khún bad ka la lyniar la lympat ia lade kat ba lah, bad ka la mareh sha katei ka ríat bad ka la pynnoh ia lade. Kumta lyngngoh ki shnong-ki-tháw baroh bad y'm lah ba'n khang mano-mano ruh, ka bat la ka wait ha ka kti. Te nadúh kata ka por ki khot "ka ksháid-noh-ka-Likai."

The Dingiei Hill.

Dingiei Hill is one of the highest peaks in the Khasi country, resembling in height and size the Shillong "Peak" which lies opposite and to the north of it. There are many villages on this hill belonging to the Shillong Siem. In olden days on the top of this hill grew a gigantic tree overshadowing the whole world, the name of that tree was "ka Dingiei." The Khasis came to a determination that if this tree were cut down (lit. destroyed) the world would become good and would have light, for as long as it (the tree) remained standing, the world remained dark and unfruitful. They accordingly came to an unanimous decision to fell it. When they cut (the tree) during the day and went back next morning, they found that the marks of cutting had been obliterated. Thus they cut each day, and next morning they found that the marks had disappeared. This was the case always. Then they marvelled why this thing was thus. They asked questions and they investigated; ka phreid (a very small bird) said "all this has happened because a tiger comes every night to (the foot of) the tree and licks the part of the tree which has been cut." Thereupon the men, having plied their axes and knives the whole day in cutting the tree (instead of carrying them away as usual), tied them to the incisions, with their edges pointing outwards. So when the tiger went as usual at night to lick the incisions, the sharp blades of the axes and knives cut his tongue. Thenceforth the tiger ceased to go to the tree; and as the tiger ceased to lick the incisions, the mark was not obliterated as before. So their work went on progressing every day until ka Dingiei fell. Thus the world received light, and cultivation throve, and there was nothing more to stand in the way of the light of the sun and the moon. It was for that reason that the name of "U Lum Dingiei" was given to the hill. Nobody knows what became of the tree, for since the time it fell its species has died out and there is no seed of it (to be found) anywhere on the earth from which it can be grown.

U Lum Dingiei.

U lum Dingiei u long u wei u lúm uba jrong shibún ha ri Khasi. U syrím ha ka jing jrong bad jingkhráw ia u lúm Shillong, bad u long marpyrshah jong u shaphang Shatei. Halor une u lúm don bún ki shnong hapoh u Siem Shillong. Mynhyndái halor une u lúm don kawei ka dieng kaba khráw shibúin eh haduh ba ka la kah dum ia ka pyrthei baroli kawei, ka kyrteng kata ka dieng ki khot ka Dingiei. Ki khún Khasi ki la ia kut jingmut ba lada yn ioh pyndüh noh ia kane ka dieng ka'n bha ka'n shái ka pyrthei, namar katba ka dang ieng, ka pyrthei ka dum bad ka'm lah ban seisoh. Kumta ki la ia ieng da kawei ka jingmut ba'n ia khet noh ia ka. Te ynda ki la pom ia ka mynsngí, ki leit pat mynstep ki shem ba la dam noh ka díen pom. Kumta ki pom biang sa ha kawei ka sngi, ynda lashái mynstep ka dam-pa-dam biang. Shu kumta barabor ka long. Hangta ki la lyngngoh, hato balei ka long kumne. Ki ia kylli ki ia tohkit; ong ka phreid (ka sim kaba rit shibun) "kane ka jinglong ha dam kumne haba phi la pom ka long namar u khla mynmiet mynmiet u wan jliah ia ka díen ba phi la pom." Te kumta ki khún bynriew ynda ki la lah pom mynsngi baroh shi sngi, mynmiet ki teh pyn-ang da ki wait ki sdí ka kata ka jaka ba ki la lah pom . Kumta u khla haba u wan mynmiet u jliah phot u thyllied haba kyndúh ha kita ki syrti wait syrti sdí. Kumtah naduh kata ka por um wan shúh; bad ynda um ioh shuh ban jliah kata ka dien pom u khun bynriew, ruh kam dam shuh. Shu nangdep ka jingtrei man ka sngi hadúh ba la kyllon ka Díngiei. Kumta sa shái phèr ka pyrthei bad sa manbha ka thung ka tep ka rep ka sei ynda ymdon ba shár shuh ia ka sngi ia u buái. Namarkata ki sa ioh ban khot kyrteng ia une a lúm "u Lúm Díngiei." Ia ka jinglong kane ka Díngiei ym don ba tip ei-ei nadúh kata ka pór hadúh mynta, namar nadúh ba la kyllon ka iapdúh [32] bad ym don symbái ba kan pynmih haei-haei ha ka pyrthei hadúh kane ka sngi.

Concerning the Origin of the Siems of Shillong.

The Siem of Shillong is a very great and powerful chief in the Khasi Hills. He is generally known throughout the Khasi Hills as the "god king". By the term "god king" is meant that God has been pleased to give over to him the largest portion of the Khasi country, i.e. the kingdom of Shillong, to rule. If you seek for the origin of these "god kings," you will find there is great uncertainty about it. At any rate there is a tradition amongst the Khasis to the following effect. In olden days a rumour got abroad that there was a woman in a cave called Marai, which is situated near the present village of Pomlakrai, at the source of the river Umiew or Umiam. She was a young and very beautiful damsel. Of the reality of the damsel's existence there is no question. Many tried to catch her, but they could not, owing to the narrowness of the cave. There came, however, a certain very clever man who went to entice her by showing her a flower called "u tiew-jalyngkteng." The damsel then came (out) near to snatch the flower, but the man went on holding back his hand until she came out into a more open place, when he seized her. He then brought her to his house and carefully tended her, and afterwards he married her. That damsel was called "*Ka Pah Syntiew*, the flower-lured one," because that man caught her by coaxing and enticing her with a flower. That man, who came from the village of Nongjri in the Bhoi country, was called the Nongjri Kongor. After she had given birth to daughters and sons, she returned, to the same place whence she had been captured, and from that time forth she never came out again, however much her husband and children called and implored her. Her children increased in stature and in wisdom and the people hearing of the wonderful origin of their mother, came from all parts of the country to look at them. The children also were very clever at showing their humility and good manners in the presence of the elders. All the people (in return) loved them and considered them to be the children of the gods and did homage to them. It occurred to the nobles and leaders of the Shillong Raj to appoint them Siems, because (they said) the children had been born of a wonderful woman, who, it seemed very clear, was the daughter of the "god Shillong." Therefore they gladly decided to appoint them Siems in the country of Shillong, (i.e., the present Khyrim and Mylliem States). The children thus became Siems, and they were called "Ki Siem-Blei" (the god kings) of Shilong. [33]

 Shaphang ba long U Siem Shillong.

 U Siem Shillong u long uwei u Siem uba khráw shibún bad uba don bór ruh ha kane ka ri lúm Khasi. Ia une u Siem la jiw bna baroh kawei ka ri ba u long u Siem-Blei. Haba ong Siem-Blei ka mut ba U Blei u la i mon sngewbha ba'n aiti ha u ban synshár ia kawei ka bynta kaba khráw ha ri Khasi. Ha une la ái ba'n synshar ha ri Shillong. Haba wád ia ka jingsdang jong kine ki Siem Blei don shibún ka jingb'ym thikna. La kumno-kumno ka don ka jingiathu-khana kum kane kaba harum ha pydeng ki Khasi hadúh kane ka sngi. Ha kaba nyngkong eh la byna ha don kawei ka bríew ha ka krem Marái, kaba hajan ka shnong Pomlakrái mynta, ha tyllong ka wah Umiew ne Umiám. Kata ka bríew kaba dang met samla kaba bhabríew shibún eh. Ia kaba ka don, ka don hangta barabor, bad bún ki ia pyrshang ban kem ia ka, kim lah namar ka long ka krem kaba khim. Te ynda la mih uwei u bríew uba kham sian u la leit khroh ia ka da kaba pyni da u syntíew uba ki khot u tiéw-ja-lyngkteng. Kumta katno ka bríew ka la wan hajan ba'n kynieh ia uta u syntiew, te uta u bríew u nangring da kaba pynran ia la ka kti khyndiat khyndiat hadúh ka'n da mih ha kaba kham kylluíd ka jaka, u sa kem ia ka. Hangta u la wallam sha la ieng, u ri u sumar bha ia ka, bad hadien-hadien u la shongkurim ia ka. Te la khot kyrteng ia kata ka bríew ka Pah-syntiew, namar ba uta u briew u ioh kem ia ka da kaba khroh ba pah da u syntiew. Uta u bríew u long uba na Nongjri Bhoi, bad ki jiw khot u Kongor Nongjri ia u. Te ynda ka la kha ki khún, kynthei bad shynrang, ka la leit phet sha kajuh ka jaka na kaba u la ioh kem ia ka, bad nadúh kata ka por ka'm wan shuh, la'u tnga ki khún ki leit khot leit pyrta katno-katno ruh. Kita ki khún ki la nangshait nang sian, bad ki bríew ruh, haba ki la bna ia ka jinglong kaba phylla ka jong ku kmie jong ki, ki la wan khnang na kylleng ki jaka ba'n khmih ia kita ki khynnah. Te kita ki khynnah ki la nang shibún ba'n leh rit ba'n leh don akór ha khmat ki tymmen bríew, ki bríew ruh baroh ki a ieit ia ki bad ki tharai ba ki long ki khún Blei. Kumta ki la ia ngúh ki la ia dem ia kita ki khynnah bad hadíen kata ka la jia ha ki dohnúd kiba khráw-batri, ki tymmen-ki-san ha ka ri Shillong ban thung Siem ia ki namar ki khynnah ki long kiba la wan kha da ka briew kaba phylla shibún, kaba imat eh ba ka long ka khún u Blei Shillong. Te kumta ki la ia kut da ka mon snowbha baroh ba'n thung Siem ia ki ha ka hima Shillong, bad kumta la long Siem kita ki khynnah, ki synsháh bad ki khot ruh ia ki Siem-Blei-Siem-Shillong.

U Loh Ryndi and Ka Lim Dohkha.

The Syntengs give the following explanation of the origin of Siems of Suhtnga. There was a man from Wár Umwi named U Loh Ryndi. He went one day to fish in the Umwi stream. When he had caught only one fish, he returned home. He roasted the fish and placed it on the *tyngir* (a swinging shelf above the hearth). He forgot that it was there, and did not remember to eat it. The next morning he went out for a walk to the hill. When he returned home in the evening, he found his house had been swept and looked after, and that the rice had been cooked. He was much surprised at this. The next day the same thing happened. When this state of things continued to occur, he made a pretence of going for a walk to the hill and he called his dog. But he concealed himself the whole day outside the village, and when it was time for cooking rice (evening), he returned home. When he saw that smoke was rising from the house, he crept up stealthily in order that he might suddenly enter the house. Finding a woman there, he said, "Who art thou?" She replied, "I am Ka Lih Dohkha. I am the fish whom thou didst catch and forget to eat. She forthwith added, "Thou must not let any one know. I have many relatives. Come, let us go and fetch them to come here." So Ka Loh Ryndi bade his mother take care of the house until his return from his journey. They went together and arrived at the place where he had caught her, and she jumped into the water and he remained on the dry land. After a while she returned, bringing with her her relatives, but how many of them there were is not known. They all went to the house of U Loh Ryndi. When Ka Lih Dohkha began to enter the house, and was about to cross the threshold, she saw a broom which his mother had placed on the threshold. She therefore abruptly turned back with all her relatives to the river. After that U Loh Ryndi saw in a dream that Ka Lih Dohkha had gone by the river Umwai

Khyrwi to a village called Suhtnga. (Since that time all the fish have left the river up to the present day.) He accordingly went to angle for her in that stream, and when he had caught her, he found that she looked after him just the same as before. After that he married Ka Lih Dohkha and she bore him twelve daughters and a son. When the children of U Loh Ryndi and Ka Lih Dohkha grew up, both of them returned to the stream Umwai Khyrwi. It is said that from the fishing rod of U Loh Ryndi, which he left on the bank of the stream, there grew up bamboos, the joints and leaves of which grow upside down to the present day.

U Loh Ryndi bad Ka Lim Dohkha.

Ki Synteng ki batai ia ka jinglong tynrai ki Siem Suhtnga kumne. La don u wei U Wár Umwi, uba kyrteng U Loh Ryndi, uba la leit khwái dohkha na ka Wah Umwi; te ynda la ngat tang kata kawai u la wan noh sba la ieng. Ynda u la syang u la buh noh halor tyngír ha ka ruh. Hangta u la klet bad um kynmáw shuh ban bám ia ka. Kumta ynda la-shái mynstep u la leit kái pat sha lum, te haba u la wan noh la jan miet u la shem ia ka iing jong u ba la sár la sumar bad ka ja ba la ih. Mynkata u la lyngngeh shibán ba ka long kumne. Te kum la-shái ka la long kumjuh. Ynda ka shu dem iailong kumne-pa-kumne la bán sín eh, ynda kumta u la leh ia lade kum u ban sa leit lúm, u da ting ia u ksew. Hinrei u la rih noh baroh shi sngi harud nong, bad ynda la poi ka por shet ja u la wan noh sha iing. Te mynba u la ioh-i ba la tydem ding ha ieng u la syntiat bha biang ba un ioh rung kynsan bluit hapoh. Hynda kumta u la shem ia ka kynthei hangta. U la ong ia ka, "Pha kaei"? Ka la ong ia u, "nga long Ka Lih-dohkha, ma nga, nga long kata ka dohkha ba me la ngat bad me la klet ban bam." Ynda kumta ka la ong ia u "me wat pyntip iano iano ruh, nga don ki kur shibún eh, ngin ia leit sháw ia ki ban wan noh shane." Kumta U Loh Ryndi u la buh ia la ka kmie ban sumar ia ka iing tad ynda un wan na ka jingleit jong u. Ynda ki la ia leit ki la poi ha kata ka jaka ba u la ngat ia ka. Ynda kumta ka la sid ha ka um, u te u nang sah ha ka ryngkew. Te la shibit ka la wan pat sha u bad ka wallam lem bad ka ia ki kur, hinrei ki long katno ngut ym lah banong, bad ki la leit baroh sha ka iing U Loh Ryndi. Te mynba Ka Lih Dohkha ka la sydang rung ha iing, hamar be kan sa jám ia ka shahksew ka la ioh-i ia u synsar ba la buh ka kmie jong u hapoh kata ka shahksew; namarkata ka la kylla dín bak bad ki kur jong ka sha kata ka wah. Hadin kata U Loh Ryndi u la phohsníw, u la ioh-i ha kata ka jingphohsniw ia Ka Lih Dohkha ba ka la leit noh sha ka shnong ba ki khot ka Suhtnga ha ka Umwai-khyrwi (naduh kata la jah noh ki dohkha ha ka wah Umwi haduh mynta). Te u ruh u la leit sha kata ka wah ban khwai ia ka, bad ynda u la ngat u la shem ba ka sumar ia u kumjuh. Ynda nangta u la shongkurim bad Ka Lih Dohkha, bad u la ioh khún khadar ngut ki kynthei uwei u shynrang. Ynda la rangbah kita ki khún u Loh Ryndi bad Ka Lih Dohkha ki la leit noh baroh ar ngut ha kata ka Umwai Khyrwi. Te ki ong ba na u ryngwiang khwai jong U Loh Ryndi, harud um ba u la ieh noh, la long ki shken kiba ka mat ka long khongpong bad ka sla de kumjuh jen haduh mynta.

Kyllang and Symper.

Kyllang is a hill which is near the village of Mawnai in Khadsawphra, and Symper is a hill which is situated in the Siemship of Maharam. The old folks say that there are gods which inhabit these hills, which are called U Kyllang and U Symper. These gods had a quarrel for some reason that we mortals do not know. They fought by throwing mud at one another. After they had fought, once or twice, U Kyllang proved victorious. So U Symper, having been humiliated, sits quietly in his own place to this day, and U Kyllang sits very proudly because be was victorious in the fight. The holes which are like tanks in U Symper's sides remain to this day; it is said that U Kyllang made those holes during the battle.

U Kyllang [34] bad U Symper.

U Kyllang u long u lúm uba hajan ka shnong Mawnái ha Khadsawphra bad U Symper u dei u lúm uba long ha ri Maharam. Ha kine ki lúm ki tymmen ki jiw tharai ba don ki blei kiba shong hangto kiba kyrteng U Kyllang bad U Symper. Kine ki blei baroh ar ngut ki la ia kajia namar kano kano ka dáw kaba ngi u bynríw ngim lah ban tip. Te ki la ialeh baroh ar ngut da kaba ia khawoh ktih. Ynda ki la ialeh shi por ar por jop U Kyllang. Kumta U Symper u shong pynrit ia lade ha la ka jaka jar-jar haduh mynta, bad U Kyllang u shong da kaba sngew khráw sngew sarong shibún ba u la jop ha ka jingialeh. Ki thlíw kiba long kum ki pukri kiba don ha ki krung u lúm Symper ki sah haduh mynta; ki ong ba la pynlong ia kito ki thlíw da U Kyllang ha ka por ialeh.

The Siem creating stone at Mawsmai.

On the outskirts of Mawsmai village, and to the west of it, stands a hill; it is a very beautiful hill. From a distance it looks like the hump of a bull. It has big trees growing on it, as people are afraid to cut them because they believe that the god "Ryngkew" is there, who takes care of and protects the country. This hill has two names, U Mawlong Siem and U Lyngkrem. U Mawlong Siem is the smaller (peak) on the southern side, and U Lyngkrem the taller one, in which there is a cave. The Mawsmai people sacrifice once or twice a year according to the god's demand. The Mawsmai people have, besides U Mawlong Siem, other village gods (called "Ryngkew"). The name of the one is "U Rangjadong," and the name of the other "U Ramsong." Sacrifices are offered to these two also. U Mawlong Siem is a very great and stern god. The other gods dare not engage in battle with him. He has a daughter called "Ka Khmat Kharai" (i.e. the mouth of the abyss). The god of the Umwai people fell in love with this daughter, but he was unable to obtain her in marrage, as U Mawlong Siem did not like him. It is not possible to know the exact reason why the name of U Mawlong Siem was given to him, but at any rate it appears that the name arose from the fact that in olden days before the death of a Siem there used to be heard at "Mawlong Siem" a great noise of beating of drums. The Mawsmai and the Mawmluh people used to hear it, and they attributed it to the god "Mawlong Siem," who beat the drum for his children to dance to. At any rate, when this sound is heard, it never fails to portend the death of a Siem. It appears that this hill was called "Mawlong Siem" for that reason.

U Mawlong Siem ha Mawsmai.

Harúd 'nong Máwsmái don u wei u lúm uba shaphang sepngi na ka shnong. Une u lúm uba i-tynnad shibún. Ban khymih na sha jingngái u long kum u syntai masi kyrtong. U don ki dieng kiba khráw ki bým jiw don ba núd ban thoh ban daiñ namar ba ki ñiew ba u long U Ryngkew u blei uba sumar uba da ia ka muluk ka jaka. Ia une u lúm ki khot ar kyrteng, U Mawlong Siem bad U Lyngkrem, U Máwlong Siem u long uta uba kham lyngkot shaphang shathi, bad U Lyngkrem u long uta uba jerong eh bad uba don ka krem Pubon hapoh. Ia une U Mawlong Siem ki Máwsmái ki jiw ai jingknia da u blang shisin shi snem ne shi sin ar snem katba u pan. Ki Mawmluh ruh ki leh kumjuh na la shnong. Nalor une U Mawlong Siem ki Máwsmái ki don shuh ki Ryngkew hajan shgong, uwei U Rangjadong bad uwei pat U Ramsong. Ia kine ki kñia. Une U Mawlong Siem u long u blei uba khráw shibún bad uba eh. Ki para blei kim núd ban ia leh thyma ia ki. U don kawai ka khún kaba kyrteng "Ka Khymat Kharái," u blei ki Umwái u i-bha ia ka, hinrei um lah poi namar U Máwlong Siem úm sngewbha ia u. Ban tip thikna ia ka dáw balei ba khot kyrteng Máwlong Siem ia u ym lah ban tip; hinrei la kumno kumno i-mat ba kane ka kyrteng ka la mih namar ba mynhyndái haba yn sa iap Siem la jiw ioh sngew hangta ha U Máwlong Siem ba don ka jingsawa tem ksing kaba khraw shibun. Ki Mawsmai bad ki Mawmluh ki jiw ioh sngew, bad ki jiw tharai ba u blei Mawlong Siem u tem ksing ban pynshád khún. Lei lei haba la ioh sngew kum kata ka jingsawa ym jiw pep ia ka ban iap Siem, bad i-mat ba na kata ka daw la khot kyrteng ia une u lum Máwlong Siem.

Why There Are Spots On The Moon.

In olden days there was a woman who had four children, three girls and one boy. Their names were these, Ka Sngi (sun), Ka Um (water), Ka Ding (fire), and U Bynai (moon). These four children belonged to rich gentle folk. The Moon was a wicked young man, for he began to make love to his elder sister, Ka Sngi. In the beginning the Moon was as bright as the Sun. When the Sun became aware of his bad intentions, she was very angry. She took some ashes in her hand and said to him, "do you harbour such an incestuous and wicked intention against me, your elder sister, who has taken care of you and held you in her arms, and carried you on her back like a mother does; now I will cover your brow with ashes, you wicked and shameless one; begone from the house." Then the Moon felt very much ashamed, and from that time he gave out a white light because the Sun had covered him with ashes. What we see like a cloud (on the Moon) when it is full, are the ashes which adhered from the time the Sun covered him with them. The three daughters, however, remained at home to take care of their mother, until she grow old and died.

Kumno ba la Thoh dak U Bynai.

La don kawei ka briew mynhyndái kaba don saw ngut ki khún, lai ngut ki kynthei bad u wei u shynrang. Ki kyrteng jong ki ki long kine, Ka Sngi, Ka Um, Ka Ding, bad U Bynái. Kine baroh saw ngut ki la long ki khún ríwbba khún don burom shisha shisha. Te une U Bynái u la long u bríew uba riwnar, u sydang ban i-bha ia la ka hynmen, Ka Sngi. Une U Bynái ruh ha kaba mynnyngkong u long uba phyrnái hi ryngkat Ka Sngi. Te ynda ka Sngi ka la sngewthuh ia ka jingmut riwnar jong u ka la sngew bittar shibún bad ka la shim u dypei ha la ka kti bad ka la ong ia u, "da kum kane ka kam kaba sang kaba sníw phi thew ia nga ka hynmen kaba la thum la bah, la sumar sukher kum ka kymie ryngkat; mynta ngan tep da u dypei ia ka shyllang-mat jong me u riwnar u khlem raiñ,—khie phet noh na iing." Te U Bynái u la sngew rem sngew raiñ shibún eh. Bad naduh kata ka por U Bynái u kylla da ka jinghái kaba líh namar ba tep Ka Sngi da u dypei. Bad uta uba ngi ioh-i ha U Bynái kum u l'oh ha ka por ba u pyllun u long u dypei keiñ uba sah naduh ba tep Ka Sngi. Te ki sah lai ngut ki para kynthei kiba sumar ia la ka kmie ba la sydot la tymmen haduh ba kan da iap.

"Sohpet Byneng" Hill.

In olden days, when the earth was very young, they say that heaven and earth were very near to one another, because the navel-string of heaven drew the earth very close to it. This navel-string of heaven, resembling flesh, linked a hill near Sumer with heaven. At that time all the subjects of the Siem of Mylliem throughout his kingdom came to one decision, i.e. to sever the navel-string from that hill. After they had cut it, the navel-string became short; and, as soon as it shortened, heaven then ascended high. It was since that time that heaven became so high, and it is for that reason that they call that hill which is near Sumer "U Sohpet Byneng."

U Lúm Sohpet Byneng.

Mynhyndái mynba dang lung ka pyrthei ki ong ba ka byneng bad ka khyndew ki ia jan sbibún namar ba U Sohpet Byneng u ring ia ka byneng ba'n wan kham hajan. Une U Sohpet Byneng u long kum ka doh kaba snoh na u wei u lum uba hajan Sumer bad ka snoh ruh ia ka byneng. Te mynkata ka pór ki khún ki raiot U Siem Mylliem baroh kawei ka hima ki ia ryntieh kawei ka buit ban ia ieng ba'n khet noh ia uta U Sohpet Byneng na uta u lum. Te ynda ki la ialeh ba'n khet ia u u la dykut, bad tang u shu dykut ka byneng ka la kiw theng sha jerong. Kumta ka shu jngái kumne ka byneng nadúh kata ka pór ba dykut U Sohpet Byneng nalór uta u lúm. Kane ruh ka long ka dáw namar balei ba la khot ia uta u lúm uba don hajan Sumer "U Lúm Sohpet Byneng."

How the Dog came to live with Man.

In olden days, when the world was young, all the beasts lived happily together, and they bought and sold together, and they jointly built markets. The largest market where all the beasts used to take their articles for sale was "Luri-Lura," in the Bhoi country. To that market the dog came to sell rotten peas. No animal would buy that stinking stuff. Whenever any beast passed by his stall, he used to say "Please buy this stuff." When they looked at it and smelt it, it gave out a bad odour. When many animals had collected together near the stall of the dog, they took offence at him, and they said to him, "Why have you come to sell this evil smelling, dirty stuff?" They then kicked his ware and trampled it under foot. The dog then complained to the principal beasts and also to the tiger, who was at that time the priest of the market. But they condemned him, saying, "You will be fined for coming to sell such dirty stuff in the market." So they acted despitefully towards him by kicking and trampling upon his wares. When the dog perceived that there was no one to give ear to his complaint, he went to man, who said, "Come and live with me, and I will arise with you to seek revenge on all the animals who have wronged you." The dog agreed and went to live with man from that time. Then man began to hunt with the assistance of the dog. The dog knows well also how to follow the tracks of the animals, because he can scent in their footprints the smell of the rotten pea stuff which they trod under foot at Luri-Lura market.

Kumno u Kseq u la wan Shong bad u Briew.

Mynhyndái, mynba dang lung ka pyrthei shibit, ki mrád ki mreng lái phew jaid ki ia suk ki ia lok para mrád, bad ki ju ia-die-ia-thied, ia tháw iew tháw hat ryngkat. Te ka iew kaba khráw tam eh kaba poi baroh ki lái phew mrád ba'n wallam la ki jingkhaii pateng ka long ka Iew "Luri-Lura" ba ri Bhoi. Ha kata ka iew u ksew u wan die 'tung rymbái, te ym man don ba pán thied satia ia kata ka ktung. La iaid kawei ka mrád u tyrwa, "To thied kane ka ktung." Haba ka la khmih bad ka la íw, kaba iwtung pynban, la iaid kawei pat ruh shu shem ba ka long kumta, kaba sniew bad kaba íwtung ka jingdie jong u ksew. Te haba ki la ialang kham bún ha ka basa jong u ki la phoi ia u ksew, ki ong "balei me wan die ia ka ktung kaba íw jakhlia?" bad ki la kynjat ia ka jingdie jong u bad ki la iúh hapoh slajat. Te u ksew u la mudui ha ki para mrád kiba kham rangbah bad ha u khla uba long lyngdoh, ha kata ka iew. Pynban ki la pynrem ia u, bad ki la ong, "yn dain kuna ia me uba wan die ia ka jakhlia ha ka iew ka hat." Kumta ki la leh bein ia u da kaba iuh kaba kynjat ia kata ka ktung. Te u ksew haba u ioh-i b'ym don ba sngap ia ka jingmudui jong u, u la wan sha u bynriew, bad u bynriew u la ong "To wan shong noh bad nga nga'n ieng ryngkat bad me ba'n wád kyput ia ki lái phew mrád kiba leh bein ia me." Te kumta u ksew u la kohnguh bad u la wan shong bad u bynriew nadúh kata ka pór. Nangta sa long ka beh mrád u bynriew ryngkat bad ka jingiarap u ksew. U ksew ruh u tip ba'n búd dien ia ki mrád, namar u sngewthúh ba ka dien ka khnap ka mrád baroh ka don ka jingíw-khong ba la sah ka jingíw nadúh kata ka pór ba ki iúh ia ka ktung rymbái jong u ha ka Iew Luri-Lura.

The "Thlen."

In olden days there was a market in the village of Langhiang Kongkhen, and there was a bridge sacred to the gods there. All the children of men used to frequent that heavenly market. They used to pass by Rangjirteh, where there is a cave which was tenanted by a gigantic "thlen." When they went to that market, as soon as they arrived at Rangjirteh they were swallowed up by the "thlen." The "thlen" did this in obedience to an order he had received. If ten people went there, five of them were swallowed up; half of them he devoured, and half of them he let go. But any one who went alone was not touched by the "thlen," for it was necessary for him to leave untouched half (of the number of those who went). When many people had been devoured, and when they saw that all the children of men would be destroyed, whether they were Khasis or plains people, they held a great durbar at Sunnai market to which both Khasis and plains people went. They considered together as to how to devise a means by which they could slay the "thlen" which had devoured the children of men. After they had deliberated for a long time they decided to adopt the following plan. In the grove that is close to Laitryngew, which is called "the grove of U Suidnoh," there was a man called "U Suidnoh." They counselled together to get "U Suidnoh" to make friends with the "thlen." This Suidnoh was a courageous man who did not care for any one. He used always to walk alone; so when he went to the "thlen," the latter did not eat him because there was no one else with him who could be let go. The people advised U Suidnoh that he should go and give the "thlen" flesh every day, either goats, or pigs, or cattle. After he had done this for a long time, the "thlen" became tame, and was great friends with U Suidnoh. When both of them became very intimate thus, the children of men advised U Suidnoh to build a smelting house. So he built a smelting house and made the iron red-hot, and, holding it with a pair of tongs, took it to the "thlen." When he arrived he said to the "thlen," "Open your mouth, open your mouth, brother-in-law, here is some flesh." As soon as he opened his mouth, he threw the red-hot iron down his throat. The monster then struggled and wriggled so violently in its death agony that the earth shook as if there had been an earthquake. When U Suidnoh saw the death struggle of the "thlen," he fainted (from excitement). The quaking of the earth startled all the children of men, and they thought that something had happened. When U Suidnoh did not return home his family went to look for him, for they knew that he had gone to feed the "thlen" with red-hot iron. They found him there lying in a faint. When they had revived him, they asked him why he had fainted thus. He replied, "When I was feeding the 'thlen' with red-hot iron, he struggled and wriggled and I fainted. Come, let us go and see what has become of him." They then went and found that the "thlen" was dead. They then published abroad all over the world that the "thlen" was dead, and they convened a durbar to decide about eating him. In the durbar they came to the following understanding, i.e. that the Khasis should eat half, and the plains people half (of the body). After they had come to this decision in the durbar, they then went to take him out of the cave, and they lifted him on to a rock. They there cut into pieces the "thlen's" carcase. The plains people from the East, being more numerous, ate up their share entirely, not leaving anything—for this reason there are no "thlens" in the plains; but the Khasis from the West, being fewer in numbers, could not eat up the whole of their share; they left a little of it. Thus, because they did not eat it all, the "thlen" has remained with them. U Suidnoh gained for himself fame and honour, which he enjoys up to the present day. The Khasis, therefore, when they find that the hair or the clothes of any one belonging to them have been cut, refer the matter to U Suidnoh, and they sacrifice to him. The Syntengs also have their "thlen," but he differs much from the Khasi "thlen." The Syntengs also believe he is a kind of serpent, and there are some families and clans who keep him and worship him like a god. They sacrifice to him a pig only; they do not propitiate him with human blood as the Khasis do. [35]

Shaphang U Thlen.

Mynhyndái la don ka iew ha Langhiang Kongkhen, ba don ka jingkieng blei hangta. Baroh ki khún bynriw ki ia wan ha kane ka iew blei. Ki iáid lynti na Rangjirteh, kaba don ka krem u thlen uba khráw eh. Te katba ki leit sha kane ka iew blei tang shu poi ha Rangjirteh la ngúid noh u thlen. U ieh kum ha kane ka rukom kat kum ka hukum ba u la ioh. Lada iáid shiphaw ngut, san ngut la ngúid noh; shiteng shiteng la bám, shiteng shiteng la pyllait noh. Hinrei ia uba iáid wei briew ym bit ba'n bám. Ka dei ba'n da pyllait shiteng shiteng. Te ynda la lut than eh ki briew, ki i ruh kum ba'n sa dúh ki khún bynriew baroh, bad Khasi bad Dykhar, hangta ki la sydang ba'n lum ka dorbar bah ha ka iew Sunnai, u Dykhar u hangta u Khasi ruh hangta. Ki ia pyrkhat ba'n ioh ka buit ka lád da kumno ki lah ba'n pyniap noh ia u thlen uba la bam dúh ia u khún bynriew. Ynda ki la dorbar kham slem ki la ioh ka lád kaba biang kumne. Ha kata ka khláw hajan Laitryngew kaba ki khot 'làw Suidnoh la don uwei uba kyrteng "U Suidnoh" ki la ong ba'n pynialok ia U Suidnoh bad U Thlen. Une U Suidnoh u long uba riwnar u b'ym jiw iáid ryngkat briew. Wei briw, wei briw, u iáid. Kumte haba u leit sha U Thlen ruh u'm bám satia namar ba U Thlen hi ruh u'm jiw bám ha b'ym don jingpyllait. Ki briew ki la sylla ia U Suidnoh ba un leit ai doh ia u hala ka sngi; u ai da ki blang, ki sniang, ki massi. Haba la leh kumta kham slem U Thlen u la júh, u la ia lok bha bad "U Suidnoh." Te ynda kine ki la ia juh bha, u khún bynriew u la bythah pat ia U Suidnoh ba u'n shna shlem, bad u la shna shlem ba'n pyrsut nar-wah. Ynda u la pyrsut ia u nar hadúh ba u la sáw bha hâin u la khap na ka lawar ding bak bad katba u dang sáw dang khluid bha u la leit lam ha U Thlen. Tang shu poi u ong "Ko kynum ang, ang, kane ka doh," bad iang u shu ang u la thep jluk ha u pydot. Hangta U Thlen u la khih u la lympat u la kyrhtat u la ksaid iap badúh ba la win ka khyndew kumba khih u jumái. Hangta U Suidnoh, haba u ioh-i ia ka jingksáid iap U Thlen, u ruh u la iaplér b'ym tip briew shúh. Te kata ka jingwin ka khyndew ka la pynkyndit ia u khún bynriew baroh ha ka pyrthei, bad ki la pyrkhat ba la jia ei ei. U Suidnoh u'm poi shúh sha la iing, te kiba ha iing jong u ki la leit wád, namar ki la tip ba u la leit ai jingbám ha U Thlen da u nar sáw: hangta ki la shem ba u la iap lér, bad ki la pynkyndit ia u bad ki la kylli ia u "Balei me iaplér kumne?" U ong, "Hamar ba nga dang ai jingbam ia U Thlen da u nar sáw ba la pyrsut bha, u la kyrthat, khih lympat U Thlen bad nga la iap lér. "Ia, ia leit khymih kumno u la long." Ynda ki la ia leit khymih ki shem ba la iap U Thlen. Hangta la pynbyna hàw ia ka pyrthei baroh be la lah iap U Thlen, bad u lùm ka dorbar ba'n bám noh ia u. Hangta ha ka dorbar ki la ia kut kumne: ki Khasi ki'n bám shiteng bad ki Dykhar ki'n bam shiteng. Ynda la ia kut kumta ha ka dorbar ki la ieng ba'n leit sei noh na ka krem, bad ki la rah halor u máwsiang. Hangta ki la ia shain ia dain ia ka doh U Thlen lyngkhot lyngkhot. Ki Dykhar na mih-ngi, namar ba ki kham bún briew ki la bám lut ia la ka bynta, kim shym pynaah ei ei, kumta ym don Thlen shúh ha pyddeng ki Dylhar. Hinrei ki Khasi, na sepngi namar ba ki kham duna briew ki'm shym lah ba'n bam lut ia la ka bynta, ki la pynsah katto katne. Kumta namar ba ki'm shym bám lut, U Thlen u dang sah. U Suidnoh u la ioh la ka nám la ka burom hadúh mynta. Namar haba ki Khasi ki shem ba la ot shniuh ne ot jáin ki pynkit halor U Suidnoh bad ki ái jingknia ia u. Ki Synteng ruh ki don la U Thlen hinrei u phér shibun na U Thlen Khasi. Ki Synteng ruh ki ngeit ba u long u kynja bysein, bad don ki iing bad ki jaid kiba jiw ri ia u bad ki mane kum u blei. Ki ai jingknia ia u tang da u sniang, hinrei kim ái da ka snám briew kumba ái ki Khasi kiba ri ia u.

About the River "Rupatylli" at Duwara.

In ancient times, when the world was still young, there were two river goddesses who lived on the Shillong Peak; perhaps really they were the daughters of the god of the Peak. These two wagered one against the other that each would be the first to arrive in the Sylhet plains by cutting a channel for herself. They agreed to start from Shillong Peak. One followed the channel of the Umngot, and the other that of Umiew or Umiam. The one that followed the channel of Umngot chose a soft and easy bed, and although the way was a longer one, she did not find it a trouble to go by a circuitous route. When she reached the Sylhet plains she was called "Shengurkhat," and she then flowed past Chhatak, and so reached Duwara. She looked round to see where Umiam was, but she could not descry her anywhere. So out of playfulness she flowed slowly, and she formed a channel like a necklace (*rupatylli*) by way of waiting to see where Umiam was. Umiew was very proud, she felt strong enough to make the channel she chose, and although it was through the midst of hills and rocks, she cared not a bit; so she wasted time by digging through the hills and boulders. When she reached Shella, she thought she could easily beat Umngot, for the course she had taken was a very straight one. When she got a little below Shella she saw Umngot shouting for joy with foaming waves in the Rupatylli channel at Duwara. She was covered with shame, and she slackened her speed and split herself up into 5 branches, namely, ka Umtong, ka Torasa, ka Pasbiria ka Kumarjani, and ka Duwara. Umiam did this so as to hide her shame from Umngot. This is how the river Rupatylli was formed at Duwara, to be a token that Umngot had been victorious in her contest with Umiew. [36]

Shaphang ka wah. Rupatylli ha Duwara.

Hyndái mynba dang lung ka pyrthei la don ár ngut ki blei um kiba shong ha lúm Shillong. Lehse shisha ki long ki khún u blei Shillong. Kine ki la ia kop ba'n ia mareh ba'n ia pynpoi kloi sha ri madan Shilot da kaba ia pom mar kawei ka wah. Kumta ki la ia kut bad ki la ia mih na Shillong kawei ka Umngot bad kawei ka Umiew ne Umiám. Kata ka Umngot ka búd ia ka lynti na ba, jem ba jem, la ka long kham jingngái ruh kam sngew salia ba'n iáid kyllain. Kumta ka la poi ha Shilot ba'n khot ka wah Shengurkhat bad ka iaid hadúh Shattok, bad ka poi ha Duwara. Ka khymih ia ka Umiam haei-haei-ruh, te ym ioh-i. Kumta ka la leh suki kái, ka tháw ka rupa tylli hangto ba'n long kumba sangeh ba'n ioh-i ia ka Umiám. Ka Umiew ka long kaba kham sarong, ka sngew khlain ba'n iaid na ka lynti kaba bit la ka long da ki lúm ne ki máw, ka'm suidniew, kumta ka la pynlut por ha kaba tih ia ki lúm bad ki máw. Ynda ka la poi ha Shella ka la shu mut ba'n jop ia ka Umngot namar ka lynti jong ka ka long kaba beit eh, te ynda ka la poi harum Shella khyndiat ka la ioh-i ia ka Umngot ba ka la risa da ka jingkhie dew ha ka wah Rupatylli ha Duwara. Kumta ka la sngew ráin suin bad ka la leh suki noh da kaba pynpait tynat ia lade san tylli, kawei ka Umtang; ár ka Umtarasa; lái ka Pasbiria; sáw ka wah Kumarjani; san ka wah Duwara. Kumne ka la leh khnang ba'n búh riah ia la ka jingkhein burom ha khymat ka Umngot. Kumta sa long ka wah Rupatylli ha Duwara namar ka long ka dak ka jingjop ka Umngot ia ka Umiew.

The Kupli (Kopili).

The Kopili river rises in the "Black Mountains," [37] and flows northwards into the Brahmaputra. It is the boundary between the country of the Syntengs and that of the Hadems. [38] Any traveller who wishes to cross this river must leave behind him the rice which he has taken for his journey, and any other food that he may have taken with him. If he does not do so, even if he crosses the river at an unforbidden point, he is liable to offer a sacrifice to the Kopili goddess. The people offer to her three fowls and three goats outside the village, i.e. one to the goddess herself, and the other two to her sons, U Shyngkram and U Jali; and five fowls, that they may all three feast together; this is the case of one transgression only. But in the case of a man who has committed more than one, it is not possible to say how many goats and fowls must be sacrificed, because the river often demands offerings on account of a man's parents or relatives having crossed the river at some time or other.

From the time of the old Siem to that of U Ram Singh Siem, they used to sacrifice to this great goddess two persons during the months of November and December at the time of offering: a sacrifice at Jaintiapur. After a ceremony performed by the Brahmins at Jaintiapur, the victims are led to the Mawshai (Shangpung) market, where they are allowed to take and eat anything they like. After that they conduct them to Sumer; but some say that the stone on which the victims are beheaded is situated below the village of Ka Lew Kai, near a stream which falls into the Kopili, and where there is a *mawkynthei* (flat table-stone) close to that sacred river.

They place the victims on that stone, where the executioner beheads them with a terrible sword. After that they throw the dead bodies their heads into the river. But in the days of U Markuhain (U Raj Indro Singh) "who was our contemporary" they have ceased to do so out of fear of East India Company. The victims are known by the name of "Mugha Khara."

At the time all the people of the territory of the twelve dolois were in great state of terror. It is said that the victim-catchers, when they inquired about the clan (of their intended victims), conducted themselves as if they did not intend to do anything. When the people told their clan, then they caught them. When they heard that the people belonged to clans from which *kongngors* [39] were selected, they did not arrest them. When it was impossible to get hold of any one else, they sacrificed some of the (king's) slaves.

Shaphang Ka Kupli, U Shyngkram bad U Jali, ki Khún jong ka.

Ka Kupli ka long ka wah na ki lúm baiong bad ka túid da artet ha ka wah Brahmaputra. Ka long ka púd ia ka ri Synteng bad ka ri. Hadem ha mihngi. Uno-uno u nongleit jingleit uba kwah ban jám ia kane ka wah Blei-Kupli u don kam ba'n bred noh ia la u kháw-ryneng ha shiliang wah, bad ia ki kynja jingbám baroh phar, te un sa klan ia ka. Lada u'm ka deb kumta, la'u klan na ka jaka ka b'ym sang ruh un háp jingaingúh ha ka. Ki khún-ki-hajár ia ka ha lum lái s'iar, lái blang kawei ia ka, marmar uwei ia U Shyngkram bad U Jali; bad san s'iar ba ki'n ia bám sngewbha baroh lái ngut shi khún shi kymie, kata ka long haba long tang kawei ka lait, hinrei haba ka'n long katba shong ka lait u briew lei-lei, ngam tip ka'n long katno blang katno siar namar haba dei ka'n wan pán ka jingkñia namar ba la klan ia ka na khlieh lane na kyjat da u kyñie u kypa kano-kano ka iing lane kano-kano ka kur. Nadúh ki sngi ki Siem Tymmen haduh ki sngi U Ram Singh Siem ia kane ka blei bah ka kymai u lei ba khraw ki kñia da ki briew ár-ngùt shi snem shi snem hamar u bynái ba ki puja ne ai ngúh ha Jaintiapur. kata, hamar u 'nái wieng bad u 'nái nohprah. Ynda ki la kñia ha Jaintiapur da ki Bramon, ki sa ia lam ia ki sha ka iew Mawshái ne ka iew Shangpung ba ki'n bám shiwa katba mon na kata ka iew. Nangta pat sha Sumer, kiwei pat ki ong ba u máw ba ki khrái khlieh ia ki Muga Khara u don harum ka shnong Iewksi hajan kawei ka wah kaba túid sha ka Kupli— sha ka jaka ba don ka máw kynthei harúd kata ka wah blei Kumta ki sa kyntiw halor kata ka maw kynthei ia ki; nangta pat wan sa u nongkhrai khlieh bad ka wait ba i-shyrkhei, u khrai ia ki hangta. Hadin kata ki sa shat ia ki met-iap sha um bad ia ki khlieh jong ki ruh de. Hinrei ha ki sngi U Markuháin ne U Raj-Indro Singh uba ha Khyjong ngi mynta ym long shúh kumta namar ba u tieng ia ka Kompani. Ia kine ki briew ba ki kñia ki khot kyrteng ia ki ki Muga Khara.

Mynkata ki bynriew shi khadár doloi sngew tieng, ki ong ba ki nongkem ki da kylli shiwa ia ka jaid, ki da leh ia lade kum ki bym mut ba'n leh ei-ei-ruh, te ynda kita ki briw ia kibe ki mut ba'n kem ki la ia thuh ia la ka jaid ki sa kem ia ki. Haba ki sngew ba ki long na ka jaid kaba jiw long kongngór ki'm jiw kem. Te haba ym ioh eh ki kñia da ki mráw Siem.

The Village of Mawpun-ka-Rytiang (Mawpunkyrtiang).

There was in olden days a woman called Ka Rytiang of the Siem clan. Whilst she was still a spinster, she used to go to catch fish in a stream over which there is to the present day a bridge made of a single stone, called Mawpun ka Rytiang. Whilst she was catching fish in the midst of the stream a fit of drowsiness overtook her. At that very moment there approached her a very handsome young man, who thus addressed her; "Take this drumful of money; do not marry, and thou shalt nevertheless bear children. Thou must throw a bridge built of a single stone across this stream, thou must build thy house entirely of stone, the beams must be all of stone. Thou must spend all the money I have given thee, and if it does not suffice for thy expenditure, I shall bring more. Thou wilt remember all that I say?" She replied "yes." As soon as he had finished speaking to her, she awoke from her fit of drowsiness, and found herself holding a drumful of money. On her way home she pondered over what he had said to her, and her heart was full of joy that she had met a god who had given her so much money, and who had spoken such words to her. She then constructed a bridge over that stream, with a single stone, which remains till this day. [40] When she was about to build her house, it happened that she got married notwithstanding; she gave birth to a blind child, and died shortly afterwards. So the people called the village "Mawpun-ka-Rytiang," or, when abbreviated, "Mawpunkyrtiang."

Ka Shnong Mawpun-ka-Rytiang (Mawpunkyrtiang).

Te la don mynhyndái kawei ka briew kaba kyrteng ka Rytiang, ka jaid Siem. Mynba ka dangsamla ka leit tong shér na kata ka wah kaba don u Máwpún uba ki khot hadúh mynta u Máwpún ka-Rytiang. Hamar ba ka dang tong shér ha pyddeng um ka lamshoh sam thiah hangta. Hamarkata ka por la mih u wei u briew uba bhabriew shibun eh, bad u ong ha ka, "Heh kane ka tyngka shi sing nalai; te pha wat shongkurim shuh ho; koit, ki khun pha'n ioh hi, bad pha'n pún uwei u máwpún na Shilliang sha shilliang kane ka wah, bad thaw iing ba phán shong da ki máw suda ki rijid ki rishot, kiei kiei baroh thaw da ki maw. Pha'n pynlut kane ka tyngka baroh, bad lada ym dap ruh ngán sa wallam pat. Phán kynmáw ho ia kaba nga la ong baroh." Ka ong "haoid." Te kumne-kumne, tang shu la dep kine ki ktin baroh ba u kren, ka la kyndit na kata ka jingshoh samthiah, bad ka tyngka ka don ha ka kti jong ka shi'sing nalai. Te ynda ka la wan sha la iing, artat artat ka lynti ka la puson ha la ka mynsim da kaba kymen ba ka la iashem ia u blei uba la ai katne ki tyngka bad uba la kren kum kine ki ktin. Te kumta ka la ring u máwpún uba don badúh mynta. Bad hamar ba ka dang sydang ba'n tháw sa ka iing ka lap ba ioh tynga noh pynban; kumta ka kha u khun da uba matlah bad tang shibit ka iap noh. Kumta ki ioh ban khot ka shnong Máwpún-ka-Rytiang, lane haba kren lyngkot Mawpunkyrtiang.

The Siem of Malyniang.

The Siem of Malyniang was one of those kings who, people said, was one of the "god-kings." He lived in the village of Madur, which is now in the Maskut doloiship. There arose from the royal family of Malyniang a king whose name was Kyllong Raja. His manner was very peculiar, but he was at the same time both stern and courageous. He made up his mind to conquer the whole of the Synteng country as well as the territory of the Siem of Shillong, in order to extend his own kingdom of Madur. This Kyllong did not require many followers when he went to war because he was a very strong man and a man whom nobody could kill, for, if he was killed he came to life again immediately. The Synteng king once chopped him up into pieces and threw his hands and feet far away, and thought he would not come to life again. Nevertheless, next morning he came to life just the same, and he walked along all the paths and by-ways to intercept his enemies. The Synteng king was in great trouble on his account, and was at a loss for a plan how to overcome him, because, having been killed once or twice, he came to life again.

When the Synteng king had thought well over matter, he hit on a device which he thought a very good one, by which he could ascertain by what manner of means he came to life again after having once been killed. The Synteng king's stratagem was the following. He selected the most beautiful girl in the Synteng country, he put on her ornaments of gold and of silver and royal raiment of great price, and he said to her, "All these will I give thee, and more besides, if thou canst obtain for me the secret of Kyllong Raja, and canst inform me how he brings himself to life again after being killed. Now I will send thee to the market there, and if Kyllong Raja takes a fancy to thee, and if he is willing to take thee to wife, thou wilt go, and thou wilt pretend to love him as far as is in thy power. Afterwards thou wilt inquire regarding all his secrets and wisdom, i.e. how he comes to life again after he has been killed; and after thou hast found out all these things, thou wilt inform me, so that I may overcome him. Then, if thou art successful in thy mission, I will give thee a great reward." He then sent her to the market. Kyllong Raja saw her and fell in love with her, and he took her to wife and kept her at Madur. Then that damsel pretended to love him exceedingly, and she repeatedly asked him his secret, how he came to life again. Then Kyllong Raja, fancying that she really loved him, confessed all to her. He said, "My life depends upon these things. I must bathe every day and must wash my entrails" (hence the appellation of "the king who washes his inside" which they gave him), "after that I take my food, and there is no one on earth who can kill me unless he obtains possession of my entrails. Thus my life hangs only on my entrails."

When, therefore, that damsel who had become his wife had learnt all these things, she sent word to the Synteng king that he should send one of his elders, to whom she might reveal the secret of U Kyllong's existence. When the Synteng king heard this, he sent his elders to her. She then told all those things that U Kyllong had confessed to her. When the Synteng king had heard everything, he gave orders to the people to be on the watch so as to get hold of U Kyllong Raja. They found him one day bathing, with his entrails placed on one side of the bathing-place, so that afterwards he might wash them. Thereupon a man from Ralliang seized the entrails and killed him. He cut the entrails into little pieces and gave them to the dogs. Thenceforth U Kyllong Raja was not able to come to life again. Madur was conquered, and all the members of the royal family of Malyniang were scattered from that time. Seven generations have passed since then. [41]

Shaphang U Siem Malyniang

U Siem Malyniang u la long uwei u Siem ba jiw byna ba u long u kynja Siem blei. Une u la shong ha ka shnong Madur kaba long mynta ha ka ilaka u doloi Maskut. Ha ka jaid Siem Malyniang la mih uwei uba kyrteng U Kyllong Raja. Une u Siem uba phylla shibun ha la ka jinglong, u briew uba eh uba shlur. U la thymu ban job ia ka ri Synteng baroh bad ia ka ri Shillong bán pynkhráw ia la ka hima Madur. Une u Kylong u'm donkam shibun ki nongbud bán leit ia leh ia kano-kano ka thyma, namar u long u briew uba khlain shibun bad u by'm jiw don uba lah ba'n pyniap ia u. La ki pyniap ruh u im pat kumne-kumne. U Siem Synteng u la pom ia u tukra-tukra, u la bred ia ki kyjat ki kti sha jingngai, bad u la tharai ba u'n ym im shuh, pynban tang la mynstep u la im hi kumjuh, u la iaid ia ki lad ki dong ban sywait ia ki nongshun. U Siem Synteng u la shitom shibun ia u bad u la duh buit ruh da kumno yn leh ba'n jop ia u, haba shi sin ar sin la pyniap u shu im pat kumjuh pakumjuh. Te haba u Siem Synteng u la pyrkhat bha u la shem kawei ka buit kaba u tharai ba ka long kaba bha tam bad kaba u lah ban tip da kano ka rukom ne ka jingstad ba u im pat haba la pyniap ia u. Ka buit jong u Siem Synteng ka la long kumne. U la shim kawei ka samla kaba bhábriew tam na ka ri Synteng baroh, u pyndeng ki jingdeng ksiar ki jingdeng rupa, bad u pynkup ki jain Siem kiba kordor eh, bad u ong ha ka "ngan ai ia pha kine baroh, bad ngan ai shuh ruh nalor kine lada pha'n ioh ia ka buit u Kyllong Raja ban iathuh ha nga da kumno u lah ban pynim pat ia lade haba pom ia u. Te mynia nga'n phah ia pha sha ieu shato, lada une u Kyllong Raja u i-bha ia pha, bad u'n shim ia-pha ban long ka tynga jong u, phan leit, bad phan leh ieit ia u katba lah. Hadin sa kylli ia ka buit ka jingstad baroh, da kumno u im pat haba la pom ruh, bad ynda pha la tip ia kita baroh sa pyntip sha nga ba nga'n sa jop ia u. Te lada pha'n leh kumta nga'n ai buskit ia pha shibun ho. Kumta u pbah iew soit ia ka. Te une U Kyllong Raja u la iohih ia ka, bad u la i-bha shisha ia ka, bad u shim iaka ba'n long ka tynga jong u. U buh ia ka ha Madur. Te kata ka samla ka la leh ieit ia u shibun eh bad ka kylli byniah ia ka buit ka jingstad ba u im pat. Hangta une u Kyllong Raja, haba u iohih ba ka leh ieit shibun u phla ia kiei-kiei baroh hak-a. U ong, "Ka jing im jong-nga ka long kumne:— nga dei ban sum ha la ka sngi bad ban sait ia la ki snir (nangta la khot ia u "U Siem sait-snir"). Hadin kata ngan sa bam ja, bad y'm don mano-mano ba lah ban pyniap ia nga lada ki'm ioh ia ki snir. Kumta ka jing-im jong nga ka sydin tang ha ki snir hi." Kumta, ynda kata ka samla, ka tynga jong u, ka la ioh tip ia kata baroh ka phah ktin sha u Siem Synteng ba'n wan uno-uno u rangbah ba ka'n iathuh ia ka jingim bad ka jingiap u Kyllong Raja. Te u Siem Synteng ynda u la sngow ia kata ka ktin shi syndon u la phah ia la ki rangbah sha ka. Te ka la iathuh ia kiei-kiei baroh katba u Kyllong Raja u la phla. Te u Siem Synteng ynda u la tip ia kane baroh u la ai hukum ia ki briew ba ki'n khiar ban ioh ia u Kyllong Raja. Te ha kawei ka sngi ki la lap ia u ba u sum bad u la buh ia ki snir ha kata ka jaka ba u sum ba u mut ban sait ia ki. Hangta uwei u briéw uba na Ralliang u la shim ia ki snir jong u bad u pom ia u; ia kita ki snir u la pyndykut lyngkot lyngkhai bad u la ai ha ki ksew. Naduh kata ka por u Kyllong Raja u'm lah shuh ba'n im pat, bad kumta la jop ia ka Madur, la pynsakyma ia ka jaid Siem Malyniang naduh kata ka por. Te naduh kata hadúh mynta la duh hinniew kyrteng bynriw.

U Manik Raitong and his Flute

In the northern portion of the Khasi Hills which borders on the Bhoi country there lived a man, by name U Manik. The people nicknamed him "U Manik Raitong," because he was an orphan, his parents, his brothers and sisters, and the whole of his clansfolk having died. He was very poor in addition. U Manik Raitong was filled with grief night and day. He used to weep and deeply groan on account of his orphanhood and state of beggary. He did not care about going out for a walk, or playing like his fellow youths. He used to smear himself with ashes and dust. He used to pass his days only in weeping and groaning, because he felt the strain of his misery to such an extent. He made a flute upon which to play a pathetic and mournful tune. By day he used to work as a ploughman, whenever he was called upon to do so. If nobody called him, he used to sit inactive at home, weeping and groaning and smearing his rags with dust and ashes. At night he used to bathe and dress himself well, and, after having eaten his food, he used to take his flute and play on it till morning. This was always his practice. He was a very skilful player. He had twelve principal tunes. There lived in the same village a queen. Her husband, the Siem, used to be absent from home for long intervals in connection with his public duties. One night, when the queen heard the strains of U Raitong's flute, she listened to them with very great pleasure, and she felt so much compassion for him that she arose from her couch at midnight and went to visit him. When she reached his house, she asked him to open the door, so that she might pay him a call. U Raitong said "I can't open the door, as this is not the time to pay visits," and he went on playing his flute and dancing to the music, with tears in his eyes. Then the queen peeped through one of the chinks of the wall and saw him, and she was beside herself, and breaking open the door she entered in. Then U Raitong, having stopped playing, was annoyed that, to add to his misfortunes, this woman had come to trouble him thus. When she tried to beguile him, U Raitong admonished her and sent her away. She departed just before daybreak. U Raitong then took off his fine clothes, and putting on his rags, sprinkled himself with dust and ashes, and went to plough as was his wont. The queen, however, ensnared him by another device, and whilst the king was still away in the plains, she gave birth to a male child. When the Siem returned, he was much surprised to find that she had borne a child during his absence, and however much he asked her to confess, she would not do so. So the king called the elders and young men to judge the case, and when no proof was found concerning this business, the king appointed another day, when all the males (in the State) should appear, each man holding a plantain. On the appointed day, all the males of the State having appeared, the king told them all to sit in a circle and to show their plantains, and said, "We will place this child in the midst, and to whomsoever the child goes, he is his father, and the adulterer. We will beat him to death with clubs according to the law." Accordingly, when all the people sat in a circle, and the child was placed in the midst, he went to no one, and, although the king called and coaxed him much, he nevertheless refused to go. Then the king said, "Remember who is absent." All replied, "There is no one else except U Manik Raitong." The Siem replied, "Call, then, U Raitong." Some of the people said, "It is useless to call that unfortunate, who is like a dog or a cat; leave him alone, oh king." The king replied, "No, go and call him, for every man must come." So they called him, and when he arrived and the child saw him, the child laughed and followed "U Raitong." Then the people shouted that it was U Raitong who had committed adultery with the queen. The king and his ministers then ordered that U Raitong should be put to death outside the village. U Raitong said, "Be pleased to prepare a funeral pyre, and I will burn myself thereon, wicked man that I am." They agreed to his request. U Raitong said to those who were preparing the funeral pyre, "When I arrive near the funeral pyre, set fire to it beforehand, and I will throw myself in, and you stand at a distance." Then U Raitong went and bathed, dressed himself well, and, taking his flute, played on it as he walked backwards to the funeral pyre; and when he arrived close to it, they lighted it as he had told them to do. He walked three times round the pyre, and then planted his flute in the earth and threw himself into the flames. The queen, too, ran quickly and threw herself on the pyre also. After U Raitong and the queen had been burned, a pool of water formed in the foundations of the pyre, and a bamboo sprang up whose leaves grew upside-down. From U Raitong's time it has become the practice to play the flute at funerals as a sign of mourning for the departed.

U Manik Raitong bad ka Sharati jong u.

La don uwei u bríw shaphang shatei ha ka ri Khasi ha khap ri Bhoi uba kyrteng U Manik. Ki bríw ki la sin ia u U Manik Raitong namar ba u long u khun swet uba la iap baroh ki kymi, ki kypa, ki hynmen, ki para bad ki kur ki jaid. U long ruh uba duk shibun. Une U Manik Raitong u dap da ki jingsngowsih synia sngi, u iam ud jilliw ha la ka mynsim namar la ka jinglong khun swet long pukir. Um jiw kwah ban iaid kai leh kai kum ki para samla; u sum da ka dypei da ka khyndew ia lade, u pynleit la ki sngi ki por tang ha ki jingud ki jingiam ba u sngowisynei ia ka pyrthei sngi ba shem shitom haduh katne. Te u la thaw kawei ka sharati ban put ka jingiam bríw bad jingriwai sngowisynei. Mynsngi mynsngi u jiw leit bylla pynlur masi haba la don ba wer, haba ym don u shong khop-khop ha la iing, u iam u ud, u sum dypei sum khyndew halor la ki jain syrdep jot. Mynmiet mynmiet u sum u sleh, u kup bha kup khuid; bad ynda u la lah bam lah dih u shim ka sharati u put haduh ban da shai. Barobor u jiw leh kumta. Ha kaba put ruh u long uba nang shibún, u don khadar jaid ki jingput kiba kongsan tam ha ka jingput jong u. Te la don ka mahadei ha kata ka shnong kaba u tynga jong ka u long u Siem Rangbah ha ka Hima. Une u Siem u leit sha Dykhar ban pyndep bun jaid ki kam Siem jong u, bad u dei ban jah slem na la iing. Kane ka mahadei ha kawei ka miet haba ka la ioh sngow ba'riew ka sharati U Raitong ka la sngowbha shibun eh ban sngap, bad haba ka la sngap ka la sngow ieit sngowisynei ia U Raitong haduh ba ka la khie joit shiteng synia ban leit kai sha U Raitong. Te haba ka la poi tiap ha khymat ka iing jong u ka la phah plie ban wan kai. U Raitong u ong ym lah ban plie namar kam long ka por ba dei ban wan kai. Kumta u put la ka jingput bad la ka jingshad nohlyngngeb pynjem ryndang jaw ummat. Te ke mahadei, haba ka la khymih na kawei ka thliew kaba pei, ka la iohih ia u; hangta lei-lei kam don pyrthei shuh haduh ba ka la kyddiah ia ki jingkhang bad ka la rung shapoh iing. Kumta U Raitong u la wai noh la ka jingput bad u sngowsib, halor ba shem kat kane ka pyrthei sngi, sa kane ruh nang wan leh ih-bein kumne. Haba ka la lam pynsboi ia u, U Raitong u la sneng ia ka bad u la phah nob ia ka, te ka la leit noh haba ka sydang ban shai pher. U Raitong u la law la ki jain bha, u la shim la ki syrdep bad, u dypei ban leh kumta u jiw leh bad u la leit pynlur masi. Hinrei kane ka mahadei ka la riam ia u da kawei pat ka buit. Te katba u Siem u nangsah ha Dykhar ka la nang kha i wei i khun shinrang, bad haba u la wan u la sngow phylla shibun eh ba ka la ioh khun haba um don. La u kylli byniah katno-katno ruh kam phla satia. Kumta U Siem u la lum ia u tymmen u san, u khynraw khyndein, baroh ban bishar, te haba ym shem sabud ei ei shaphang kane ka kam, kumta u buh ha kawei ka sngi ba yn wan u shinrang bríw baroh katha don, kin wallam bad lakait kawei-kawei man u bríw. Ynda la poi kata ka sngi, baroh ki la wan na ka hima, bad U Siem u ong, phin shonq tawiar baroh, pynih la ka kait, ngin buh ia une u khunlung ha pyddeng, jar haba une a khunlung un leit uta dei u kypa bad uba klim, ia uta yn shoh tangon ha bynda iap kum ka ain ka jiw long. Kumta te haba la shong tawiar u paitbah byllin, la bah ia uta u khunlung ha pyddeng. Uta u khunlung um leit hano-hano ruh, la khot la khroh. U Siem katno katno ruh um treh. "To ia ia kynmaw sa man u bym don hangne" ong U Siem. Baroh ki ong, "ym don shuh, sa tang U Raitong." "Khot te ia U Raitong," ong U Siem. Don katto katne na pyddeng uta a paitbah kiba ong. "Ym khot makna ia uba pli, uba kum u ksew, u miaw, yn nai Siem." "Em shu khot wei u kynja shinrang briw dei ban wan." Te la khot is u, bad haba u la poi tiap uta u khunlung u khymih u sam rykhie bad u leit bud ia U Raitong. Kumta risa shar u paitbah baroh ba U Raitong u la klim ia ka mahadei. Te U Siem bad la ki Myntri ki la ai hukum ban leit pyniap noh ia U Raitong sharud nong. Te u ong "phi da sngowbha shu thaw da la ka jingthang ngan thang hi ia lade wei nga u riwnar ruser. Kumta ki la shah ia kata ka jingpan jong u. Te U Raitong u la ong ha kita kiba thaw jingthang. "Ynda nga poi sha jan jingthang sa nang ai ding lypa ngan sa nang thang hi, phi kynriah noh sha jingngai. Kumta U Raitong u wan sum wan sleh, u kup bha sem bha, u shim ka sharati u put, u leit da kaba iaid dadin shaduh jingthang. Te ynda u la poi ha jan ki la buh ding kumta u la ong; ynda poi ha jingthang u iaid tawiar lai sin ia ka, u sih ka sharati ha khyndew, bad u thang ia lade. Ka Mahadei ruh da kaba kyrkieh ka la mareh sha kata ka jingthang bad ka ruh ka la thang lem hangta ia lade. Kumta ynda la ing U Raitong bad kata Ka Mahadei, long da ka um ha kata ka nongrim jingthang, bad mih u shken uba long ka mat sha khongpong. Naduh U Raitong sa long ka sharati haduh mynta ban put iam briw ban pynih la ki jingsngowsih na ka bynta kiba la iap.

CHAPTER VI

Miscellaneous

Teknonomy.

The Khasis, like the Alfoors of Poso in Celebes, seem to be somewhat reluctant to utter the names of their own immediate relations, and of other people's also. Parents are very frequently called the mother of so and so (the child's name being mentioned), or the father of so and so, cf. *Ka kmi ka Weri*, *U kpa u Philip*. The actual names of the parents, after falling into desuetude, are often entirely forgotten. The origin of the practice may be that the Khasis, like the Alfoors, were reluctant to mention their parents by name for fear of attracting the notice of evil spirits. The practice of teknonomy, however, is not confined to the Khasis or the Alfoors of Celebes (see footnote to page 412 of the "Golden Bough"). The custom is also believed to have been prevalent to some extent not long ago in some parts of Ireland.

The advent of the Welsh Missionaries and the partial dissemination of English education has in some cases produced rather peculiar names. I quote some instances:—

U Water Kingdom, Ka Mediterranean Sea, Ka Red Sea; U Shakewell Bones, U Overland, Ka Brindisi, Ka Medina, Ka Mary Jones, U Mission, and Ka India.

Khasi Method of Calculating Time.

The Khasis adopt the lunar month, *u bynai*, twelve of which go to the year *ka snem*. They have no system of reckoning cycles, as is the custom with some of the Shan tribes. The following are the names of the months:—

U kylla-lyngkot, corresponding to January. This month in the Khasi Hills is the coldest in the year. The Khasis turn (*kylla*) the fire brand (*lyngkot*) in order to keep themselves warm in this month, hence its name *kylla-lyngkot*.

U Rymphang, the windy month, corresponding with February.

U Lyber, March. In this month the hills are again clothed with verdure, and the grass sprouts up (*lyber*), hence the name of the month, *u Lyber*.

U Iaiong, April. This name may possibly be a corruption of u *bynai-iong*, i.e. the black moon, the changeable weather month.

U Jymmang, May. This is the month when the plant called by the Khasis *ut'ieu jymmang*, or snake-plant, blooms, hence the name.

U Jyllieu. The deep water month, the word *jyllieu* meaning deep. This corresponds to June.

U náitung. The evil-smelling month; when the vegetation rots owing to excessive moisture. This corresponds with July.

U'náilar. The month when the weather is supposed to become clear, *synlar*, and when the plant called *ja'nailar* blooms. This is August.

U'nái-lur. September. The month for weeding the ground.

U Ri-sáw. The month when the Autumn tints first appear, literally, when the country, *ri*, becomes red, *saw*. This is October.

U'nái wieng. The month when cultivators fry the produce of their fields in *wieng* or earthen pots, corresponding with November.

U Noh-práh. The month when the *práh* or baskets for carrying the crops are put away (*buh noh*). Another interpretation given by Bivar is "the month of the fall of the leaf." December.

The Khasi week has the peculiarity that it almost universally consists of eight days. The reason of the eight-day week is because the markets are usually held every eighth day. The names of the days of the week are not those of planets, but of places where the principal markets are held, or used to be held, in the Khasi and Jaintia Hills. The following are the names of the days of the week and of the principal markets in the district:—

Khasi Hills. Jaintia Hills.

1.	Lynkah (Barpani or Khawang) (Suhtnga).	Kylino.
2.	Nongkrem	Pynaing.
3.	Um-Iong (Maolong the hat at Luban)	Maolong.(Nartiang).
4.	Ranghop (Ieu-bah at Cherra) (Mawtawar in Mylliem) (Unsaw in Nongkhlaw)	Maosiang. (Jowai).
5.	Shillong (Laitlyngkot)	Maoshai. (Shangpung).
6.	Pomtih or Pomtiah (Mawkhar, small market)	Pynkat. (Mynao).
7.	Umnih	Thym-blein.
8.	Yeo-duh (Mawkhar, large market)	Ka-hat. (Jaintiapur).

In the Wár country, markets are usually held every fourth day, e.g. at Nongjri, Mawbang, Tyllap, and Shella. At Theria the market is held every Friday, and at Hat-majai, or Rholagunj, every Tuesday.

The Lynngams.

Although mention has been made incidentally in various parts of this monograph of Lynngam customs, it has been thought necessary to give the Lynngams a separate chapter, as these people differ so very greatly from the Khasis in their manner of life, and in their customs. *Lynngam* is the Khasi name; the Garo name for the Lynngams is *Megam*. There are several *Megam* villages in the north-eastern corner of the Garo Hills district, and there is regular communication kept up between these villages and the Lynngam inhabitants of the Khasi Hills district. The Lynngams must not be confused with the *Háná* or *Námdaniya* Garos who inhabit the low hills to the north of the Khasi Hills district, and are called by the Khasis *Dko*. All Lynngams claim to be Khasis, they dislike being called Garos; but although it is true they speak what may be called a dialect of Khasi, and observe some of the Khasi customs, the Lynngams are more Garo than Khasi. Before proceeding further, it should be stated that the Assamese of Boko call the Lynngams *Núniyá* Garos, all hill people being Garos to the Assamese of that region, without distinction or difference. It is owing to these three different names being used for the same people that there has been so much confusion about Lynngams previously; e.g. at one census they were named *Lynngam*, at another they received the appellation of Garo, and at a third enumeration they were called Khasis. In Section I. the habitat of the Lynngams has been roughly defined. It is impossible to define the Lynngam country exactly, because these people are continually shifting their village sites owing to the exigencies of *jhum* cultivation, which has been described in Section II. Some of the Lynngams preserve a tradition that they originally came from the Kamrup plains. It is interesting that a people, like the Garos in so many respects, should have the same idea as the Garos as to the hills on the south bank of the Brahmaputra not always having been their abode. The Garo legend is that they dwelt for some years in the Goalpara and Kamrup plains after they descended from Thibet, and before they moved to the Garo Hills; and there is unmistakable evidence of their occupation of both districts in the shape of certain Garo villages on both banks of the Brahmaputra for some little distance up the river. If, as I suspect, the Lynngams are an offshoot of the Garos, it is, perhaps, possible that they entered the Khasi Hills much in the same way as the Garos entered the hill district to which they have given their name. The Lynngams are much darker than the Khasis, and possess the Thibeto-Burman type of feature often to a marked degree. It is not extraordinary that they should have adopted some of the Khasi customs; for the Khasis, being the stronger people, would in course of time be bound to influence them in this respect. That the Lynngams observe the matriarchate and erect (some clans) memorial stones is not peculiar, because the Garos, like the Khasis, are also a matriarchal people (to a limited degree), and the custom of erecting memorial stones is not confined to the Khasis, for other hill tribes in Assam observe the practice, e.g. certain Naga tribes and the Mikirs; and the Garos themselves put up carved posts, called *kima*, in honour of the departed. Although there is not much intermarriage between the Khasis and the Lynngams nowadays, perhaps in days gone by there was a mixture of blood, the result being the hybrid race we are now considering. Some of the leading characteristics of the Lynngams will now be detailed. The Lynngams are by complexion swarthy, with features of Mongolian type. The men are of middle height and the women remarkably short, both sexes being not nearly so robust as the Khasis, a result due probably to climatic influences, for the Lynngams live in fever-haunted jungles. The men have very little hair about the face, although a scanty moustache is sometimes seen, the hairs in the centre being carefully plucked out, the result being two tufts on either side. Beards are never seen. The women are ill-favoured, and wear very little clothing. The men wear the sleeveless coat of the Khasi and Mikir pattern, called *phongmarong*, which is made of cotton dyed red, blue, and white. This custom may have been borrowed from the Khasi. They do not grow their own cotton, but obtain it from the plains. They make their own dyes, *changlong* (red) and *hur sai-iong* (black). A cotton cloth, barely enough for purposes of decency, is tied between the legs, the ends being allowed to hang down in front and behind. Sometimes an apron is worn in front. At the present day the men wear knitted woollen caps, generally black or red, of the Nongstoin pattern (a sort of fisherman's cap), but the elderly men and head-men wear turbans. The females wear a cotton cloth about eighteen inches broad round the loins, sometimes striped red and blue, but more often only dark blue. A blue or red cloth is thrown loosely across the shoulders by unmarried girls, but married women only wear the waist-cloth, like the Garos. A cloth is tied round the head by married women, sometimes, Garo fashion. The women wear quantities of blue beads as necklaces, like their Garo sisters. They obtain the beads from the Garo markets at the foot of the hills. Brass ear-rings are worn by both sexes; the women, like the Garos, load their ears to such an extent with brass rings as to distend the lobes greatly. Silver armlets are worn by the head-men only, or by those who possess the means to give a great feast to the villagers. This is the custom of the Garo *nokmas*, or head-men. Both sexes wear bracelets. The men also wear necklaces of beads. The rich wear necklaces of cornelian and another stone which is thought by the Lynngams to be valuable. A necklace of such stones is called *u'pieng blei* (god's necklace). This stone is apparently some rough gem which may be picked up by the Lynngams in the river beds. A rich man amongst them, however, is one who possesses a number of metal gongs, which they call *wiang*. For these they pay very high prices, Rs. 100 being quite a moderate sum for one of them. Being curious to see one of these gongs, I asked a *sirdar*, or head-man, to show me one. He replied that he would do so, but it would take time, as he always buried his gongs in the jungle for fear of thieves. Next morning he brought me a gong of bell metal, with carvings of animals engraved thereon. The gong when struck gave out a rich deep note like that of Burmese or Thibetan gongs. These gongs have a regular currency in this part of the hills, and represent to the Lynngams "Bank of England" notes. It would be interesting to try to ascertain what is their history, for no one in the Lynngam country makes them in these days. Is it possible that the Garos brought them with them when they migrated from Thibet? The gongs are well known in the Garo Hills, and I hear that when a *nokma*, or head-man, there dies his corpse is laid out upon them. They thus possess also an element of sanctity, besides being valuable for what they will fetch to the Garos or Lynngams. We may hope to hear more about them in Captain Playfair's account of the Garos.

The Lynngams do not tattoo. Their weapons are the large-headed Garo spear, the dao, and the shield. They do not usually carry bows and arrows, although there are some who possess them. They are by occupation cultivators. They sow two kinds of hill rice, red and white, on the hill-sides. They have no wet paddy cultivation, and they do not cultivate in terraces like the Nagas. They burn the jungle about February, after cutting down some of the trees and clearing away some of the debris, and then sow the paddy broadcast, without cultivating the ground in any way. They also cultivate millet and Jobs-tears in the same way. With the paddy chillies are sown the first year. The egg plant, arum, ginger, turmeric, and sweet potatoes of several varieties are grown by them in a similar manner. Those that rear the lac insect plant *landoo* tress (Hindi *arhal dal*) in the forest clearings, and rear the insect thereon. Some of these people, however, are prohibited by a custom of their own from cultivating the *landoo*, in which case they plant certain other trees favourable to the growth of the lac insect. The villages are situated near their patches of cultivation in the forest. The villages are constantly shifting, owing to the necessity of burning fresh tracts of forest every two years. The houses are entirely built of bamboo, and, for such temporary structures, are very well built. In front, the houses are raised some 3 or 4 ft. from the ground on platforms, being generally built on the side of a fairly steep hill, one end of the house resting on the ground, and the other on bamboo posts. The back end of the house is sometimes some 8 or 9 ft. from the ground. At the end of the house farthest away from the village path is a platform used for sitting out in the evening, and for spreading chillies and other articles to dry. Some Lynngam houses have only one room in which men, women, and children an all huddled together, the hearth being in the centre, and, underneath the platform, the pigs. Well-to-do people, however, possess a retiring room, where husband and wife sleep. A house I measured at Nongsohbar village was of the following dimensions:—Length, 42 ft; breadth, 16 ft.; height of house from the ground to the eaves, front, 9 ft.; back 18 ft. Houses are built with a portion of the thatch hanging over the eaves in front. No explanation could be given me for this. It is probably a Garo custom. In some Lynngam villages there are houses in the centre of the village where the young unmarried men sleep, where male guests are accommodated, and where the village festivities go on. These are similar to the *dekachang* or bachelors' club-houses of the Mikirs, Garos, and Lalungs, and to the *morang* of the Nagas. This is a custom of the Thibeto-Burman tribes in Assam, and is not a Khasi institution. There are also high platforms, some 12 ft. or 15 ft. in height, in Lynngam villages, where the elders sit of an evening in the hot weather and take the air. Lynngam houses and villages are usually much cleaner than the ordinary Khasi villages, and although the Lynngams keep pigs, they do not seems to be so much en *évidence* as in the Khasi village. There is little or no furniture in a Lynngam house. The Lynngam sleeps on a mat on the floor, and in odd weather covers himself with a quilt, made out of the bark of a tree, which is beaten out and then carefully woven, several layers of flattened bark being used before the right thickness is attained. This quilt is called by the Lynngam "*Ka syllar*" (Garo *simpak*). Food is cooked in earthen pots, but no plates are used, the broad leaves of the *mariang* tree taking their place. The leaves are thrown away after use, a fresh supply being required for each meal.

 The Lynngams brew rice beer, they do no distil spirit; the beer is brewed according to the Khasi method. Games they have none, and there are no jovial archery meetings like those of the Khasis. The Lynngam methods of hunting are setting spring guns and digging pitfalls for game. The people say that now the Government and the Siem of Nongstoin have prohibited both of these methods of destroying game, they no longer employ them. But I came across a pitfall for deer not long ago in the neighbourhood of a village in the Lynngam country. The people declared it to be a very old one; but this I very much doubt, and I fear that these objectionable methods of hunting are still used. The Lynngams fish to a small extent with nets, but their idea of fishing, *par excellence*, is poisoning the streams, an account of which has already been given in this monograph. The Lynngams are omnivorous feeders, they may be said to eat everything except dogs, snakes, the *huluk* monkey, and lizards. They like rice, when they can get it; for sometimes the out-turn of their fields does not last them more than a few months. They then have to fall back on Jobstears and millet. They eat arums largely, and for vegetables they cook wild plantains and the young shoots of bamboos and cane plants. The Lynngams are divided up into exogamous clans in the same manner as the Khasis. The clans are overgrown families. The Lynngams have some stories regarding the founders of these clans, of which the following is a specimen:—"A woman was asleep under a *sohbar* tree in the jungle, a flower from which fell on her, and she conceived and bore a female child who was the ancestress of the Nongsohbar clan." Some of the stories of the origins of other clans do not bear repeating. There do not appear to be any hypergamous groups. As with the Khasis, it is a deadly sin to marry any one belonging to your own *kur*, or clan. Unlike the Khasis, however, a Lynngam can marry two sisters at a time. The Lynngam marriages are arranged by *ksiangs*, or go-betweens much in the same way as Khasi marriages; but the ritual observed is less elaborate, and shows a mixture of Khasi and Garo customs (see section III.). The Lynngams intermarry with the Garos. It appears that sometimes the parents of girls exact bride-money, and marriages by capture have been heard of. Both of these customs are more characteristic of the Bodo tribes of the plains than of the Khasis. There are no special birth customs, as with the Khasis, except that when the umbilical cord falls a fowl is sacrificed, and the child is brought outside the house. Children are named without any special ceremony. The death customs of the Lynngams have been described in Section III. A peculiar characteristic is the keeping of the dead body in the house for days, sometimes even for several months, before it is burnt. The putrefying corpse inside the house seems to cause these people no inconvenience, for whilst it remains there, they eat, carry on their ordinary avocations, and sleep there, regardless of what would be considered by others an intolerable nuisance. The religion of these people consists of a mixture of ancestor-worship and the propitiation of the spirits of fell and fall, which are, most of them, believed to be of evil influence, as is the case with other savage races. As with the people of Nongstoin, the primaeval ancestress, "*ka Iaw bei*," is worshipped for the welfare of the clan, a sow being sacrificed to her, with a gourd of rice-beer, and leaves of the oak, or *dieng-sning* tree. The leaves of the oak are afterwards hung up inside the house, together with the jaw bone of the pig. Sacrifices are offered to a forest demon, *U Bang-jang* (a god who brings illness), by the roadside; also to *Ka Miang Bylli U Majymma*, the god of cultivation, at seed time, on the path to the forest clearing where the seed is sown. Models of paddy stone-houses, baskets and agricultural implements are made, sand being used to indicate the grain. These are placed by the roadside, the skulls of the sacrificial animals and the feathers of fowls being hung up on bamboo about the place where the has been performed. There are no priests or *lyngdohs*, the fathers of the hamlet performing the various ceremonies. The Lynngams possess no head-hunting customs, as far as it has been possible to ascertain. These people are still wild and uncivilized. Although they do not, as a rule, give trouble, from an administrative point of view, a very serious dacoity, accompanied by murder, was committed by certain Lynngams at an Assamese village on the outskirts of the Lynngam country a few years ago. The victims were two Merwari merchants and their servant, as well as another man. These people were brutally murdered by the Lynngams, and robbed of their property. The offenders were, however, successfully traced and arrested by Inspector Raj Mohan Das, and several of them suffered capital punishment, the remainder being transported for life.

CHAPTER VII

Language

Before commencing to describe the more salient features of the Khasi language, its grammar, and syntax, it seems to be of importance to show how intimately connected Khasi is with some of the languages of Further India. In the middle of the last century Logan pointed out affinity between Khasi and these languages, but it has been left to Professor Kuhn to prove this connection to demonstration. The examples of comparative vocabularies which follow are taken from Kuhn's "*Beiträge zur Sprachenkunde Hinterindiens*," Sir George Scott's "Upper Burma Gazetteer," and Sir George Campbell's lists. It will be seen from the collections of words that follow how Khasi possesses many words in common with Mon or Talaing, Khmêr, Suk, Stieng, Bahnar, Annam, Khamen-Boram, Xong, Samre, Khmu, Lemet, Palaung, and Wa. There is some correspondence, although perhaps to a lesser degree, between Khasi and the Ho-Munda languages and those of Malacca and the Nancowry language of the Nicobar Islands.

Let us now examine the table of numerals. The Khasi word for 1 is *wei*, but in the Amwi dialect of Khasi it is *mi*. In Khmu the word is *mui*, also in Suk; in Mon *mwoi* and in Xong *moi*. The word for 2 is identical in Khasi and Lemet, viz., *ar*. The word for 3, viz. *lai*, is identical in Khasi and Wa: also compare Lemet *lohe*. Khasi *saw* and Lakadong *thaw* for 4 are, however, deviating forms. In the case of 5, if we cut out the prefix *m* in the Mon word *m'san*, we have fairly close agreement with the Khasi *san*. In the numeral 6, if we cut out the prefix *hin* of the Khasi (*hin*)*riw*, and the initial *t* of Mon and Suk *t'rou*, *trou*, we have close agreement. In the Khasi words for 7 and 8 the syllable *hin* is but a prefix. This is also probably the case in the Khasi word (*khyn*)*dai* for 9, and the *shi* in the Khasi word *shiphew*, 10, merely means one.

Numerals

Numerals.

	Sue.	Mon or Talaing.	Suk.	Stieng.	Bahnar.	Annam.	Khmen Boran.	Xong.	Samre.
1	mue	mwoi	mui	muoi	moin, ming	mot	mnay	moi	moe
2	bar	ba	bar	bar	bar	hai	bar	pra	pra
3	pei	pi	pe	pei	peng	ba	peh	pe	pe
4	puon	pan	puon	puon	puon	bon	pon	pon	pon
5	sung	m'sun	sung	pram	(po)dam	nam	pram	pram	pram
6	thpat	t'rou	trou	prou	(to)trou	sau	krong	dam	kadon
7	thpol	t'pah	pho	poh	(to)po	bay	grul	kanul	kanul
8	thkol	dc'am	tam	pham	(to)ngam	tam	kati	kati	katai
9	thke	d'ceit	kin	en	(to)xin	chin	kansar	kasa	katea
10	muchit	cah	chit	jemat jet	jit	muoi chuk	rai	rai	rai

	Khan.	Lomei.	Palaung.	Wa.	Khasi.	Dialects of Khasi.		
or Jirang.					Lakadong.	Amwi.	Synteng.	Mymar
1 mui	mus(mos)	le	te	wei	bi	mi	wi	mi
2 bar	ar	e(a)	ra(a)	ar	a	o	ar	ir
3 pe	lohe	oe	lai	loi	peh	la	la	lei
4 puon	pun(pon)	phun	pon	saw	pon	sia	so	so
5 pfuong	pan	phan	hpawn(fan)	san	than	san	san	san
6 tol	tal	to	laiya(lia)	(hin)riw	thro	thrau	ynro	threi
7 kul	pul	phu	a-laiya	(hin)iew	(hum)thloi	ynthla	ynniaw	
8 ti ynthlei	ta	ta	(alia) s'te(su'te)	phra	humpya	humphyo	phra	
9 humpyir kash	tim	tim	s'ti(su'ti)	(khyn)dai	hunsulai	hunshia	khyndo	
10 khyndai kan	kel	ken(ko)	kao	(shi)phew	shiphai	shipho	(shi)phaw	shiphi

It will be seen that there is considerable similarity in the numerals of the different languages up to six, the correspondence being most strongly marked in the numerals 1, 2, 5, and 6. If we remember that primitive people seldom can count higher than the number of digits of one hand, the dissimilarity in the numerals, as the end of the decade is approached, is probably explained. As the different people speaking these languages advanced in civilization they learned to count further; but by this time they had become in some cases like those of the Khasis, the Palaungs, and Mons, widely separated from one another. As they advanced in civilization, and found the necessity of an improved notation, they manufactured numerals which differed from one another, although they retained the first few numerals they had made use of in their days of savagery. Let us now study some extracts from Kuhn's interesting comparative vocabulary. [42] We find many instances of agreement. I give some examples:—

Heaven.—Palaung, *pleng*; Khmêr, *plieng* (rain); Xong, *pleng*; Khasi, *bneng*. Mynnar (Jirang) *phanliang* seems to be very near Khmer *phlieng*, and Palaung, and Xong *pleng*.

Day (Sun)—Khmêr, *thngay*; Mon, *tuyai*; Annam; *ngay*; Lemet, *ngay pri*; Palaung, *sengei*; Khasi, *sngi*; Lakadong, *sngoi*; Kol *singi*.

Year.—Mon, *snam*; Annam, *nam*; Stieng, *so'nam*; Bahnar, *sandm*; Khasi, *snem*.

Lightning:—Mon, *l'li*; Khasi, *leilih*.

Stone, Rock.—Mon, *tma, k'maw*; Stieng, *to'mâu*; Bahn, *tmo, temo*; Khmêr, *thma*; Xong, *tmo*; Palaung, *mau*; Ba, *maou*; Khasi, *maw*; Wa, *hsi-mo, hsi-mao*. Also compare Mynnar (Jirang) *smaw*.

Water.—Palaung, *em*; Khasi, *um*; Lakadong, *am*; Amwi, *am*; Mynnar (Jirang), *um*; Rumai, *om*. Probably the Stieng *um*, to bathe, can be connected with the Khasi word for water.

Sea, pond, or *tank*—Khmêr, *ping*; Khasi, *pung*.

Rice.—Mon, *sro*, paddy, seems to be in connection with Khmer, *srur* (spoken *srau* or *srou*). Xong *ruko* is in Palaung *rekao, sakao,* or *takao*. These words remind us of the Khasi *khaw*, which seems to be borrowed from the Shan *khaw* (*hkao hsau*).

Dog.—The common word for this animal will be found to be nearly the same in sound in many of these languages, e.g. Suk. *cho*; Stieng, *sou*; Bahnar, *ko, cho*; Annam, *cho*; Xong, *tcho*; Mi, *khmu*; Lemet, *so*; Palaung, *tsao, hsao*; Khasi; *ksew*. The Mon *khluiw* is the same as the Khasi *ksew*, if *l* is changed into *s*. The Lakadong and Synteng dialects of Khasi have *ksaw*, and Mynnar (Jirang) *ksow*.

Rat, mouse.—Mon, *kni, gni*; Stieng, *ko'nei*; Bahnar, *kone*; Khasi, *khnai*.

Swine.—Bahnar *niung* is evidently Khasi *'niang*, the abbreviated form of *sniang*.

Tiger.—Mon, *kla*; Stieng, *klah*; Bahnar, *kla*; Khmêr, *khla* and Khasi, *khla* are evidently the same. With this compare the Kol *kula, kula, kula*.

Bird.—Sue, *kiem*; Mon, *g'cem, ka-teim*; Hüei, *chiem*; Stieng, *chum*; Bahnar, Annam, *chim*; Xong, *chiem*; Palaung and Wa, *hsim*, and Khasi *sim* are clearly the same. Also compare Mynnar (Jiraug), *ksem* which is very near to Mon, *g'cem*.

Fowl.—Hüei, *kat, yar*; Suk, *yer*; Bahnar, *ir*;. Stieng *iêr*; Khmu, *yer*; Lemet, *er*; Palaung, *her*, and Khasi, *siar*, abbreviated into *'iar*, are probably the same.

Fish.—The word *ka* or *kha* runs through the following languages:—Mon, Stieng, Bahnar, Annam, Khmu, Lemet, Palaung, Wa; and if we cut off the first syllable of the Khasi word for fish, *dohkha*, we find *'kha*, which is the same word as in the languages above mentioned, with an aspirate added. The Khasi *doh* merely means flesh, and the word *dokkha* is very frequently abbreviated, cf. *'kha saw*, *'kha iong*.

Crab.—Mon, *kh'tam*; Khmêr, *ktam*; Khasi, *tham*. If we add the gender sign to the Khasi word, it becomes *ka tham*, and we have exact correspondence.

Woman.—Mon, *brou* or *brao*. Is this the same as the Khasi (*ka*) *briw*?

Child.—So, *kón*; Suk, *kon*; Mon, *kon*; Hüei, *kuon*; Annan, *kon*; Khmêr, *kun*; Khasi, *khun*. Compare Nancowry, *kon*.

Eye.—The word *mat, mat, mat*, run through several of these languages, e.g. Mon, *mat*; Huei, *mat*; Stieng; *mat*; Bahnar *mat*; Annam, *mat*; Khasi, *khmat* (dialectic *mat*). In Nancowry compare *olmat*, eye, and *okmat*, eyebrow, and (*e*)*mat* (*hen*) *mat* (*drug*), *mat*, of the Nicobar dialects, also Semang *mat, met, med*. Kuhn remarks that the word *mat* is common for "*sight*," and "eye" all over the Malay Archipelago. It should be remarked that in the Amwi and Lakadong dialects of Khasi the word is *mat*.

Nose.—If we cut off the aspirate *kh* from the Khasi *khmut*, which thus becomes *mut*, we find some correspondence between Mon, *muh* (*mu*); Stieng (*tro*), *muh*; Bahnar, *muh*. Here also compare Ho *mua, muta*; Mundari, *mun*; Uraon, *moy*. In the Anwi and Lakadong dialects of Khasi the word is *mur-kong*.

Hand.—Xong, *ti*; Mon, *toi*; Annam, *tay*, Khmer, *te* (from *sang te*, finger); Palaung, *tae, tai*, and Khasi, *kti* (with prefix *k*) closely correspond. The forms *ta* and *toi* of Amwi, and Lakadong, respectively, still more closely correspond with the Mon-Khmer languages than with Khasi. Here compare Nancowry *tei* and *ti*, or *ti* of the Kol languages.

Blood.—Palaung *hnam*, and Wa *nam* closely correspond with Khasi *snám*; here compare Khmêr *iham*.

Horn:—Mon, *grang*, the horn of an animal, may be compared with the Khasi *reng*.

Far.—Distant. Bahnar, *hangai*; Annam, *ngai*; Khmêr, *chhngay*; Lemet, *sngay*; Sue *chngai* may be compared with the Khasi *jing-ngai*. Amwi *shnjngoi* seems to be a closer form to the above than Khasi *jing-ngai*. But compare Mynnar (Jirang), *chngi*, which is clearly very close to Sue *chngai*, and Khmer *chhngay*.

To weep, to cry.—Mon, *yam*; Khmer, *yam*; Khmu Lemet and Palaung, *yam*, are clearly the same as Khasi *iam*, with which also may be compared Ho *yam*.

It is interesting to note that the Amwi and Lakadong dialects of Khasi, which are spoken by the people who dwell on the southern slopes of the Jaintia Hills, seem more closely to correspond with the Mon-Khmer forms than even with Khasi. The Mynnar or Jirang dialect of Khasi, spoken on the extreme north of the hills, also appears to possess some words which are very similar indeed to some of the Mon-Khmer forms given by Professor Kuhn. Unfortunately, I had time to collect but a few words of this interesting dialect, as I arrived in the portion of the country inhabited by these people only a short time before submitting this monograph to Government. The Mynnar dialect appears to be akin to the Synteng, Lakadong, and Amwi forms of speech. The Mynnars observe also the Synteng ceremony of "*Beh-ding-khlam,*" or driving away the demon of cholera, so that although now inhabiting a part of the country a considerable distance away from that of the Synteng, it is not unlikely that they were originally connected with the latter more closely.

Professor Kuhn comes to the conclusion that there is a distinct connection between Khasi, Mon or Talaing, Khmêr, and the other languages of Indo-China that have been mentioned, which is to be seen not only from similarities in some of the numerals, but from the convincing conformities of many other words of these languages. He goes on to add that more important than these contacts of the mono-syllabic languages of Indo-China with mono-syllabic Khasi is their affinity with the Kol, and Nancowry poly-syllabic languages and with that of the aboriginal inhabitants of Malacca, i.e. the languages of the so-called Orang-Outang, or men of tile woods, Sakei, Semung, Orang-Benua, and others; and that although it is not, perhaps, permissible to derive at once from this connection the relation of the Khasi Mon-Khmêr mono-syllabic group with these poly-syllabic languages, it seems to be certain that a common substratum lies below a great portion of the Indo-Chinese languages as well as those of the Kol and Ho-Munda group. More important than connections between words is, as Dr. Grierson points out in his introduction to the Mon-Khmêr family, the order of the words in the sentence. In both Khasi and Mon that order is subject, verb, object. Taking this fact in conjunction with the similarities of the Khasi and Mon vocabularies, we may conclude that it is proof positive of the connection between Khasi and Mon, or Talaing. In Munda, however, this order is subject, object, verb. Tiffs is a very important difference, for, as Dr. Grierson points out, "the order of words in a sentence follows the order of thought of the speaker; it follows therefore that the Mundas think in an order of ideas different from those of the Khasis and the Mons." Dr. Grierson comes to the stone conclusion with respect to these languages as Professor Kuhn, which is as follows:—"Owing to the existence of these differences we should not be justified in assuming a common origin for the Mon-Khmêr languages on the one hand, and for the Munda, Nancowry, and Malacca languages on the other. We may, however, safely assume that there is at the bottom of all these tongues a common substratum, over which there have settled layers of the speeches of other peoples, differing in different localities. Nevertheless, this substratum was so firmly, established as to prevent its being entirely hidden by them, and frequent undeniable traces of it are still discernible in languages spoken in widely distant tracts of Nearer and Further India. Of what language this original substratum consisted we are not yet in a position to say. Whatever it was, it covered a wide area, larger than the area covered by many families of languages in India at the present day. Languages With this common substratum are now spoken, not only in the modern Province of Assam, in Burma, Siam, Cambodia, and Anam, but also over the whole of Central India, as far west as the Berars." Grierson, having agreed regarding the existence of this common substratum, does not finally determine whether the ancient substratum was the parent of the present Munda language, or of the Mon-Khmêr language. He says, "It cannot have been the parent of both, but it is possible that it was the parent of neither." We are thus still in a state of uncertainty as to what was the origin of these languages.

The brief description which follows of some of the more prominent characteristics of the Khasi language is based chiefly on Sir Charles Lyall's skeleton Grammar contained in Vol. II. of Dr. Grierson's "Linguistic Survey of India." It does not pretend to be an exhaustive treatise on the language; for this students are referred to the excellent grammar compiled by the Rev. H. Roberts.

The Article.—There are four articles in Khasi; three in the singular, *u*, (masculine), *ka* (feminine), and *i* (diminutive of both genders); and one in the plural for both genders, *ki*.

All Khasi nouns take a pronominal prefix to denote the gender, i.e. the third personal pronoun, *u* (masculine), *ka* (feminine), *i* (diminutive). The great majority of inanimate nouns are feminine, and all abstract nouns. The sun (day), *ka sngi*, is feminine, the moon (month), *u b'nai*, is masculine. Sometimes the word varies in meaning according to the gender, e,g. *u ngap*, a bee; *ka ngap*, honey.

Genders.—Names of mountains, stones, plants, fruits, stem, and the moon, are masculine, e.g.:—
U *kyllang*, the Kyllang rock.
U *mawlein*, quartz.
U *phan*, potato.
U *soh niamtra*, orange.
U *'lur duti*, the morning star.
U *'tiw kulap*, rose.
U *b'nai*, the moon.

Names of rivers, lakes, books, places, the sun, and' all abstract nouns are feminine, e.g.:—
Ka *wah*, river.
Ka *nan*, lake.
Ka *kitap*, book.
Ka *Shillong*, Shillong.
Ka *sngi*, sun
Ka *jingsneng*, advice.

The article *i* is used either as a diminutive, as *i khunlung*, a baby, or for denoting endearment, as *i mei*, mother.

Number.—U, *ka*, and *i* stand for the singular number, e.g. *u khla* (a tiger), *ka khoh* (a Khasi basket), *i khun* (a child). *Ki* is the sign of the plural, as *Ki maw*, the stones. *Ki* in some few instances is used honorifically, as *ki Siem*, the king, *ki kthaw*, the father-in-law.

Cases are eight in number, and are denoted by prefixes. The declension of the noun *lum* (hill) is given below by way of example:—

	Singular.	Plural
Nominative	*u lum*	*ki lum*
Accusative	*ia u lum*	*ia ki lum*
Instrumental	*da u lum*	*da ki lum*
Dative	*ia, ha,* or	*ia, ha,* or
	sha u lum	*sha ki lum*
Ablative	*na u lum*	*na ki lum*
Genitive	*jong u lum*	*jong ki lum*
Locative	*ha u lum*	*ha ki lum*
Vocative	*ko lum*	*ko phi ki lum*

The sign of the genitive case, *jong,* is sometimes omitted for the sake of brevity, e.g. *u ksew nga* (my dog) for *u ksew jong nga.* The preposition *la* gives also the force of the possessive case, e.g. *la ka jong ka jong* (their own). There are some nouns which change their form, or rather are abbreviated when used in the vocative case, e.g. *ko mei,* not *ko kmei* = Oh mother; *ko pa,* not *ko kpa* = Oh father. These, however, are all of them nouns showing relationships.

Pronouns.—Personal pronouns are *nga* (I), *ngi* (we), *me* (thou, masculine) *pha* (thou, feminine), *phi,* (you, masculine or feminine), *u* (he, it), *ka* (she, it), *i* (diminutive form of *u* or *ka*), and *ki* (they).

The emphatic form of the personal pronoun is formed by prefixing *ma,* e.g. *ma-nga, ma-u,* after a verb, but not after a preposition, e.g. *dei-ma-nga* = it is I. But *ai, ia ma nga* is an incorrect form.

The *Reflexive Pronoun* is formed by the word *lade* (self) being suffixed to the personal pronoun, as *u leh sniu ia lade* = he does himself harm, or by the addition of the word *hi* (self) to the personal pronoun, as *phi hi phi ong* (you yourself).

The *Relative Pronoun* is formed by the suffix *ba,* added to any of the personal pronouns, as *kaba, uba, kiba* (who, which).

The *Demonstrative Pronoun* is formed by the addition of the particles denoting the position of things with reference to the speaker, e.g. (1) near = this, *ne* (*u-ne, kane, i-ne, ki-ne*); (2) in sight, but further off = that, *to* (*uto,* &c.); (3) further away, but still visible = that *tai* (*u-tai,* &c.); (4) out of sight or only contemplated in the mind = that, *ta* (*u-ta,* &c.); (5) above = that, *tei* (*u-tei,* &c.); (6) below = this, *thi* (*ka-thi,* &c.); *katai-tai, katei-tei, kathie-thie* point to an object at a great distance but within sight.

The *Interrogative Pronoun* is the article followed by *no* or *ei* (e.g. *u-no, kano,* who), *u-ei, ka-ei* (who, which). *Ei* is often used without the "article," and *no* (which is restricted to persons) when declined, regularly drops the "article," e.g. *jong-no* whose? *ia-no,* whom? *sha-no,* to whom? What? neuter, is *aiuh,* and also *kaei.*

Adjectives are formed by prefixing *ba* to the root, thus *bha* goodness; *ba-bha,* good; *sniu,* badness; *ba-sniu,* bad. When *ba* is dropped, the word in no longer an adjective but a verb, and in some cases a noun, e.g. *uba khraw* (adj.) = big, great; *u khraw* = he becomes great. An adjective may be formed without any of the prefixes *ba, uba,* &c., e.g. *ka miau-tuh* = a thieving cat.

An adjective follows the noun it qualifies, and agrees with the noun it qualifies in gender and number.

Comparison.—The comparative is formed by adding *kham* before an adjective, followed by *ban ia* (than), or simply *ia*, and the superlative by adding such adverbs of intensity as *tam, eh, eh than, tam eh, shikaddei,* which are followed generelly by *ia* or *ban ia*.

Numerals.—In Khasi the cardinal number always precedes the noun (e.g. *lai sin,* three times,) The following are the first ten numerals.

1	*Wei*
2	*Ar*
3	*Lai*
4	*Sau*
5	*San*
6	*Hinriu*
7	*Hinnieu*
8	*Phra*
9	*Khyndai*
10	*Shipheu*

The word *khad* is prefixed for forming the numerals from 11 to 19, e.g. *khad-wei, khad-ar,* eleven, twelve, &c.

The verbal root (which never varies) may be simple or compound. The compound roots are (1) *Causals,* formed by prefixing *pyn* to the simple root; as *iap,* die; *pyniap,* kill. (2) *Frequentatives,* formed by prefixing *iai*; as *iam,* weep; *iai iam,* weep continually. (3) *Inceptives,* by prefixing *man*; as *stad,* be wise; *manstad,* grow wise. (4) *Reciprocals,* by prefixing *ia*; as *ieit,* love; *ia-ieit,* love one another. (5) *Intensives,* by prefixing tim particle *kyn, lyn, syn, tyn.* Any noun or adjective may be treated as a verbal root by means of a prefix of these five classes. Thus *kajia,* a quarrel (Hindustani loan word, *qazia*;) *ia kajio,* to quarrel with one another; *bynta,* share; *pyn-ia-bynta* (reciprocal catmal), to divide between several persons. It should be mentioned with reference to the second class or frequentative verbs, that they sometimes take the prefixes, or particles as Roberts prefers to call them, *dem, dup, nang, shait, ksaw* in place of *iai*, e.g. *dem-wan,* to come after; *dup-teh,* to practise; *nang-wad,* to go on searching; *shait pang,* to be always ill; *ksaw-bam,* to be in the habit of devouring. There are two verbs for "to be," *long,* implying existence absolutely, and *don,* implying limited existence, and also meaning "to have." There is only one form of conjugation for all verbs. Tense and mood are indicated by prefixes, number and person by the subject. When the subject is a noun the pronoun is inserted before the verb. The following is the conjugation of the verb "to be" in the present, past, and future tenses:—

	Present.		Past.		Future.	
	Singular.	Plural.	Singular.	Plural.	Singular.	Plural.
	1	2	3	4	5	6
	Nga long	*Ngi long*	*Nga la long*	*Ngi la long*	*Ngan long*	*Ngin long*
	I am	We are	I was	We were	I shall be	We shall be
	Me (mas.) or *pha* (fem.) *long*	*Phi long*	*Me* or *pha la long*	*Phi la long*	*Men or* phan *long*	*Phin long*
	Thou art	Ye are	Thou wast	Ye were	Thou shalt be	You shall be
	U (mas.) or *ka* (fem.) *long*	*Ki long*	*U* or *ka la long*	*Ki la long*	*U'n or* ka'n *long*	*Kin long*
	He or she is	They are	He or she was	They were	He or she will be	They will be

The above simple tenses are made definite or emphatic by various means. *La*, sign of the past, when added to *lah*, sign of the potential, has the sense of the pluperfect, e.g. *nga la lah long*, I had been. *Yn* abbreviated into *'n* emphasizes the future, the particle *sa* also indicates the future; *da* is the usual sign of the subjunctive mood, *lada, la, lymda, tad, ynda, ban, da* are other signs of this mood. The sign of the infinitive is *ba'n*. The imperative is either (1) the simple root, or (2) the root compounded with some word such as *to*.

Participles.—The present participle is formed by prefixing *ba* to the root, e.g. *ba long*, being. The imperfect participle is formed by prefixing such words as *ba u, ka da, da kaba,* &c. The perfect participle is formed by putting such particles as *ba la, haba la, da kaba la* before the verb. Verbal nouns of agency are formed by prefixing *nong* to the root, e.g. *u nong knia* (the sacrificer). The *Passive Voice* is formed by using the verb impersonally, and putting the subject into the Accusative case with *ia*.

Potentiality is indicated by the verb *lah*, necessity by the verb *dei; dang* and *da* show the indefinite present.

The *negative* is indicated by the particles *ym*, contracted into *'m, shym,* and *pat*. *Ym* is put before the verb, e.g. *'ym don briew* = there is no one; with a pronoun it is contracted, e.g. *u'm wan*, he does not come. It follows the sign of the future, e.g. *phi'n y'm man*, you will not come. *Shym* and *pat* are neptive particles, and are used with *negative verbs* in the past tense, e.g. *u'm shymla man*, he did not come.

The use of the word "jing."—One of the most striking features of the language is the use of the word *jing*, which is employed to create a verbal noun out of a verb: for instance, take the verb *bam*, to eat; if we prefix *jing* we have *jingbam*, food. *Bat*, to hold; *jing-bat*, a handle. The use of the word *nong* has already been noticed under the heading "verbs." As an example of another common prefix, it may again be mentioned here. Thus, *nong-ai-jingbam* means a table servant, literally one who gives food. Again, *nong-bat*, a holder, literally, one who holds.

Syntax.—The order of words in the sentence is usually (1) subject, (2) verb, and (3) object, in fact, the same as in English, and in this respect it differs entirely from the order in the languages derived from Sanskrit, and that of the languages of the Thibeto-Burman group, as far as I have been able to ascertain. For instance, in the Kachari or Boro language the order in the sentence is (1) subject, (2) object, (3) verb. In Khasi when emphasis is needed, however, the object occasionally precedes the berb, e.g. *ia u soh u la die*, he has sold the fruit, literally, the fruit he has sold. As stated before, adjectives follow the nouns they qualify, e.g. *u lum bajyrong*, a high mountain, literally, the hill that is high. Interrogative adverbs may either precede or follow the verb, e.g. *naei phi wan*, or *phi wan naei*, where do you come from?

No account of the Khasi language would be complete without some reference to the adverbs which are so very numerous in Khasi. U Nissor Singh, in his admirable little book of "Hints on the Study of the Khasi Language," writes, "Adverbs are so numerous in the Khasi language that I shall not attempt to enumerate them all in this small book. Many of the adverbs, indeed, belong to the untranslatables of the language. We are never in want of a specific term to express the appropriate degree of any quality." To learn how to use the right adverb at the right time is one of the niceties of the language. There is a peculiarity about some of the adverbs of place which should be mentioned: e.g. *Hangto*, there (within sight); *hangne*, here; *hangta*, there (out of sight); *hangai*, there (at some distance); *hangtei*, there (upwards); *hangthi*, there (downwards); also the interrogative adverbs *hangno, nangno*, whence, contain the inherent root *nga*, and it seems possible that this *nga* is the first personal pronoun I. If this is so, *hangto* would mean literally "to me there," *hangthi* "to me down there," and similarly *nangno, nangne* would mean "from where to me there" and "from there to me here."

Adverbs generally follow the words they modify, as *u'n leit mynta* = he will go now, but there are exceptions to the above rule, such as interrogative adverbs. The following come before those they modify: *tang shu, la dang* (as soon as, when); *kham, shait* (used to, ever); *pat* or *put* (yet) ; and *shym* (not); but *shuh* (more) goes last. Adverbs of past time are formed by prefixing *myn*, e.g. *mynhynne*, a short time ago. Adverbs of future time are formed by prefixing *la*. The particles *man, man la*, and *hala* denote repetition.

The Khasis are exceedingly fond of using double words [43] which add much to the finish and polish of a sentence. Old people especially have a predilection this way. It is one of the great diffuculties of the language to learn how to use such double words correctly. The following are some examples:—

Nouns.

kajain ka nep	cloth.
ka kot ka sla	paper.
ka lynti ka syngking	road.

ka iing ka sem	house.
u babu, u phabu	babu.
u tymen u san	elder.
ka stih, ka wait	arms (lit.: shield and sword).
u badon ba em	a well to do person.
ka spah ka phew	wealth
u kha-u-man	a relation on the father's side.

Verbs.

pynsyk-pynsain	to comfort.
ia shoh ia dat	to scuffle.
byrngem-byrait	to threaten.
shepting-shepsmiej	to be afraid.
ihthuh-ihthaw	to be familiar.
kyrpad-kyrpon	to beg.
ia lum-ia lang	to assemble.

Adjectives.

basniw-basmeh	bad.
basmat-basting	active.
donbor-donsor	powerful.
don burom-don surom	noble.
bakhraw-batri	pertaining to a noble family.
baduk-basuk	poor, needy.
babok-basot	righteous.
bariwbha-riwmiat.	wealthy.

Adverbs.

hur-hur	delicately.
hain-hain	brilliantly (red).
prum-prum, prem-prem	prominently.
rymbiaw-rymboin	shrikingly.
nior-nior, iar-iar	weakly.
parum-pareh	many.
sip-sip, sap-sap	having no taste.

The Mikirs appear to have borrowed a small portion of their vocabulary from the Khasis. The following are quoted as examples of possible common roots:—

	Mikir.	Khasi.
belly	pòk	kpoh.

strike (*v.*)	chòk	shoh.
father	po	kpa.
come (*v.*)	vàng	wán.
rice beer	hor	hiar.
maternal uncle	ni-lur	kni.

The Lynngam dialect differs so much from the standard Khasi that some remarks regarding the former will not be out of place. Dr. Grierson, on pages 17 to 19 of his Volume II. of the "Linguistic Survey of India," has indicated some of these differences, which may be recapitulated here as follows. Some of the commonest verbs vary considerably from those used in the standard dialect. There are also many minor differences of pronunciation. A man is *u breo*, not *u briew*, a son is a *u khon*, not *u khun*. Standard *ng* is often represented by *nj*. Thus *doinj* for *ding*, fire. A final *h* often appears as *k*, and an initial *b* as *p*. Thus, *baroh* (Standard), all, becomes in Lynngam *prok*. Standard *ei* becomes *aw*. Thus *wei* = *waw*, one; *dei* = *daw*, necessary. The articles are frequently omitted. The pronoun *u* is used for the plural as well as the singular, instead of the Standard plural *ki*. The diminutive *i* is used with inanimate nouns. This is also sometimes the case in the Standard form.

Nouns.—The prefix of the Accusative-dative is *se* or *sa*, often contracted to *s'* instead of *ia* (Standard). The prefix of the Dative is *hanam, hnam*, or *tnam*. The Standard Dative-locative prefix *ha* is also used, and may be spelt *he* or *hy*. *Ta* or *te* are also found. For the genitive, besides the Standard *jong*, are found *ha, am-ba, am*, and *am-nam*. *Am-nam* and *am* also mean "from."

The plural sometimes takes the suffix *met*.

Adjectives.—The usual word for male is *korang*, and for "female" *konthaw*, in place of the Standard *shynrang* and *kynthei* respectively. The following are examples of comparisons:—*Re-myrriang*, good; *Mai-myrriang*, better; *U re-myrriang*, best. The Standard *tam* is also used for the superlative.

Pronouns.—The Personal Pronouns are:—

	Singular	Plural
1st Person,	ne	biaw, iaw.
2nd Person,	mi, mei	phiaw.
3rd Person	u, ju, u-ju	kiw.

The Nominative of the pronoun of the second person singular is given once as *ba-mi*, and once as *ma-mi*. The *ma* or *ba* is the Standard emphatic prefix *ma*.

Demonstrative Pronouns appear to be *be, tei* that, and *uni*, or *nih*, this. *Be* is used as a definite article in the phrase *be jawmai*, the earthquake.

The Relative Pronoun is *u-lah*, who.

Interrogative Pronouns are *net, u-iet*, who? and *met*, what?

Verbs.—The pronoun which is the subject of a verb may either precede or follow it. Thus *ne rip*, I strike; *rip biaw*, we strike. The words meaning to be are *re, im*, and *meit* in addition to the Standard *long*. Like the Standard *don, im*, corresponding to Synteng *em*, also means to have. As in the Standard, the Present Tense is formed by using the bare root.

The Past Tense is formed in one of five ways, viz.:—

1. By suffixing *let*, as in *ong-let*, said. 2. By suffixing *lah-let*, as in *dih-lah-let*, went. 3. By prefixing *lah*, and suffixing *let*, as in *lah-ong-let*, said. 4. By prefixing *lah*, as in *lah-kyllei*, asked. 5. By prefixing *yn* (*yng, ym*), as in *yn-nai*, gave; *yng-kheit*, shook; *um-pait*, broke; *yn-jai*, fell.

The Future is formed in a very peculiar way. The Standard *yn* is inserted into the middle of the root, immediately after the first consenant. Thus *rip*, strike; *rynip*, will strike. If the root is a compound, it is inserted between the two members, as in *pan-yn-sop*, will fill. Here observe that the Standard causative prefix *pyn* becomes *pan* in Lynngam. The Infinitive the same form as the Future.

Dr. Grierson points out the following most noteworthy fact with reference to the formation of the Lynngam Future and Infinitive, i.e., that similar infixes occur in Malay in the Nancowry dialect of Nicobar, and the Malacca aboriginal languages.

The prefix of the Imperative is *nei*, as in *nei-ai*, give; *nei-lam*, bring. The usual negative particle is *ji*, which is suffixed, e.g. *um-ji* is not.

Numerals.

Lynngam	Standard (Khasi).
1. Waw, shi	Wei, shi.
2. Ar-re or a-re	Ar.
3. Lai-re	Lai.
4. Saw-re	Saw.
5. San-de	San.
6 Hyrrew-re	Hinriw.
7. Hynnju-re	Hinniew.
8. Phra-re	Phra.
9. Khondai-re	Khyndai.
10. Shi-phu	Shi-phew.

The peculiarity about the Lynngam numerals is the suffix *re*, and the numeral "five" *de*. None of the other dialects of Khasi posess this peculiarity. Dr. Grierson's Volume may be referred to for a Lynngam Vocabulary. I make the following additions:—

English	Lynngam	Khasi (Standard).
Hearth	paw ka	dypei
Earthen pot	kheow	u khiw
Flesh	mim	ka doh
Spoon	jamplai	ka siang
Sleeping-room	syrkut	ka'rumpei
Drinking-gourd	longtang	u skaw
,, ,,	longjak	u klong dih-um

Broom	shipuat	u synsar

Clothing

Turban	khabong jain brung	ka jain spong
Ear-ring	kurneng	ka shohshkor
Apron	shiliang	ka jymphong
Haversack	jolonjwa [44]	ka pla
Cap	pokhia	ka tupia
Girdle	pun-poh	u saipan
Under Garment (female)	jain tongpan	ka jympin

Domestic Terms.

Pestle	synraw	u synrei
Door	phyrdaw	ka jingkhang
Fowl house	kjor syar	ka sem siar
Portion of house in front of the hearth	nengiaw	ka nongpei
Do. behind the hearth	shangla	ka rumpei
Store-house	siang	ka ieng buh kyba
Millet	jrai	u krai
Indian corn	soh rikhawu	riw hadem
Arum	chew	ka shiriew

Agricultural Implements.

Spade	wakhew	u mokhiew
Bill-hook	wait-bah	ka wait Lynngam
Do.	wait-koh	ka wait khmut
Axe	dapam	u sdi
Basket used in reaping and sowing	khyrnai	ka koh rit.

CHAPTER A

Exogamous Clans in the Cherra State

1. Basa-iew-moit
   Intermarriage with Majaw and Hynniewta clans prohibited.
2. Diengdoh
   Intermarriage with Lalu, Diengdohbah and Diengdohkylla clans prohibited.
3. 'Dkhar
4. Dohling
5. Dulai
6. Dunai
7. Hura
8. Hynniewta
9. Jala
10. Jyrwa
11. Khar Jarain
12. „ Khlem
13. „ Khrang
14. „ Kongor
15. „ Kyni
16. „ Lukhi
17. „ Maw
18. „ Mawphlang
19. „ Mu
20. „ Muid
21. „ Muti
22. „ Mylliem
23. „ Naior
24. „ Shi-ieng
25. „ Synteng
26. — —
27. Khong-bri
28. „ hat
29. „ ji
30. „ joh
31. „ kwang
32. „ kynshen
33. „ kyntiaj
34. „ kyshah
35. „ lam
36. „ liar
37. „ longioi

38. „ lynnong
39. „ mawpat
40. „ mukon
41. „ ngain
42. „ riat
43. „ rymmai
44. „ sdir
45. „ shir
46. „ sit
47. „ sngi
48. „ sya
49. „ war
50. „ wet
51. „ wir
52. Lyngdoh-Nonglwai
53. Lynden
54. Lynrah
55. Majaw
56. Marbaniang
   This is one of the myntri clans of Mawsynram State.
57. Malngiang
   Originally from Maskut in the Jowai Sub-division.
58. Marpna
59. Mawlong
60. Marboh
   Formerly one of the Khadar Kur clans. Has now become extinct.
61. Mawdkhap
62. Mohkhiew
63. Mynrieng
64. Myrthong
65. Nongbri
66. Nongkynrih
   One of the myntri clans of the Khyrim State.
67. Nonglait
68. Nongtran
69. Nonglathiang
70. Nongrum
   One of the myntri clans of the Khyrim State.
71. Nontariang
   These two clans cannot intermarry. Nongtariang is now one of the Khadar Kur clans in place of the Marboh clan which has become extinct.
72. Padoh
73. Parariang
74. Pohnong

75. Prawai
76. Puria
77. Pompyrthat
78. Rani
79. Rapthap
80. Rynjah
   One of the myntri clans of the Khyrim State.
81. Samai
82. Shabong
83. Shanpru
84. Shrieh
   Shrieh means a monkey. Possibly totemistic.
85. Siem Lyngng
86. Sohkhlet
87. Shyngpliang
88. Sumer
89. Swer
90. Syiem
91. Syngai
92. Synrem
93. Thabah
94. Tham
   Tham means a crab. Possibly totemistic.
95. Tohtih
96. Umdor
97. Walang
98. Warkon
99 Khyrwang
100. Ksing

CHAPTER B

Exogamous Clans in the Khyrim State

1. Awri
2. Bariang
3. Basa-iew-moit
4. Bhoi
5. Bithai
6. Diengdoh (2)
    Intermarriage with Masar clan prohibited.
7. 'Dkhar
8. Dumpep
9. Hadem
10. Jasia
11. Khang-shei
12. Khar baino
13. „ baki
14. „ bangar
    Intermarriage with Nong-lwai clan prohibited.
15. Khar bih-khiew
    Intermarriage prohibited with Khar-umnuid clan
16. Khar bonniud
17. „ bud
18. „ buli
19. „ dint
20. „ dohling
21. „ dumpep
22. „ hi-dint
23. „ iap
24. „ Kamni
25. „ Kongor
26. „ Kset
27. „ kynang
28. „ long
29. „ luni
30. „ Malki
31. „ Masar
32. „ mawlieh
    Intermarriage with Khar pomtiah clan prohibited.
33. Khar mihpein
34. „ mithai
35. „ mudai
36. „ mujai

37. „ mukhi
38. „ muti
39. „ mylliem
40. „ patti
41. „ pein
42. „ phan
43. „ phur
44. „ pohlong
45. „ pohshiah
46. „ pomtiah
    Intermarriage with Khar mawlieh clan prohibited.
47. Khar pomtih
48. „ pran
49. „ ryngi
50. „ rynta
51. „ Sati
52. „ shan
53. „ shi-ieng
54. „ shilot
55. „ shong
56. „ shrieh
57. „ sohnoh
58. „ sugi
59. „ Umnuid
    Intermarriage with Khar-bihkhiew clan prohibited.
60. Khar urmut
61. „ War
62. Khier
63. Khmah
64. Khong-binam
65. „ blah
66. „ buh
67. „ buhphang
68. „ 'dkhar
69. „ dup
    Intermarriage prohibited with Rongsai and Khongree clans.
70. Khong [45] iap
71. „ iong
72. „ ji
    Intermarriage with Pongrup clan prohibited.
73. Khong joh
74. „ kai
75. „ khar
76. „ kiang
77. „ kib

78. ,, kylla
79. ,, kyndiah
80. ,, lam
81. ,, liam
82. ,, likong
83. ,, litung
84. ,, luni
85. ,, malai
86. ,, mawlow
87. ,, niur
88. ,, noh
89. ,, pdei
90. ,, pnam
91. ,, pnan
92. ,, sdoh
93. ,, siting
94. ,, slit
95. ,, sugi }
96. ,, sni }
97. ,, sti }
    Intermarriage prohibited also with Lyngdoh clan
98. Khong stia
99. ,, sylla (2)
100. ,, thaw
101. ,, tiang
102. ,, thorem
103. ,, wanduh (2)
104. ,, wet
105. ,, wir
106. Khriam
107. Khynriam
108. Khynriem
109. Khynriem miyat
110. Khynriem mawshorok
   Intermarriage with Pongrup, Lyndoh and Mawthoh clans prohibited.
111. Khynriem wahksieng
112. Kur Kalang.
113. Lamin
114. Lawai
   Intermarriage with Lyngdoh clan prohibited.
115. Lawaisawkher
116. Lingshing
117. Liting
118. Lyngbah

119. Lyngdoh
   Intermarriage with Pongrup and Mawthoh clans prohibited.
120. Lyngiar
121. Mairang
122. Majaid
123. Manar
124. Masar
   Intermarriage with Diengdoh clan prohibited.
125. Mawiong
126. Mawphlang
127. Mawsharoh
128. Mawthoh
   Intermarriage with Pongrup and Lyngdoh clans prohibited.
129. Mawwa
130. Morbah
131. Mormein
132. Mukhin
133. Muroh
134. Mylliem
135. Mylliem muthong }
136. ,, Ngap   }
137. ,, pdah   }
   Intermarriage between these clans prohibited also with Sohtum clan
138. Mynsong
139. Niengnong
140. Nieng-suh
142. Nongbri
   Intermarriage with Nong-kynrih clans prohibited.
143. Nongbri Partuh
144. Nonghulew
145. Nong-khlieh
146. Nong-kynrieh
   Intermarriage with Nongbri clan prohibited.
147. Nong-lwai
   Intermarriage with Khar-Bangar clan prohibited.
148. Nong-lyer
149. Nong-pinir
150. Nong-pluh
151. Nongrum
152. Nongspung
153. Nongsteng
154. Nongstein
155. Nongtlub
156. Pdei

157. Pohkhla
158. Pohthmi
159. Pongrup
   Intermarriage with Mawthoh and Lyngdoh clans prohibited.
160. Rumkheng
161. Ruson
162. Rymkheng
163. Ryndong (2)
164. Ryngksai
165. Rynjah
   Intermarriage with Mawroh clan prohibited.
166. Rynjem
167. Ryntong
168. Ryngngi
169. Shabong
170. Shadap
171. Singting
172. Sohkhleb
173. Sohtum
   Intermarriage with Mylliemngap, Mylliempdah and Mylliem-muttong clans prohibited.
174. Sonjri
175. Songthiang
176. Sumer
177. Surong
178. Suting
179. Swali
180. Swer
181. Synnah
182. Synteng
183. Synteng-hen
184. Tadong
185. Tangper
186. Tangsang
187. Tarieng
188. Trai-iew
189. Tyngsier
190. Tynsil (2)
191. Tyngsong
192. Umsong
193. Uri-ieng
194. Wallang
195. Warbah
   Intermarriage with War-shong prohibited.
196. War-Jnem

197. „ jri
198. „ khyllew
199. War-malai
200. „ moi
201. „ Nongjri
202. Wan-khar
203. War-shong
   Intermarriage with Warbah prohibited.

CHAPTER C

Divination by Egg-Breaking

The *dieng shat pylleng*, or egg-breaking board, is shaped as indicated in the diagram. Having placed a little heap of red earth on the board at point *p*, the egg-breaker sits facing the board in the position shown in the diagram. He first of all makes a little heap of rice in the middle of the board sufficient to support the egg. He places the egg there. He then takes it up and smears it with red earth, muttering incantations the while. Having finished the invocation to the spirits, the egg-breaker sweeps the grains of rice off the board, stands up, and dashes the egg on the board with considerable force. The large portion of the egg-shell is made to fall in the middle of the board, as at X in the diagram. This portion of the shell is called *ka lieng*, or the boat. The small bits of egg-shell which fall around the boat are either good or evil prognostics, according to the following rules:—

1. The bits of shell which fall on the right of the boat are called *ki jinglar*, and those on the left *ki jingkem*. Supposing fragments of shell fall as at *b, c, d, e*, with their insides downwards, this is a good sign, but if one of the fragments lies with its outside downwards, this is a bad omen, and signifies *ka sang long kha*, or sin on the father's or the children's part. It may also signify *ka daw lum*, or "cause from the hill," i.e, that the illness or other affliction has been caused by a god of some hill.

2. If the fragments of shell lie on the left side of the boat as at *g, k, i, j* in the diagram, they are named *ki jingkem*. If they lie with their insides downwards, they indicate a favourable sign. If *g* lies with its outside downwards, this is an evil omen. If *g* and *h* lie with their insides downwards, this is favourable, even if *i* lies with its outside downwards. If, however, *j* lies with its outside downwards, this is not a good sign.

3. If there are a number of pieces of egg-shell lying in a line, as at *k*, this is an evil prognostic, the line of shell fragments indicating the road to the funeral pyre. Such a line of shell fragments is called *ki'leng rah thang*. This sign is a harbinger of death.

4. If all the fragments of shell on both sides of the board, excepting the boat, lie with their insides downwards, the question asked by the egg-breaker is not answered. If *a* or *l* fall with their outsides downwards, this is a bad sign.

5. If the portion of a shell at *f* falls with the outside downwards, this indicates that some god needs appearing by sacrifice.

6. If there are a number of small fragments lying around the boat, as in the diagram, these mean that there are many reasons for the illness, which cannot be ascertained.

7. If the portion of shell marked *s* is detsehed from the boat, this indicates that the goddess is very angry.

8. If four fragments lie around the boat so as to form a square, as *c, e, h, j,* these mean that the patient is at the point of death. These are called *ki leng sher thang.*

8. If there are no fragments, as at *d, e, f, g, h, i,* it is a puzzle, *ka leng kymtip.*

Note.—The above information was obtained from U Sarup Singh, of Mairong; U Them, of Laitlyngkot, and U Bud, of Jowai. Different egg-breakers have somewhat different methods of reading the signs, but the main points are usually the same.

NOTES

[1] The previous history of the Khasi state of Jaintia, so far as it can be traced will be found related in Mr. E. A. Gait's *History of Assam* (1906), pp. 253-262.

[2] P. 211.

[3] Vol. iii., p. 168, 177, &c.

[4] These cloths, which Lindsay calls "*moongadutties*," were really the produce of Assam, and were *dhutis* or waist-cloths of *muga* silk.

[5] Pp. 218-220., It appears from p. 219 that Mr. Scott's report is responsible for the erroneous statement (often repeated) that the mountaineers "called by us Cossyahs, denominate themselves Khyee." This second name is in fact the pronunciation current in Sylhet of the word *Khasi*, *h* being substituted for *s*, and should be written as *Khahi*.

[6] In Mr. Scott's time it was usual to speak of such a place as a "Sanatary."

[7] Vol. ix, pp. 833 sqq.

[8] Vol. xiii., pp. 612 sqq.

[9] Pp. 272 sqq.

[10] Called]w|oskop'ia: one of the lost books of the Orphic cycle was entitled t`a]w|oskopik'a.

[11] The figures for Khasi population in the Khasi and Jaintia Hills district will be found under "Habitat."

[12] The average rainfall at the Cherrapunji Police Station during the last twenty years, from figures obtained from the office of the Director of Land Records and Agriculture, has been 118 inches. The greatest rainfall registered in any one year during the period was in 1899, when it amounted to 641 inches.

[13] It is interesting to compare the remarks of M. Aymonier in his volume iii of "Le Cambodge." He writes as follows:—"Mais en Indo-Chine on trouve, partout disseminé, ce que les indigènes, au Cambodge du moins, appellant, comme les peuples les plus éloignés du globe les traits de foudre.' Ce sont ici des haches de l'âge néolithique ou de la pierre polie, dont la plupart appartiennent au type repandu en toute la terre. D'autres de ces celtes, dits épaulés, parcequ'ils possèdent un talon d'une forme particulière, paraissent appartenir en propre à l'Indo-Chine et à la presqu'ile dekkhanique. Its fourniraient donc un premier indice, non négligeable, d'une communauté d'origine des populations primitives des deux péninsules, cis et trans gangétiques."

[14] Mawkhar is a suburb of Shillong, the headquarters station.

[15] The maund is 82 lbs.

[16] See Bulletin No. 5 of the Agricultural Department of Assam, 1898, pp. 4 and 5.

[17] Khasi *u sak-riew*.

[18] Colocasia osculenta, Beng. *Kachu*.

[19] About threepence.

[20] For the story in detail see the Folk-lore section of the monograph.

[21] Simsong is the Garo name for the river Someshwari.

[22] Officer.
[23] See page 13, "Ka Niam Khasi" (U Jeebon Roy.)
[24] What follows is a literal translation of the Khasi.
[25] This cave is at Pomdalai, some five miles west of Cherrapunji, close to a great waterfall called *Noh Ka Likai*, i.e. the place where Ka Likai jumped down the precipice (for a full account of this story see Section V. of the monograph), where there is a large block of stone, with some cuts over it, known as *Dain Thlen*, i.e. the snake cutting (place).
[26] In another account it is said to have been U Suid-noh himself who did this.
[27] Sir Charles Lyall has pointed out that the Mikirs possess this custom; it is probably borrowed from the Khasis.
[28] Karl Pearson's essay on "mother age civilization."
[29] Lit.: Cut by magic.
[30] In Ahom *kái* = fowl, *chán* = beautiful, *mung* = country. Therefore *Kái-chán-mung* = fowl of a beautiful country (heaven).
[31] A spirit which is supposed to have the power of causing a disease of the navel of a child.
[32] *Iapduh* is the regular word used for a clan, and in this case a species dying out.
[33] The Shillong Peak is thought to be the seat of a powerful *blei* or god who has his abode in the wood close to the top of the "Peak." Another folk-tale will be found concerning this god.
[34] another version is that it was U Kyrphei, another hill in Nongspung territory, who fought with U Symper.
[35] For further details regarding the Khasi superstition of the "thlen," the reader is referred to the portion of the monograph dealing with human sacrifices. It may be mentioned that the "thlen's" cave is at a place called Pom Doloi in the territory of the Siem of Cherra, where there is also a rock called "Dain Thlen" (the cutting of the "thlen"). Another version of the story explaining why there are still "thlens" in the Khasi Hills is that there was an old woman who lived at a placed called Mawphu, a village in a valley to the west of Cherrapunji. This old woman forgot to eat her share of the "thlen's" flesh, the result being that the species became repropagated.
[36] Both rivers, Umngot and Umiew, or Umiam, have their sources in or close to the Shillong Peak. The word "Rupatylli" signifies in Khasi a solid silver necklace of a peculiar shape. In order to appreciate this pretty tale thoroughly, the reader ought to view the river "Rupatylli" from the heights of the Laitkynsew, or Mahadeo, whence it is to be seen glistening in the sun like a veritable rupatylli or silver necklace.
[37] Those mountains are the high hills which lie to the east of the Jowai Sub-Division, and which form part of the boundary line between the Khasi and Jaintia Hills District and North Cachar.
[38] The word Hadem is possibly a corruption of "Hidimba," the old name for North Cachar.

[39] A Kongngor is one who has married a Khasi princess.

[40] This stone bridge, situated on the Theria road about a mile below Cherra, existed up to the Earthquake of 1897, which demolished it. The large slab of stone which formed the roadway of the bridge, is however, still to be seen lying in the bed of the stream.

[41] The above story is said to have been taken down word for word from the mouth of an old woman of the Malyniang clan who lived at Mawlong.—P.R.G.

[42] Kuhn's "Beiträge zur Sprachenkunde Hinterindiens."

[43] Khasi *ktin kynnoh*.

[44] Assamese loan word, a corruption of "julungá."

[45] The word *khong* has probably connection with the Synteng word *jong* meaning a clan.

Echo Library
www.echo-library.com

Echo Library uses advanced digital print-on-demand technology to build and preserve an exciting world class collection of rare and out-of-print books, making them readily available for everyone to enjoy.

Situated just yards from Teddington Lock on the River Thames, Echo Library was founded in 2005 by Tom Cherrington, a specialist dealer in rare and antiquarian books with a passion for literature.

Please visit our website for a complete catalogue of our books, which includes foreign language titles.

The Right to Read

Echo Library actively supports the Royal National Institute of the Blind's Right to Read initiative by publishing a comprehensive range of large print and clear print titles.

Large Print titles are in 16 point Tiresias font as recommended by the RNIB.

Clear Print titles are in 13 point Tiresias font and designed for those who find standard print difficult to read.

Customer Service

If there is a serious error in the text or layout please send details to feedback@echo-library.com and we will supply a corrected copy. If there is a printing fault or the book is damaged please refer to your supplier.

Printed in the United States
117355LV00010B/223/A